C000129644

The Crisis Behind Our Crisis

Alexander Boot

Foreword by Theodore Dalrymple

Copyright © Alexander Boot 2010
All rights reserved

No part of this book may be reproduced or transmitted in any form
or by any means, electronic or mechanical, including photocopying,
recording, or by any information storage and retrieval system,
without permission in writing from the publishers.

ISBN 978 1901 546 385

Front cover design
Bernard Burridge
Photography by Joanne Burridge

St. Matthew Publishing Ltd
1 Barnfield, Common Lane, Hemingford Abbots
Huntingdon PE28 9AX   UK
01480 399098
Email: PF.SMP@dial.pipex.com
www.stmatthewpublishing.co.uk

For Peter, the least I can do.

TABLE OF CONTENTS

FOREWORD

The advertising slogan of a credit card that was launched when I was still a young man said that the card would take the waiting out of wanting.

Unfortunately, a good advertising slogan does not necessarily reflect sound economic policy, let alone a good philosophy of life; but it would hardly be too much to say that the current economic crisis in the west has been caused by the removal of waiting from wanting, that is to say a mass desire to consume more than is earned, all at the expense of the future. Debt, both private and public, has increased rapidly, indeed incontinently; few western countries pay their way in the world, but fund their current expenditure by resort to borrowing abroad.

In this brilliant book, Alexander Boot delves far deeper than anyone else into the origins of the current crisis – a crisis that, incidentally, he demonstrates is very far from being over. With implacable logic and a grasp of history far superior to that of other commentators, he shows that the economic crisis is not merely economic, but spiritual.

Economics cannot be divorced from human behaviour, nor human behaviour from the thought behind it, nor the thought behind it from its philosophical or metaphysical roots, whether they are acknowledged or not. As a matter of empirical fact, a man who believes that human life has a meaning external to itself is likely to behave differently from a man who believes that his three score years and ten (or now twenty) on earth is all that there is.

Why do people, not merely a few individuals but millions and tens of millions of them, continually live beyond their means by the resort to credit, a resort which is often dishonourable if not dishonest? Why do those in authority encourage them to do so, and why do governments always promise more than they have the duty, right or economic means to supply?

I do not want to anticipate Mr Boot's answer: to do that would be like introducing a whodunit by giving the name of the culprit. Suffice it to say that my late friend, the great development economist, Peter Bauer, used to say that one of the characteristics of our age was a great supply of information on every imaginable subject on the one hand, and the complete absence of connected thought on the other. This is not a complaint he could make of Mr Boot, who has not only absorbed a huge amount of information, but understood its interconnectedness, its meaning.

Dr Theodore Dalrymple

ACKNOWLEDGEMENTS

What you are about to read is not merely a book on economics, though you will find quite a bit of it there. Nor is it a metaphysical essay, though at times it may read like one. Neither is it just social and political commentary, though it is that among other things. It is not history, though I do take an historical approach. My aim here is to bring all of those together in order to analyse our present ordeal from various angles, some not yet covered by other writers.

To have a sporting chance of pulling this off I had to draw on multiple sources that can be broadly divided into three groups: personal experience of life in general and business in particular, books, talks with friends. The less said about the first the better: living is a private business, even though in my case never a solitary one. But the other two merit a comment.

This being an essay rather than a scholarly treatise, I have decided against providing a complete bibliography at the end. Whenever a book has had a direct bearing on my thinking, I mention it in the text. Hundreds, possibly thousands of others go unmentioned precisely because there are hundreds, possibly thousands of them. If you happen to be interested in the background of any subject I touch upon, it will be easier for you to look it up on the net than to decide which of the books appearing in an endless bibliography are worth digging up.

Living, as I said, is not a solitary business for me. But writing certainly is, and there is inevitably much stewing in one's own juice. The danger is that the stew may run dry, unless one's friends add a splash of wisdom here, a dollop of knowledge there, a touch of erudition at the end. And I am blessed with friends who are both sage enough to be able to offer such help and generous enough to be willing to do so.

Two must be thanked first. The Rev. Dr Peter Mullen is a deep religious thinker and metaphysical philosopher, and also a busy author of some thirty books: theology, philosophy, essays, collections of sermons, novels, poetry. Yet he has taken time away from his pastoral duties and his own prodigious writing to go over this text in minute detail, keeping me on the straight and narrow in his areas of expertise. If you spot some lapses in those areas, put them down to my stubbornness, not to Peter's advice. Even more important, in the ten years that we have been friends, Peter has always offered much needed encouragement and much exaggerated praise. In the latter, one has to make allowances for his natural kindness reinforced by his priestly sense of duty; the former is always invaluable.

Dr Anthony Daniels has been a close friend for some twenty years, and all that time we have had daily conversations, mostly by phone, feeding off each other. I do not know if Tony has derived any benefit from this, but I know for sure that I have. The author of God knows how many books, and more articles than even He knows, Tony writes the most penetrating and stylish social commentary in English, and he is a relentlessly logical polemicist. I can testify to that, having found myself on the losing end of many a ferocious exchange. Yet there was victory in those defeats, in that as a result I refined my own arguments, ridding them of the more gaping holes. There is hardly a secular point in this essay that Tony and I had not discussed many times over long before I put my fingers on the keyboard. And speaking of encouragement, it was Tony who first suggested that I should write books. So, if you hate this one, he must take a little of the blame – and if you like it, much of the credit.

Dr Andrew Hegarty has not been a friend for as long, but he too has kindly offered some comments on theology that have made this essay more sound. Adam Parkin and Michael Berry, both financiers of enviable attainment, have read the relevant chapters and pointed out ways in which they could be improved. Clifford Middleton and Nicola Beckley also offered helpful comments. Philip Foster of SMP is a publisher who has learned to perfection the two hardest things about editing: when to leave alone, and when not to.

And of course no list of those to whom I owe gratitude would be complete without my wife, the sublime pianist Penelope Blackie. As always, she lovingly went over the text, adding to it her artist's sense of form and her womanly sense of moderation. And she even kept down the volume of her practising when I was writing, a tremendous and much appreciated sacrifice.

'A society that pursues wealth rather than morality will end up using this wealth against itself.' Aristotle

'I could not dig: I dared not rob: Therefore I lied to please the mob. Now all my lies are proved untrue, and I must face the men I slew.' Rudyard Kipling

'Poverty, again, makes men appreciate reality... It is of no direct advantage, but I am sure it is of advantage in the long run, for if you ignore reality you will come sooner or later against it, like a ship against a rock in a fog, and you will suffer as the ship will suffer.' Hilaire Belloc

'None of it can be helped, but all of it can be despised.' Seneca

THE NON-SCIENCE OF ECONOMICS

When water is seeping through the bathroom wall, the problem is neither the dark stain on the paintwork nor the puddle on the floor. It is the hole in the pipe. If we ignore this simple logic, we shall be spending more and more time on our knees, trying to mop up the water. Our efforts will be in vain: the problem will get progressively worse and the house will be flooded.

Obviously you realise that what concerns me at the moment is not plumbing. This is but a metaphor for something I do care about: the present crisis that is tearing the world apart. For, to extend the metaphor, it is we who are the hapless house dwellers brought to our knees by a problem we do not understand.

The implication is that you and I together can reach such understanding, which must mean we are qualified to diagnose the condition first. But is this true? After all, the crisis is supposed to be economic, and one suspects most of you are not economists. I know for a fact that I am not, though I have read quite a few books on the subject, as I am sure you have. But not to worry: we have just begun to establish proper credentials. If any of us were indeed professional economists, we would be tempted to see the world in general, and certainly the present crisis in particular, in terms of our speciality. That would be a mistake, for the problem we are facing is not really economic at all. The economy is not the hole in the pipe. It is the puddle on the tiles – a symptom, not the cause.

Because most economists fail to realise this, so many of them are remiss in living up to their *raison d'être* in the business world: predicting economic developments. Few, for example, saw the present crisis coming, just as few of their intellectual ancestors predicted the Great Depression 80 years earlier. This goes to show that the economy is too fragile to be left to the economists, for all their graphs, charts and equations.

Not that this conclusion has not been reached by other analysts. It has been, by quite a few. In fact, a small library of books on the current crisis have already been published, some good, some not so good.[1] Many of the authors have commented upon the irresponsibility of our banks and the profligacy of our governments, both indiscretions playing into the hand of the people's hedonism. Others have pointed out that a society weaned on the pursuit of instant gratification (otherwise known as happiness) would be hard-pressed trying to keep a fiscal lid on the people's bubbling expectations.

One must admit that, by suggesting it is human folly that lies at the core of the issue, this kind of approach doubtless goes further than cold-blooded calculations of debt-to-revenue ratios and some such arcana. But it does not go far enough: we have placed the blame at the people's door without taking the next step inside the house. We have not explained why our banks are irresponsible, our governments profligate and our people hedonistic. That is to say we have not got to the cause of the trouble.

Part, or perhaps the beginning, of the problem is linguistic. When we use terms like 'irresponsible' or 'profligate' to describe banks, governments and other institutions, we seem to be assigning to them characteristics normally associated with individuals. In a way, by doing so we anthropomorphise inanimate bodies, removing them from the flesh-and-blood people who run them. We seem to imply that institutions act of their own accord, and their actions are beyond anybody's control.

This is loose phrasing that betokens loose thinking. There are no such things as irresponsible banks or profligate governments; there are only irresponsible bankers and profligate politicians. Now if we correct this linguistic solecism and begin to express ourselves with more rigour, before long we shall be talking not about bankers or politicians – and not even about consumers – but about people in

---

1. Obviously, I think that this book will elucidate the situation in ways others have not. If I did not think so, I would have written one of those other books or, more likely, none at all. Whether my claim is based on sober assessment or sheer hubris will be up to you to decide.

general. We would begin by contemplating human nature, and only then see how it is reflected in various facets of life. And if we were to prioritise these facets, then perhaps we would agree that economic activity comes fairly low down on the list. That is understandable: after all, it is people who manage economies, not the other way around.

This thought is elementary to the point of being platitudinous. Yet it is amazing how many people it escapes. Somehow, the Marxist – or shall we say virtual? – idea of the primacy of disembodied economics has taken hold, and it unites the seemingly incompatible political extremes. Nationalise the means of production, claim the socialists, and everything else will follow. Socialism good, capitalism bad. Privatise the means of production, object the libertarians, and everything else will follow. Capitalism good, socialism bad. Like Orwell's animals, both species reduce everything to a single issue. They just cannot agree on the number of legs.

However, people, even those who appear simple, are far from simple. No single activity can plausibly express all they are about; no single aspiration is the sum total of their desires. Moreover, in those rare instances when an individual can be credibly described in monistic terms, we tend to feel, usually with ample justification, that he has left the realm explainable by psychology for one only reachable by psychiatry. People whose whole being hangs on the peg of a single issue are neither focused nor dedicated. They are mad.

Economic activity reflects merely a small part of an individual's essence, and it would be far-fetched to believe that it is divorced from all other parts. Of course it is not, but that should not be understood simplistically. When performing on the economic stage most people will behave differently from the way they act at home or with their friends. However, if we know a person well, we shall have no difficulty in finding a link between the two behavioural modes. The link is the person himself, his character, culture, ideas, religion or lack thereof, aspirations, temperament – even at times appearance and other physical characteristics. And if we consider the totality of what makes a human being human, then we may well reach the conclusion that his economic performance is the easiest, though by no means easy, part to understand.

If we go on in that manner, we shall perhaps decide that economics is the simplest of all the sciences devoted to the study of human behaviour. Just consider this. Psychologists, neuro-physiologists and other such scientists have spent billions in whatever currency you care to name on trying to understand the human mind. Yet, after all those Decades of the Brain and Genome Projects, they still do not even know what the mind is, how it works, what produces and constitutes a thought, or whether consciousness ever will be wholly describable in any physical or biological terms.

When it comes to such fundamentals, all they have found so far is that those dark sections on their scanner displays sometimes light up and sometimes they do not. In other words, the neuroscientists have neither begun to acquire the most rudimentary knowledge of their object of study nor given any indication that they will ever do so. At best they are nibbling at the periphery of understanding without ever approaching its core.

This stands to reason, at least for someone who does not live by reason alone. And yet the results are not all negative. At the very least all those neurosciences, though largely failing in their declared mission, have succeeded in proving that they are indeed sciences. They have passed the critical test of going beyond common sense. Real, especially modern, science always does.[2] If we look at photons getting to us from faraway stars by unerringly and, on the face of it, rationally choosing the shortest path of least resistance for millions of years; if we even begin, to the best of our limited ability, to consider the implications of quantum mechanics and the theory of relativity (and how the two may be at odds), universal constants or modern

2. I owe this thought to Prof. Lewis Wolpert, who invariably makes sense on science, though not necessarily on some other things he explores in his popular books explaining why there is no God.

genetics with its undecipherable codes, we shall see that common sense will help us grasp none of these. It will mislead, not lead.

Economics is different. It not only does not go beyond common sense but invariably and miserably fails when trying to do so. Whenever a professional economist starts using terms and concepts that go beyond the understanding of someone with a decent secondary (or better still, primary) education, then we know that the wool is being pulled over our eyes. The chap is not trying to elucidate the problem. He is trying to obscure it, and probably for nefarious reasons. The father of modern economics, Adam Smith, never had to do this. His books rely on plain common sense to explain a very simple problem: how to get out of people's hair and let them get on with what they know how to do best – make a living. For modern economists, economics is too simple to understand.

One can draw two (naturally, commonsensical) conclusions from this. First, if our definition of a science includes as a necessary constituent its going beyond common sense, and if economics not only does not but indeed must not do so, then economics is not a science. Second, economics has an off-chance of becoming a science if it is treated as a study of merely a single aspect of life, one that is closely intertwined with others, and only ever pursued in conjunction with them.

Various aspects of an individual's life reflect his, and more generally human, nature. But they do so not only synchronically, at present, but also diachronically, over history. Not only are they linked horizontally with other aspects of human nature, culture and civilisation, but they are also linked vertically with the historical development of man since the Creation (if you happen to believe in it) or at least since time immemorial (if you do not). That is why, if we wish to get to the bottom of the present economic crisis, economics can be but a small part of things to consider. Therefore we either abandon the project before we have even started or we must delve deeper.

If you have read my 2006 book *How the West Was Lost*, you will know that I can only regard the current crisis not as an aberration but as a logical development of modernity. The problem is systemic, not merely symptomatic. As such, it can be reversed only when modernity is. When things have gone hopelessly wrong, we can only do by undoing.

By modernity I do not mean modern times – only God can reverse those. What I mean is a society dominated by the sociocultural type I described in that earlier book as 'Modman' (I referred to the traditional type ousted by Modman as 'Westman'). Now, under normal circumstances quoting from oneself is in dangerously poor taste. But our circumstances are far from being normal, and, as Guy Fawkes once said, a desperate disease requires a dangerous remedy. So this is what I wrote towards the end of that book:

'God only knows what mayhem Modmen will trigger off next. One thing for sure, neither they nor their deified happiness will survive it. The architectural monstrosities they have plonked in the middle of what used to be Westman's world will collapse like a house of cards. And when that happens, nothing of Modman will be left standing except the nastiness that he has so diligently cultivated. The same fire will consume Modmen's non-music, non-paintings, non-books. For Modmen have produced nothing of lasting value but 'happiness', and we know on the example of the last century how perishable this commodity can be. When happiness turns to misery, as history teaches it is sooner or later bound to, Modman will have nothing to fall back on. And so he will die as he has lived.'

Considering that 'Modman' was my shorthand for the modern world, this was rather apocalyptic stuff indeed. Of course, most present-day Cassandras harbour secret hopes that the more macabre of their predictions will not come true, at least not in their lifetime. I, the most reluctant Cassandra you are ever likely to meet, am no exception.

Thus, while my dim view of modernity has always remained heartfelt, at the time of writing I was still craving a miracle. Against every available fact and contrary to every bit of logic I was hoping a world that had taken leave of its senses would come back. Alas, as if to vindicate every available fact and every bit of logic, that hope has turned out to be misplaced, while the reluctant prediction has turned out to be right. The catastrophe has struck, and our world is indeed in danger of collapsing like a house of cards.

But if it is true that there is an opportunity in every crisis, then we have in the West today one of the biggest opportunities ever. This book is an attempt to understand the crisis and consider the opportunities. But it comes with a warning: Those of you who seek earth-shaking discoveries expressible in columns of numbers will be disappointed. I have always found the mechanics of finance to be as dull as they are easy to grasp, to the point of triviality. And even if I suddenly changed this view, I doubt I could add much to many a book that distinguished economists have written on the crisis since it began. I could recommend several titles (*Empire of Debt* by Bill Bonner and Addison Wiggin would perhaps be the first to come up, as it was one of the few that had actually predicted the crisis before it happened), but a leisurely stroll through the net will make any such recommendation superfluous.

What does interest me is not so much the nuts and bolts of the crisis as the historical, philosophical and psychological reasons for it – the causes more than the effects. After all, we cannot cure any disease unless we come to grips with its aetiology, instead of just observing and trying to relieve its symptoms. If you share this interest, then perhaps you will find enough in this book to stimulate your own thinking and plan your own actions.

Before you go any further, it would be only fair to let you know what you are in for. Since I regard the present crisis as a logical development of modernity, and modernity itself as a negation of the only reality possible in the West, we shall have to take an historical view. We shall follow the gradual replacement of actual reality in the West with the virtual kind. The main phases of this process are Renaissance humanism, the Reformation, the Enlightenment, the Industrial Revolution and the twentieth century.

We shall walk through all of those at a brisk pace, trying to understand how the formative ideas of each phase ushered in the virtual world in which we are living now. Along the way we shall be considering the economic implications of each development, for people's economic behaviour has always been sensitive to shifts of a theological, philosophical and sociological nature. Comparing, say, how Westerners conducted their economic affairs in the fifteenth century and how they conduct them today, we can see today's crisis, if not necessarily the fifteenth century, in a new light.

Then, in the second half of the book, we shall observe how all these factors have come together in our twenty-first century to produce the current near-meltdown in the West's economies. Here we shall leave the realm of matters philosophical and concentrate on some economic specifics. While at it we may have to look at a few figures, statistics and projections, so I hope you will bear with me.

In search of illustrative examples I shall look primarily, though not exclusively, to the USA and Britain – for two reasons. First, I have more personal experience of these countries than of any other in the West. Second, and more important, the USA deserves most of the blame for the crisis, and, in Western Europe, the UK is suffering perhaps the gravest consequences of it.

This will conclude the diagnostic part of this essay, by which time, one hopes, the aetiology of the disease will no longer remain a mystery. And finally, in the good tradition of Anglo-Saxon pragmatism, something to which I am privy only vicariously, I shall try to ponder what, if anything, we can do about the present situation. The conclusions I reach may be painful, but one hopes this will be the kind of pain produced by a surgeon's scalpel, rather than an assassin's knife.

If at the end of it all we have advanced our understanding, I shall have achieved what I set out to do. If not, I can only hope that at least you will enjoy reading this essay as much as I have enjoyed writing it.

'BROTHER CAN YOU PARADIGM?'

The general assumption at present is that there is no way to go but up. When the economy is in meltdown, things cannot get any worse. Any change would be for the better – or at least that is what the inveterate optimists are saying. More sober heads cite history to remind us that things can *always* get worse, and not every change can be automatically presumed to be for the better even when we start from an abysmally low point. But nobody listens to those naysayers.

Both the optimists and the naysayers tend to draw a parallel between the present situation and the Great Depression precipitated by the stock market crash of 1929, so this is as good a place to start as any. These days we have been trained by savants of every ideological hue to regard such events as *force majeure*, a sort of natural disaster. For example, our previous Prime Minister once referred to the present crisis as a 'hurricane', or in other words something for which no individual, and certainly not the PM himself, could be held responsible.

He forgot to mention that this particular hurricane was started and fanned into a disaster by him and people like him. Understandably he and his ilk would rather keep the human factor out of it. As far as they are concerned, the sun also ariseth, and the sun goeth down, and so doth the economy, driven by its own inner logic. This cyclical, naturalistic view of economic development is shared by many scholars, regardless of whether they express the inner logic in terms of class struggle or market forces.

Adam Smith only hinted at this when he first attributed demiurge powers to the market, whose invisible hand unerringly guides unwitting private individuals to public virtue. We shall return to this later, but for now let us just say that there is an obvious difference between nature and markets. The first is impersonal, the second is made up of people. Tremors in the ground are a result of a tectonic shift. Tremors in the market are a result of a shift in human behaviour, not in some nebulous paradigms so beloved of economists. If we continue to listen to them, soon we shall all have to march to the soup kitchens, singing in chorus, 'Brother, can you paradigm?'

When an earthquake strikes, it is no one's fault. But when an economy crashes, someone is always to blame. While looking for today's culprits, let us accept the obvious parallel with the Great Depression and see how far it will take us.

In that instance the fault lay mainly with the US government, specifically the quasi-independent Federal Reserve system, that had throughout the 1920s been increasing the money supply. The banks, awash with banknotes, were lending easily and cheaply, the people were borrowing avidly and mindlessly. Charleston contortions were turning mushrooming speakeasies into whirlwinds, torrents of illegal booze were flooding the Prohibition. As the 'roaring twenties' roared away, the dinner jacket became the uniform of 'happiness', the lacquered Packard its carrier. Alas, the proof came, if any was needed, that, when millions of people live on borrowed money, society lives on borrowed time.

Predictably, the virtual value of the market became disproportionately greater than its underlying real value. By the time the Federal Reserve tightened the money supply, it was too late and too much – they squeezed it to the point of strangulation. The crash followed, and massive deflation after that. Prices and incomes tumbled, industrial output went down by a third, an economy that had throughout the twenties been overdosing on cash now was starved of it to the point of fiscal anorexia.

The business world desperately craved to be propped up with wads of short-term money. Action was called for, yet this time the Fed did nothing; it twiddled its thumbs while the economy burnt. The ensuing massive panic led to a run on banks; many customers withdrew their deposits, thus further contracting the money supply. Nor would the money get back into circulation soon thereafter: more and more panic-stricken people simply stuffed their cash into coffee jars and buried them in their gardens.

What could have ended up as another slow-down, no better or worse than many others, turned into the Great Depression. The Charleston seamlessly segued into a millions-strong chorus of 'Brother, Can You Spare a Dime?' (adjusting for inflation, but staying in the same rhythm, that would be 'two bucks' today), the dinner suit gave way to dirty overalls, the lacquer peeled off the Packards. The world went bust.

Yet at first glance it would be churlish to deny that Western economies recovered after that calamity. It would seem undeniable that Western governments, first having caused the problem, then solved it. They battened down the hatches, did what they deemed necessary, and the world's economy came back with a vengeance. One has to agree: Western governments, led by the US administration, definitely did what they deemed necessary. But what exactly was it that they regarded as necessary, what did they actually do, and who was at the receiving end of that vengeance?

After the stock market crash of 1929, the world economy tottered. In response, the US administration acted on the aforementioned Guy Fawkes recipe and introduced a raft of protectionist legislation, followed a few years later by Roosevelt's New Deal. Those were dangerous remedies all right. But did they succeed in curing the desperate disease?

Here we would do well to remember that the stock market crash, supposedly the trigger of the calamity, barely made the front pages of the papers at the time. Only about two percent of all Americans owned any shares, and, people being people, those overachievers were unlikely to be viewed by the rest with excessive sympathy. In fact, when the value of those shares plummeted, most of the non-holders probably responded in a very human way by displaying the emotion that the Germans (and the more pretentious of us) call *Schadenfreude*. The crash was none of most people's concern, and the papers reacted with commensurate restraint.

The depression only began to bite after the protectionist measures went into effect. And that makes sense. As von Mises, Hayek or any Chicago economist worth his salt would have told you, the success of a reasonably free economy is determined by the consumer, which is to say by a strong, voracious demand. And what boosts the demand is free competition among suppliers, regardless of which country they come from. In such conditions they are forced to offer better products, lower prices and more efficient services. Supply-side ideas, so popular back in the 1980s, do not change this fact. Supply-side is just a way of stimulating demand. Manufacturers and other suppliers take the lead by offering the goods and services they bet people will want to buy. If the bet pays off, they win. If it does not, they lose.[3] But ultimately it is demand that decides the issue. You can only help the economy by helping the consumers, says the conventional wisdom. You cannot do so by hurting them.

This can only mean that protectionism cannot help the economy. It almost certainly will cause untold damage, by mollycoddling domestic production behind a protective wall of near-monopoly. That anyone should deem this necessary can only mean that domestic production was ineffective to begin with. Yet when its incompetence is artificially protected from more competent rivals, it will have little incentive to get its act together. Quality will go down, prices will head in the opposite direction, funds will be channelled into the least – and away from the most – productive areas, and consumers will bear the consequences.

There is now, or was at the time of the Great Depression, nothing new about any of this. Bright economists from Anne-Robert-Jacques Turgot, Adam Smith and David Ricardo onwards had

3. A century before the Great Depression, the French economist Jean-Baptiste Say formulated his law: supply generates demand. I, along with many modern economists, would be tempted to add, 'though sometimes it does not.'

known it and written about it. Thus, for example, Smith[4]: 'To give the monopoly of the home-market to the produce of domestic industry... must, in almost all cases, be either a useless or a hurtful regulation. If the produce of domestic can be brought there as cheap as that of foreign industry, the regulation is evidently useless. If it cannot, it must generally be hurtful.'

Having thus contributed to, or perhaps founded, classical *laissez-faire* economics, both Smith and Ricardo then unwittingly contributed to Marxism by espousing the labour theory of value. According to that theory, the price of a product must reflect the cash value of the labour that has gone into making it. Marx's inference took him to such harebrained ideas as surplus value and capitalist exploitation of labour as universally pertinent conditions of wealth generation. That theory has since been proved comprehensively wrong, but it is beyond my scope here to show how or why.

As with most things economic, this is self-explanatory anyway: the price of anything is determined by how much people are prepared to pay for it. All other considerations, including labour costs, are immaterial. And of course, by replacing products with brands, our virtual world has buried whatever was left of the labour theory of value ten feet under, along, alas, with better economic ideas that had until then stood the test of time. After all, it takes roughly the same amount of labour to make two identical scarves. Yet if one of them has a designer label on the back and the other has not, the difference in price may be ten-fold. Only in an insane virtual world would something like this make sense, labour theory or no labour theory.

Unfortunately, sanity was in short supply in the US administration of the time, as it is now, and its protectionist measures led to a precipitous decline in international trade. This spread the crisis all over the Western world, for – just as Smith

4. I hope my seriousness of purpose will not be undermined by a frivolous aside. A little boy once asked his mother who Adam Smith was. 'An economist,' explained the woman. 'Just like Daddy?' persisted the youngster. 'No, silly,' said the mother. 'Daddy is a *Senior* Economist.' Then again, considering the mayhem recently perpetrated by all those Senior Economists working for governments and major financial institutions, perhaps this aside is not so frivolous after all.

predicted always would be the case – other countries began to retaliate by imposing tariffs on American imports, thus hurting the USA a little and their own consumers a lot.

By 1933, the year both Franklin D. Roosevelt and Adolf Hitler came to power, the recession had turned into a worldwide depression, which was catastrophic for many in the short term. The long-term damage was done by the New Deal that for ever legitimised governmental activism in economic matters. No one heeded Edmund Burke's warning that 'the moment that government appears at market, the principles of the market will be subverted.'

Henceforth, enterprise in the West would never again be strictly, or in most countries even predominantly, private. Capitalism, if that term has ever had any serious meaning at all, was taken away from the capitalists. It was hijacked by the state in whose hands it appears to be more akin to corporatism and socialism.

For example, in the UK, the government at the time of writing controls 60 percent of the GDP, a proportion that is steadily rising. And in Northern Ireland and Wales, along with some other large chunks of today's, supposedly capitalist, Britain, the state already owns or controls about three quarters of the economy. The corresponding figure for Stalin's Russia was only about 85 percent (a mere 40 percent in today's KGB-run Russia, if you believe their data, which you probably should not), not that much higher, and yet no one ever blamed the Soviet monster for being a crypto-capitalist.

Sure enough, the New Deal did provide some temporary relief. All those giant construction projects financed out of the public purse relieved unemployment, or so it seemed. In fact, the relief fell in the domain of the virtual world, and few noticed that Roosevelt had gone far along the road towards creating the 'labour armies' so dear to Marx's heart. The scale was not so grandiose as Marx and Trotsky had wished, but already quite respectable. By the beginning of 1934 five million unemployed youngsters had been forced, on pain of losing their benefits, to toil in backbreaking labour for $1 a day (about $450 a month in 2009 dollars).

But by the standards of the virtual world this conscription drive did work for a short while, accompanied as it was by the post-natal kicking of a vast welfare state, massive bailouts of failing firms, introduction of a farrago of regulation, creation of an alphabet soup of new agencies and prodigious growth in money supply. Just like the similar measures adopted by Hitler, they got the economy going. It did not, however, go very far.

The implied parallel between Roosevelt's economics and Hitler's may upset some. After all, our press, much given to paroxysms of worship (often to be replaced by anticlimactic derision in tomorrow's issue), likes to compare the current US president with FDR. The public follows suit with its usual docile obedience, and, whenever it is brainwashed to adore someone, any scathing criticism can only be treated as blasphemy, at least initially. So in their eyes comparisons of Roosevelt's, and by inference the current president's, policies with the Nazis' go even further than simple blasphemy. If both A and B equal C, then whoever indulges in such parallels ought to be locked up for committing the ultimate sacrilege. Send out for the men in white coats. However, even as I am being dragged away kicking and screaming, allow me to defend myself by suggesting a simple experiment. Put Roosevelt's New Deal on the left, Hitler's New Order on the right and compare.

Chances are you would not be able to tell the difference. Herbert Hoover certainly could not, which is why he described the New Deal as a 'fascist measure'. And actually he was not the only one. When the programme was first introduced, the conservatives cringed, the Nazis gloated, the socialists cheered – and none of them failed to see the parallels. No wonder. The two programmes are strikingly similar, and this is only partly because they were both designed at roughly the same time and by mostly the same well-travelled people.[5] The real reason the programmes were so alike was that they were rooted in similar desiderata. For all modern governments, be that democracies, tyrannies or democratic tyrannies, have an innate need to expand their reach and increase their power, both internal and external. This need takes precedence over everything else, regardless of what the politicians' declared slogans are.

Those may be liberty, equality and brotherhood (France), dictatorship of the proletariat (USSR), supremacy of the Arian race (Nazi Germany), or pursuit of happiness, which is to say money (USA). No matter. The desire for maximum power either supersedes or at least underpins such PR ends served up for public consumption.

In other words, for all modern purposes, statism is the ultimate purpose of any state, regardless of its ideological bent, real or proclaimed. And the New Deal along with the Nazi New Order (let us not forget the Soviet Five-Year Plans either, this would be most unfair) was the ultimate extension of statism into the social and economic realms. This proved yet again that the more the state does for the economy, the more it controls it – and the more power it wields.

Put another way, the more the state does for the people, the more it will do to them. Both FDR and Hitler knew it, and hence the similarity between their economic programmes. (There are also obvious differences, such as that civil liberties were treated with more respect by FDR than by Hitler or Mussolini. But, being common

5. One such busy co-author was Gerard Swopes of General Electric, a company that distinguished itself by assisting both the Bolsheviks and the Nazis. Swopes more or less formulated Roosevelt's New Deal policy while sitting on the board of A.E.G., the German subsidiary of GE and a major backer of Hitler. Another busy programme designer was Paul Warburg of the Federal Reserve Bank of New York who was on the board of the American I. G. Farben, while his brother Max sat on the German board of the same company. The company's product line later included the Zyklon B gas, but there is no need to go into this now. And then there was Walter Teagle, also of the Federal Reserve Bank of New York, Chairman of Standard Oil of New Jersey, the company whose German subsidiary *Deutsche-Amerikanische Gesellschaft* had intimate links with the Nazis. This known Nazi sympathiser was one of the principal authors of FDR's New Deal package and also acted as economic consultant to the authors of Hitler's New Order.

knowledge, these are hardly worth mentioning. The similarities, however, are often ignored.)

From then on, modern governments have no longer been willing merely to officiate economic battles. They crave to fight them, to decide their outcome. Alas, if history teaches us anything, it is that modern states can only affect long-term economic outcomes adversely. Adam Smith knew this:

'What is the species of domestic industry which his capital can employ , every individual, it is evident, can... judge much better than any statesman or lawgiver can do for him. The statesman, who should attempt to direct private people in what manner they ought to employ their capitals, would not only load himself with a most unnecessary attention, but assume an authority which could safely be trusted, not only to no single person but to council or state whatever, and which nowhere be so dangerous as in the hands of a man who had folly and presumption enough to fancy himself fit to exercise it.'

Modern governments, specifically those that ran Western economies in the 1930s and are running them now, embody this 'dangerous folly and presumption'. But, as Smith only knew the barely post-natal modern state, he could not see in his worst nightmares the shape it would acquire in maturity. The Scot had no way of knowing that 150 years later such 'folly and presumption' would no longer be an unfortunate failing of the state, but its intended *modus operandi*. By the 1930s it was John Maynard Keynes, not Smith, who had become the economic prophet. And what mattered to the American state was the endless sea of its own power, not the dire straits into which it had steered the people.

It has to be said that the straits were as dire as they came. All in all 11,000 US banks failed in the nineteen-thirties, almost half of the total number. (Roosevelt celebrated his inauguration by adding a whole new meaning to the concept of bank holiday. He shut down all US banks for four days, to see which of them would be fit to resume trading.) Their failures led to the loss of billions of dollars in assets. In desperation bankers tried to administer their own dangerous remedy by calling in loans – only to find that most borrowers did not have money to repay. As a result, the few surviving banks stopped lending.

With no credit on offer, capital investment and construction either slowed down or completely dried up. Prices dipped again, as did incomes. Only personal debts did not, especially, and this is a paradox, when some conscientious people did try to repay them. Inflation was just round the corner, but for the time being deflation reigned supreme, and the value of every dollar still owed was going up by the day. The harder people tried to repay their debts, the greater was the deflationary pressure. In other words, the more people paid back, the more they owed in real terms.

When he became President in 1933, Roosevelt pushed government interference to an unprecedented level. He knew of course that, just as statism had largely caused the 1929 crash, so had interventionist measures made things much worse. The 'dust bowl' effect emptied the farms. Up to 25 percent of the people became unemployed. Industrial manufacturing fell by almost half, as did average family incomes. Housing starts dipped by 80 percent.

Predictably, Roosevelt's answer was to fight statism with more statism. The situation was ideally suited to the kind of social meddling for which his power-hungry loins ached. And he sensed unerringly that social and economic turmoil of crisis proportions is exactly the troubled waters in which an ideological statist can fish for more power.

Roosevelt responded to the challenge aggressively, by introducing the sort of measures I mentioned earlier and by borrowing almost as much as all previous presidents put together (by the end of his presidency the federal debt stood at $260 billion, not all of which is ascribable to the war). He also responded to it rhetorically, by launching vituperative attacks against big business that, he claimed, was solely responsible for the crisis.

The people who had displayed *Schadenfreude* earlier were now encouraged to indulge in a related emotion: envy. For most of us this unenviable sentiment is not far beneath the surface at the best of times. At the worst of times it often splashes out, scorching innocent bystanders with hot-headed action. A wave of strikes, tacitly encouraged by the government, shook the country and the rest of the Western world (apart from Germany and Italy, where their governments tended to discourage industrial action, and not just tacitly). The battle was heating up, but Roosevelt, waving the megalomaniac Tennessee Valley Authority (TVA)[6] in one hand and the National Relief Administration (NRA) in the other, rode in on his white steed and saved the day. Or at least that is what many thought.

They were wrong though. After Roosevelt's hasty and ill-advised measures had run out of steam, trouble came back in force. By 1938 unemployment was again nearing 20 percent, recession returned, and suddenly even the intellectually challenged realised that the depression had not really gone away. It had merely been camouflaged, and confirmation of this came from unexpected quarters.

Henry Morgenthau, Roosevelt's Treasury Secretary and one of the principal architects of the New Deal, admitted before the House Ways and Means Committee that the New Deal had failed: 'We have tried spending money,' he commiserated. 'We are spending more than we have ever spent before and it does not work. I say after eight years of this administration, we have just as much unemployment as when we started And an enormous debt to boot!'

Roosevelt's response was again characteristic. Rather than admitting that it had been raids on private enterprise and free trade that were at the root of the problem, he exacerbated the problem by

---

6. When Henry Wallace, America's near-communist Vice-President, accompanied by Mrs FDR, was once given a state tour of Soviet concentration camps, he compared them to 'our TVA'. He had a point, though not the one he intended. Unlike GULAG death camps 'our TVA' was not murderous – but it was indeed driven by the same statist impulse.

stepping up the attacks. In parallel he abandoned his half-hearted efforts to balance the budget and launched an even bigger spending programme, trying, in the language that has become so familiar to us, to spend his way out of trouble. Having dug himself into a hole, he spurned conventional wisdom and went on digging. The printing presses went into high gear, banknotes rolled off, government expenditure, as a percentage of GDP, tripled compared to the 1929 level. But it was all in vain – or rather it would have been all in vain, but for one widely publicised event. The Second World War.

Here I must remark that people and governments tend to feel about wars differently. Most people do not like them, but most governments do. This is not hard to understand for, as I have mentioned earlier, modern states pursue statism, and statism thrives on social and economic turmoil. The same goes, ten-fold, for war. War is the ultimate expression of the innate statism of modern states, the sustenance on which they build up their muscle mass.

Like babies, all modern states were born covered in blood. No modern state, whenever it came to life, was delivered without the midwifery of a formative war. In England, it was the Civil War. In the USA, ditto – more so even than the Revolutionary War. In Russia, ditto. In Spain, ditto. In France, the post-revolutionary Napoleonic wars. In Germany, the Franco-Prussian War. In Italy, the war of liberation from Austria. And collectively, modern statism vanquished finally and irreversibly as a result of what was perhaps Western man's greatest, and definitely stupidest, crime: the First World War. In all instances, people died so that the modern state might be born and then grow, weaned on the congealing red liquor.

Swords may sometimes be beaten into ploughshares, but this only occurs when the modern state feels it can increase, or at least maintain, its strength without having to fight a war. When it feels differently, the ploughshares will be quickly beaten back into swords. And once they have vanquished, the weapons can then be recast into the strongest chains binding the individual hand and foot.

War is the most reliable and time-proven way for a state to increase its power. That is why one ought to be on guard whenever a mighty modern state makes pacifist noises. Sheep must never take the wolf's protestations of vegetarianism at face value. If they do so, at first they are likely to be hailed by other peace-loving sheep and indeed by the wolf. For a short while they will become the model for all progressive animals to follow. But thereafter they are likely to become supper.

There exist only two reasons for modern states to refrain from fighting wars. One, they feel they do not need a war to increase their power at the time. Two, they fear they may not remain in power as a result. Neither of those conditions pertained in late-1930s America, and Roosevelt worked hard to drag the country into the war against the express wishes of the very *demos* in whose name he supposedly governed. In that FDR followed the example of Woodrow Wilson, who 20-odd years earlier had performed a similar trick for, one suspects, similar reasons.

Woodrow 'He-Kept-Us-Out-of-the-War' Wilson knew America would not become the world's dominant empire after the war unless she flexed her muscles during it. But he also knew that he could never get a declaration of war through Congress, however pliant, without risking a backlash from the electorate.

Wilson's better bet was to provoke Germany into precipitous action, so that the people would feel they were the wronged party that had to retaliate. That purpose was achieved by encouraging the House of Morgan to float war loans for Britain and by sending a steady flow of supplies across the Atlantic, which left the Kaiser's Germany no choice but to launch unrestricted submarine warfare. In that sense, one can say it was the *Lusitania* that carried Gen. Pershing to war, if by delayed action.

With that precedent to learn from, Roosevelt knew exactly how to manage a similar situation. If the Congress and the people were likely to prefer peace to war, they had to be left with no choice. To that end Roosevelt desperately hoped that either Germany or Japan would launch a pre-emptive strike, the sooner the better. Germany would not come out and play. Japan, being starved of essential raw materials by the American blockade, would.

She really did not have much choice: when in the summer of 1941 the US government suddenly froze all Japanese assets in American banks, simultaneously imposing an embargo on the export of oil, Japan's foreign trade instantly shrank by 75 percent and her oil imports by 90 percent.

Did Roosevelt merely hope for something like Pearl Harbour, or did he deliberately provoke it? This is no place to come down on either side of the debates that have raged ever since on FDR's exact role in those tragic events. Suffice it to say that, no matter how much we despise conspiracy theories, it would be hard to deny that quite a few perfectly non-theoretical conspiracies have been hatched in modern history. Russian bolshevism, for example, was one. So was Italian fascism. So was German nazism.

While Roosevelt was obviously a more benign politician than Messrs Lenin, Mussolini or Hitler, nothing in his track record or character suggests he was incapable of deviousness. And, while his methods were of necessity different from those used by his more extreme colleagues in other countries, he pursued the same ends all modern politicians do: great, preferably unlimited, power.

Roosevelt remembered that it was usually wartime leaders who went down in history as great (which is to say the most powerful) statesmen. And his place in history was important for FDR, as it is for any egotistic politician. So I would be inclined to think that in this instance the conspiracy theorists just may have a point, especially since they have a corpus of circumstantial evidence going for them[7], not to mention the old *cui bono* principle. It is also useful to

7. One such bit of evidence is the memorandum that Arthur H. McCollum, a senior officer in naval intelligence, sent to Captain Knox, Roosevelt's top military advisor, on 7 October, 1940. Having outlined the possible ways of provoking Japan into war, McCollum concludes, 'If by these mean Japan could be led to commit an overt act of war, so much the better.' Intelligence officers seldom submit reports, or especially reach conclusions, they do not think their superiors want to see. What I find amusing is that earlier in the memo McCollum describes Russia as neutral. In fact the USSR was

remember that, as I shall argue later, by then the real world was on the way out, and the virtual world on the way in.

Seeming had become the new being, appearance the new reality. More important, misconceived expediency was ousting old morality. In such circumstances people like Roosevelt, or for that matter most modern politicians, tend to be in the vanguard of a changing world. Thus, though I have no way of knowing if FDR indeed acted the way conspiracy theorists claim he did, I am unaware of any ethical barriers that could have prevented him from doing so.

By then Nazi Germany had shown the way to virtual riches by stimulating her own economy with massive infusions of capital into rearmament and public works. Following suit, Britain steadily reduced her unemployment and, once the war started, eliminated it altogether. In the USA the war also got rid of unemployment and doubled the GDP, burying the depression under an avalanche of tanks, planes and lorries.

Moreover, even the comparatively modest deprivation that Americans suffered during the war gave them a huge appetite for the good things in life directly the war ended. The appetite eventually turned into gluttony, and now we are all suffering from the ensuing reflux.

But what is important in the context of this chapter is the parallels between the Great Depression and our present difficulties. Such parallels are clearly visible in various aspects of the two calamities, both on and underneath the surface.

at the time Hitler's closest ally. It was the misnamed Non-Aggression Pact that had kicked off the Second World War. It was the two predators who had divided Europe between them. It was their two-pronged attack that had defeated Poland in 1939. Even as McCollum put pen to paper, it was planes flying on Soviet fuel that were raining on London bombs made in Russia. And it was endless trainloads of Russian strategic materials that were flowing into the veins of the Nazi military monster. But then Western intelligence services always have been inept when dealing with Russia.

We have already seen that large-scale action by the state, for as long as it remained peaceful, only succeeded in masking the depression for a while – not in ending it. It took a murderous war to do that, with almost 300,000 Americans sacrificing their lives at the altar of statism.[8]

Some of them no doubt had noble motives, but most, one suspects, just did their jobs without asking themselves the kind of questions they knew they would be unable to answer. However, whatever their motives, the net geopolitical result of their sacrifice was far from noble. By laudably assisting in the defeat of brown and black fascism, they were lamentably instrumental in handing half the world over to the red variety. Though the chromatic distinction is clear enough, one struggles to see any difference between the two in principle.

We could argue about this rather uncompromising conclusion till the economists come home. But one conclusion is indisputable: it was the war that ended the Great Depression and created a wave of consumer demand whipped up by the government's fiscal policies. This unbridled optimism, expressed in monetary terms, has carried the West on the crest of its wave ever since. Until, that is, the time when the penny dropped.

Now, if we go back a couple of pages and look at the features of the Great Depression, its causes and the measures Western governments took to combat it, we shall find more than enough grist for the mill of those who see the parallel between the 1930s and now. If you doubt that our present downfall is as precipitous, just look at the decline in the market value of the West's major financial institutions between 2007 and 2009 (in billions of dollars):

Royal Bank of Scotland: from 120 to 4.6; UBS: from 116 to 35; HSBC: from 215 to 97; BNB Paribas: from 108 to 32.5; Citigroup: from 255 to 19 (!); Goldman Sachs: from 100 to 35; Deutsche Bank: from 76 to 10.3; Credit Suisse: from 75 to 27; JP Morgan: from 165 to 85;

---

8. The Russians, who lost at least 27 million, along with the Germans, Poles and even Brits, who all suffered greater casualties than the Americans, sometimes sneer at this number. It says much about modernity that over a quarter of a million deaths can be dismissed as trifling losses.

Santander: from 116 to 64. And of course Lehman Brothers, a company holding $600 billion in assets, collapsed in September, 2008.

And the US motor industry, traditionally the bedrock of the country's economy and still accounting for 20 percent of all manufacturing jobs, was not doing much better. By the middle of 2009 both General Motors and Chrysler had filed for bankruptcy protection, having shed thousands of jobs and lost billions of dollars. It took a massive government bailout, funded by the Fed's printing press, to save the whole industry from going to the wall – for the time being.

I could extend the list of disasters *ad infinitum*, but there is no need: the picture is clear. Also clear is that both the causes of the two crises and the countermeasures taken by the governments are similar. What was then frankly called printing money is now coyly referred to as 'quantitative easing', but that is a change in words, not in meaning. The question is, how far do we think this similarity will go? Will the two parallel lines remain staunchly Euclidian and never meet at the crucible of a major war? Or can one argue that they will do a Lobachevsky and overlap at that point, with sparks flying all over the place?

I described myself earlier as a most reluctant Cassandra. In keeping with that self-image, I shall refrain from supporting either side of this argument. Let us just say for now that, given the similarity of the situation and the much publicised kinship between the key personalities involved, logic would suggest that the possibility of a similar outcome cannot be dismissed out of hand. This is to say it is entirely possible that we are risking a misfortune somewhat more grave than the routing of our pension funds.

If that is true, then we clearly have much more to fear than fear itself, in FDR's phrase. Given the technological advances of which modernity is so justly proud, the possible results of human folly can now be more catastrophic than anything we have ever seen or indeed imagined in the past. But it is not the results but the folly that interests me here. For it is human irresponsibility that has been pushing us to the brink of disaster with the kind of persistence that beggars belief and – as we are finding out the hard way – not just belief. Contemplating our irresponsibility, one is tempted to fear that Hilaire Belloc's macabre forecast of decades ago applies to our time: 'Like all our modern evils, this evil will not get better. It will get worse. The only remedy for modern evils is catastrophe.'

Now, the word 'responsibility' is etymologically linked to 'response', having to answer for one's actions. But this concept is meaningless in the absence of an authority to which we can proffer such answers. It is from this angle that I shall now consider our present ordeal.

METAPHYSICS COMES BEFORE PHYSICS

Some eternal optimists may deny that we are heading for a catastrophe. But no matter how upbeat or misguided they are, even the fully paid-up members of that club will have to admit that we are in quite some trouble already. To refuse to do so would be defying the evidence before our very eyes, and normal people seldom do this. The mess is here and it is up to us to clean it up. Yet obviously we cannot even begin to think how to do so before we have understood how we got into trouble in the first place.

Just as obviously, we shall have to consider both history and man's nature as the possible causes. The latter is more or less immutable, the former is not, and, depending on how history develops, human nature reveals itself in various ways. The way it reveals itself these days has created the empirical problem we are trying to analyse and, ideally, would like to solve.

Alas, while trying to solve the empirical problem, we run headlong into an intellectual one. For neither history nor especially man's nature lends itself to simplistic reductions. The drama of human existence is not a single theme played against the background accompaniment of history. It is rather a fugue where multiple strands meet at counterpoint – only to go their separate ways later and then reunite to end up weaving a uniform aural canvas. The problem is that in an actual fugue this complexity contains the entirety of the infinite sub-complexities springing from the imagination of a great composer. But in the metaphorical fugue of life, the multiple strands at best only hint at the mystery behind them.

In attempting to advance their respective fields of study, a musicologist enjoys a considerable advantage over a philosopher in that he has to contend with one idiom only. Analysing the technical aspect of a fugue thus presents a difficult task, but not one likely to defeat an expert.

However, such analysis alone will not explain why some fugues, say by Vivaldi, are merely competent, while some others, say by Bach, are sublime. Seeking such an explanation, the musicologist would have to leave the technical world of notes and grapple with the origin of inspiration. Put another way, he would have to swap physics for metaphysics, a task that has historically defeated all but a handful of musical analysts. Most do not even take it on, feeling they do not have to.

A philosopher does not have this luxury. The challenge confronting him is much tougher – both in the physics and metaphysics of his task. Not only does he deal with temporal and spatial relationships horizontally, but he also must understand their vertical development and interconnection over history. Nor does he deal with a mystery wholly contained within tones, an entity describable in physical terms. His material is man, and we know now that science alone does not come close to uncovering the mystery of this creature.

Thus, before he has even begun to step any further away from his immediate object of study than a musicologist has to step away from the letter of the score, a philosopher has already run into metaphysical conundrums, of the kind that stonewalled all those Decades of the Brain and Genome Projects. The philosopher finds himself at sixes and sevens before he has even had time to consider the inspiration behind man's actions, which asks so many metaphysical questions that only metaphysics could possibly answer them.

This is why whenever we attempt to analyse any aspect of human behaviour we realise that we constantly have to backtrack step by step to human nature. Economics too makes us do so, as does any other discipline that deals with human behaviour.

We have agreed that the present crisis, just like its predecessors, has been caused by blunders. This holds true with whichever group we nominate as our main culprits: those government officials who claim that spending, indefinitely and infinitely, more than the state earns makes sound economic sense; those central bankers who thoughtlessly increase money supply and keep interest rates artificially low to encourage household borrowing; those commercial bankers who think they can get away for ever with accumulating risky debts a hundred times greater than their total capital; those upwardly mobile desperados who mortgage themselves to the hilt and borrow to the limit of their numerous credit cards with nary a thought for the future.

But why are they so reckless these days specifically? Why did they not act in the same way, or at least on the same scale, a mere 100 years ago, or, at a stretch, 50 or even 30? Why would a Florentine banker of the fifteenth century never have offered an unsecured loan to pay for someone's holiday, and a British banker of the twenty-first century would? Why did the statesmen and economists of the eighteenth century know it is silly to run the state on one set of economic principles and their own households on another? And not just the eighteenth – here is what Abraham Lincoln wrote in 1859:

'You cannot bring prosperity by discouraging thrift. You cannot strengthen the weak by weakening the strong. You cannot help the poor by destroying the rich. You cannot establish sound security on borrowed money. You cannot keep out of trouble by spending more than you earn.'

In other words the little rules of good housekeeping apply at the grand level of an overall economy. Why do our economists, armed with their computer models and the jargon of macros, micros and ratios, not know this, or at least refuse to acknowledge it?

In fact, they throw their hands up in horror whenever they hear something along the lines of the words of Adam Smith, who was armed only with sound common sense: 'What is prudence in the conduct of every private family, can scarce be folly in that of a great kingdom.' As far as modern economists are concerned, the old man did not know his micros from his macros. A remedial course at Wharton or the LSE would have done him no end of good.

Witness, for example, a typical statement by Samuel Brittan, the *Financial Times* economics guru: 'Since my undergraduate days, I have been pointing out that a government budget is not the same as that of an individual ' He is right about that; it is not, not these days. That is precisely the trouble. Before making his pronouncements Sir Samuel would have been well-advised to reread his David Copperfield, where Mr Micawber gets it just right: 'Annual income twenty pounds, annual expenditure nineteen pounds nineteen and six, result happiness. Annual income twenty pounds, annual expenditure twenty pounds ought and six, result misery.' Why did Dickens, untrained in the recondite wisdom of the economic science, understand what the modern economist does not?

As each subsequent 'why' takes us further and further back, subdividing into uncountable smaller questions along the way, we have two options only. One would be to abandon our pursuit altogether before we either go mad or else get so tangled up that we shall end up tying ourselves in knots. The other would be to try to reduce all those exponentially multiplying 'whys' to an umbrella question: Why has the world, which is to say man's behaviour, changed so much over the last few centuries, and especially the last few decades? The first option is tantamount to admitting defeat without even putting up a fight. This being too cowardly for words, let us try the second option and see if things become any clearer.

I have mentioned earlier that every attempt to describe man in purely physical terms has hitherto failed so comprehensively as to suggest it will never succeed. The answer to the mystery of man must lie in metaphysics,[9] that elusive something without which man's actions would be as indistinguishable from a chimpanzee's as are their biochemical, molecular and genetic make-ups. In fact, an

---

9. The word 'metaphysics' originally meant simply 'after Physics'. It was first used by Aristotle as the title of a chapter that in his book followed one entitled 'Physics'. Using the word as I do now, it would be closer in meaning to 'before physics'

answer to any serious question has to be launched from the platform of a sound metaphysical premise, the starting point of any ratiocination that in philosophy sometimes acts the way an axiom acts in mathematics, and sometimes the way a hypothesis acts in science.

We can indeed go so far as to suggest that even the underlying hypotheses from which science proceeds are usually based on a metaphysical premise rather than empirical observation. One such premise is the unshakeable belief in causality, the certainty that every physical event has a physical cause. Another is that the world is uniform, which is why scientific laws operate, and mathematics applies, universally.

That understanding did not exist in the Hellenic world, where, presaging Turgot's and Smith's thoughts on the division of labour, people had to have a Pantheon full of gods, each responsible for a small part of nature. Yet without this understanding Galileo would not have been able to claim that, 'The book of nature is written by God in the language of mathematics.' That aphorism sounds perfectly plausible, and yet it came not from a series of observations but from a metaphysical premise.

Metaphysics does not have to spring from faith in any confessional sense. It does, however, have to be correct, for a faulty metaphysical premise invariably undermines even secular ideas. In fact, it is practical results that can as often as not either vindicate the premise or disprove it. The proof of the metaphysical pudding is in the empirical eating. Conversely, if we look deeply enough, we shall realise that the most spectacular practical errors mankind ever makes all come from a metaphysical blunder that then triggers off a chain reaction of folly. Our present crisis is no exception.

In his *Essay on Metaphysics* the philosopher R.G. Collingwood (d. 1943) goes so far as to ascribe the fall of the Roman Empire to this cause. A clash between an increasingly monotheistic philosophy and an obstinately polytheistic people deprived the Romans of their spiritual backbone. They began to question the very convictions on which their society was based, and before too long they were no longer sure what those convictions were.

The Romans no longer understood their own society. They no longer knew what role they themselves had to play in their community, or what role their community played in the general scheme of things. Mired in confusion, they resorted to decadence. Misguided in their overall direction, they got lost in a warren of blind alleys. They tried to probe every which way, but there was no way out – they were running in place. Fatigue set in. Step by step, the stuffing went out of their previously taut muscles, and they fell prey to barbarian attacks. That is the aetiology of the senility and erosion of will to which historians usually, and correctly, attribute the demise of Rome.

Collingwood concludes (in *The Principles of Art*): 'Civilisations sometimes perish because they are forcibly broken up by the armed attack of enemies without or revolutionaries within; but never from this cause alone. Such attacks never succeed unless the thing that is attacked is weakened by doubt as to whether the end which it sets before itself, the form of life which it tries to realise, is worth achieving. On the other hand, this doubt is quite capable of destroying a civilisation without any help whatever. If the people who share a civilisation are no longer on the whole convinced that the form of life which it tries to realise is worth realising, nothing can save it.'

Parallels with our own situation cry out to be made, and many writers have responded to that cry. Like Rome, we too are reaping the poisoned harvest of metaphysical folly. It is the grave error we made in having jettisoned the sound theocentric metaphysics on which Western civilisation was based in the first place.

In its stead we have put forth the anthropocentric metaphysics that began with Renaissance humanism, developed through the Reformation and Enlightenment, and culminated in the manic-depressive relativism of post-modernity. Moving man from the periphery of God's world to the centre of his own, this hubristic elevation of self to a God-like status destroyed the precarious metaphysical balance on which the West rested – with consequences similar to those suffered by the Romans.

We too are no longer certain of our fundamental convictions. We too have replaced stern resolve with decadence. We too have lost the will to defend ourselves against even a theoretically weaker enemy. The major difference so far is that we have not yet had this point hammered home by a barbarian onslaught. But few are the optimists who maintain that such a development is improbable. Even fewer are the realists who point out that the barbarians have already attacked and won. Except that in our case the vandals came from inside, not outside, our city walls.

Metaphysics is the basis of all knowledge of life, for non-believers as much as for the faithful. This is a statement of fact, not of faith. For, even during its most violent swerves, human life never skids too far away from human nature. The two are irrevocably linked by a metaphysical chain, and that makes metaphysics an historical science. There have existed many determinist philosophies and creeds trying to obscure that link behind what they described as historical inevitability. But a closer look through the murky glass of history will always discern human nature shining through. That is why sound understanding of it is essential to organising this life and, if you happen to believe in it, preparing for the next.

The understanding of anything is at base a satisfactory answer to a question, either overt or implied. Thus, it is impossible to understand music without first answering the question, 'What is music?' We shall never understand morals unless we answer the question, 'What is morality?' And any cohesive understanding of man's nature has to be an answer to the question, 'What is man?' All such answers can only be metaphysical because the questions are metaphysical. That is why even the likes of Richard Dawkins and other such turgidly strident God-haters make a metaphysical statement in their very denial of metaphysics.

In that sense materialism is not really atheism, and certainly not faithlessness. The very concept of matter infinite in space and time is an article of faith, not knowledge.[10] However paradoxical this may sound to people brainwashed to believe that atheism is more scientific than faith, belief in the non-existence of God is as fideistic as belief in his existence. As neither is empirically provable, 'evolutionism' is no less hypothetical than 'creationism' – it is impossible for us to observe the root processes. All we can do is arrive at certain suppositions on the basis of the empirical data observable at present.

Moreover, unlike metaphysical philosophers, materialists seem ever more prepared not to let facts interfere with their beliefs. Ideological Darwinists lead the way, but anyone who reads any popular book even on modern physics will find ample support for this observation. Let us just take one such book, *The Trouble with Physics* by the American scientist Lee Smolin (Allen Lane 2006).

What makes this work particularly telling is that Prof. Smolin makes no bones about his being a dedicated atheist. Throughout the book he mocks religion, what with its reliance on blind faith rather than hard data. And yet, strewn over every chapter are little pearls along these lines (the emphases are mine): 'Unfortunately, M-theory remains a tantalising conjecture. It's tempting to believe it. At the same time, in the absence of a real formulation, it is not really a theory – *it is a conjecture about a theory we would love to believe in.*'

10. This particular faith is not only irreligious but also downright anti-scientific. After all, the First Law of Thermodynamics (and it is a law, not, like Darwinism, a theory) says that energy, and consequently matter, cannot appear out of nowhere. It cannot therefore be infinite – nothing comes out of nothing (*ex nihilo nihil fit*), as Christians used to say and physicists confirm. In general, materialists claiming to worship at the altar of reason show consistent and most lamentable lapses of logic. This is understandable, for the metaphysical premise from which they proceed is a logical (and scientific) solecism.

Or, if you will forgive a slightly longer passage elsewhere in the book, 'In the two string revolutions, *observation played almost no role*. As the number of string theories grew, most string theorists *continued to believe* in the original vision of a unique theory that gave unique predictions for experiments, but *there were no results that pointed in that direction*, and a few theorists had worried all along that the unique theory would never emerge. Meanwhile, the optimists insisted that *we must have faith...*'

The message of this and countless other books is clear enough. The supposed conflict between faith and science is not so straight-forward as we have been led to believe.

Thus, the opposition of the two metaphysical poles is opposition not between religion and science but between two faiths. One of them is based on God's revelation given by methods both natural (through the possibility of perceiving much of his creation experimentally) and supernatural (through the Scripture and church tradition). The other is based on nothing but man's own fanciful speculation. As such, it is not even so much faith as superstition.

As I have mentioned earlier, even scientists declaring them-selves to be atheists, and trying to use science to vindicate their atheism, nonetheless start from the metaphysical premise of accept-ing the existence of rational natural laws. If they wish to be logical, then, while rejecting the existence of a rational law-giver, they are forced to ascribe rational behaviour to nature itself. That is the most primitive pantheism, and only in our virtual world can it pass for serious thought. Strip their frenzied harangues bare of scientific cant, and they descend to the intellectual level of a prehistoric shaman.

It would be foolhardy to deny that, whichever metaphysical option we may choose, we are guided in our choice by emotional need, not just a cold-blooded weighing of intellectual pros and cons. But theocentric metaphysics offers much greater rewards in either area.

The idea of having been created and guided through life by a loving, merciful and self-sacrificial God has to appeal to most people's emotions more readily that the notion of man's descent from a single-cell organism via an unsavoury mammal that looks like a ghastly caricature of a human being. And intellectually, a thinker who starts from the theocentric premise will be able to explain next to everything that matters, while his anthropocentric counterpart will explain next to nothing.

The theist will be able to get closer to an understanding of what makes us human. For man is demonstrably not just so many atoms arranged in a recognisable physical shape. He is not merely an animal obsessed with the passing on of his genes. He is not only a brighter primate than an ape or a smarter mammal than a dog. He is the sole creature on earth endowed with what believers describe as the immortal soul and others may see as 'consciousness', 'mentality', 'spirit' 'mind' or other variations on that theme. A metaphysical aspect, in other words. And even when scientists show, credibly, that other creatures may also possess something similar, they have to admit that only man's life is governed by it.

Unlike other parts of nature, we do not merely function according to the law of causality. Man's history cannot be predetermined because man himself is not. (I shall spend some time discussing the issue of predestination later, as this is critical to our understanding of modern economics.) An animal, vegetable or mineral has no choice in its destiny. It cannot break out of the predetermined rut of its chemical or biochemical makeup. Man can do so because he possesses both the will and the ability to make free choices. In a world ruled by causality he seems to be an envoy from another world, one governed by freedom.

Consequently, the freer the man the more human he is, and in order to remain free he not only has to have freedom to choose but also valid options to choose from – and a reliable idea of which options are indeed valid and worth pursuing. It follows logically that a theist is freer than a materialist. For in every situation the former has the free choice of following either God's commandments or his own passions, which freedom is denied the latter.

Freedom of choice is what distinguishes man from beast, making all physical similarities between them a matter of trivial curiosity for those interested in petty atavisms. The nature of this uniqueness of man means it is metaphysics that determines his behaviour both now and in history. And it is man's behaviour (assisted or not, depending on your beliefs, by divine providence) that determines everything else, certainly including economics. Thus if we do not understand metaphysics, we understand nothing. And neither shall we ever learn anything worth knowing – anything that will help us to avoid making the same mistakes we have always made.

After four centuries of intensive enquiry, scientists are only now arriving at a comprehensive picture of how the various physical aspects of man fit together. But when it comes to man's unique driving force, they are no closer to such understanding now than they were centuries ago. To those scientists who value integrity above ideology, it has been clear for quite some time that not only man but also animals and even some particles of matter are at least partly driven by factors for which there cannot be a physical explanation.

For example, the zoologist Konrad Lorenz observed that a gosling just breaking out of its eggshell regards as its mother not the goose that had laid the egg but the first creature it sees – including a human. That means the bird is born with an inbred abstract concept of a mother, which it then relates to a concrete being. If even a bird seems to be born equipped with abstract givens, then it is impossible to accept any theory attributing man's behaviour solely to his physical make-up and environment.

Therefore, any true knowledge of man, and by inference of his economic behaviour, has to be based on a sound metaphysical premise. We had this knowledge in the past but have since lost it – partly because we have wrongly relied on the scientists to lead the way, and they have proved unable to do so. It follows that, if we wish to regain our erstwhile knowledge, metaphysics is worth another look, especially after history, both ancient and recent, has shown how brutally ignorance of it can be punished.

In pursuing our analysis we shall have to rely increasingly on the mental tools that go beyond common sense. Common sense cannot lead us to as many answers in metaphysics as it can in economics. For common sense can only tell us that, if A equals B, and B equals C, then A equals C. It cannot tell us what the A, B and C really mean.

The simple syllogism can be worked out logically and understood commonsensically. But the ultimate meaning behind it can only be grasped at a higher level, although we can still use common sense as a ladder to get halfway there. As we climb up, the important thing to remember is that, though one can get away with an empirical miscalculation every now and then, a metaphysical error will never go unpunished.

THERE ARE ONLY TWO WAYS TO GO

So what are the metaphysical options available to us in the West as answers to the all-important question: What is man? Historically, there have been many, but over the last few centuries they have been noticeably reduced to two. Each of them, however, is an umbrella covering multiple gradations; each can act as the starting point of our life's choices.

Option One is Christian, or Judaeo-Christian if you would rather: we were created in God's image. This makes man qualitatively different from all other animals. Although other creatures also have a role to play in the general scheme of things, man alone was singled out to fulfil a mission assigned by God. As this mission is eternal, it does not end with physical death. Thus there is no such thing as a happy end to one's life. If it is to be happy, it is not the end. I shall henceforth refer to this option as *the first metaphysical premise.*

Option Two is materialist: the living cell, which over billions of years was to become man, appeared as a biochemical accident of some kind, we are not quite sure which. A man lives his three-score and ten and then becomes fertiliser. In that he is no different from other living organisms, though while still alive he is manifestly cleverer than most. Let us call this option *the second metaphysical premise.*

Although the East offers other options as well, these are the only two positive metaphysical premises available to us in the West. We can safely disregard others, such as agnosticism. The agnostic has not really made a choice different from our two; his claim is that he has wisely refrained from making any. However, in most cases our agnostic friend is not being honest. In reality, he has made a choice but tries to hedge his bets by not owning up to it.

An agnostic is at heart an anthropocentric who lacks nerve, or else an atheist who lacks logic. There is no difference between them, only a distinction. But even if we accept an agnostic at his word, the difference between him and a self-admitted materialist is negligible in practical terms. Neither is sure how the world came into being, though the atheist may foolishly claim that he is; both reject the first metaphysical premise. What separates them is style, not substance; temperament rather than essence.

At this point one is reminded of a youngster who is lost somewhere in the countryside. By chance he runs into a crusty local smoking his pipe by the roadside. The old man mulls over a desperate plea for directions and then answers, 'Well, I wouldn't start from here.' If you fear we have found ourselves in a similar situation, in this instance being unable to get to our present economic plight from the starting point of a metaphysical premise, consider this. Our behaviour in general, and our economic behaviour in particular, depends largely, in many cases entirely, on the option we choose.

Accepting this has nothing to do with religion. We do not have to believe in divine providence to know that if we take the M1 out of London, we shall be travelling north, while the M4 will take us west. We are free to choose either road, but once we have made our choice we can only travel one way. Similarly we may choose one metaphysical premise or the other, but we must do so in the knowledge that the choice will not stay merely theoretical for long. Metaphysics has far-reaching practical ramifications, for it is in a way an applied science. What I am attempting to do here is to apply it to economics, and the task is not unduly hard.

If we believe that, once born, we shall never die but live for ever, then this belief has to change our views not only on death but also on life. Our attitude to life becomes that of a freeholder, not a temporary lodger; we are less likely to treat it with neglect. In a way, life becomes more frightening than death. After all, nothing we do is secret; every one of our actions is judged by an authority who may not allow us to cop a plea.

Though, compared to eternity, our existence on earth is risibly short, every little thing we do may mould our life in infinity – a daunting thought. Yet it is also a glorious thought: life will never end. It will only be transformed into a different kind of life and, if we do not mess up too badly while still here, it will be blissfully happy. There is death in life, but then there is also life in death.

Thus our economic activity, though variously important, cannot become *all*-important. If it does, we shall run into many moral dilemmas that will surely gore us with their horns. Yes, we want to live without much deprivation, we would rather be reasonably comfortable while still on earth – but only if the pursuit of such comfort does not jeopardise our life in eternity.

As our earthly life is to us no more than the dress rehearsal, with death as the first night, then this has to influence our behaviour either wholly or at least partly. Going against this belief would be not only blasphemous but actually stupid. Indeed, who in his right mind would sacrifice eternal bliss for a few passing pleasures? Or, more generally, who would jeopardise a higher value for the sake of a lower one?

If, on the other hand, we believe that our life starts at birth and ends at death, then we may very well act in a different way. We shall not be able to see our time on earth as the dress rehearsal – it will constitute not just the first night but the whole run. Our lives will be committed not to serving an outside authority infinitely higher than ourselves, but only to satisfying our own passions. Thus it will be natural for most of us to seek as much pleasure as we can cram into a limited lifespan.

If our existence is an accident ending in death, then it is the *process* of life that is its highest meaning. The aim then is to squeeze as much as possible out of every moment. Any self-limitation of passions becomes illogical. Anything that restricts one's pleasures goes against the essence of one's life. The polarity of good and bad is replaced by useful and useless. The worst sin stops being sinful if it brings much pleasure. And since, contrary to the popular truism, what we shall define as the best things in life are far from free, we shall have to pursue aggressively the kind of happiness that is expressible in money.

This is not to deny that the specifics of such egotistical aspirations may vary within a broad range. For some their notion of happiness may include nothing but fast cars, for others fast women, for others fast food, for still others first editions of Byron's poems. No matter. Whatever our passions are, however base or elevated they may be, we neither will nor can impose any conscious restraint upon them.

We may sense that some passions are less praiseworthy than others, but such petty concerns would not slow us down for long. Life is too short for self-laceration. As we only live once, we need to put ourselves in a position where the thirst of our passions will be slaked, and ideally at as young an age as possible.

This philosophy of life will certainly affect, if not necessarily determine, our economic behaviour. In one sense money is now the means: by exchanging it for physical necessities and pleasure we fulfil the chief desideratum of life. In another sense money also becomes the end. For one thing, the amount of pleasure to be had in this world seems limitless (it really is not, but we seldom learn this early in life), and so the amount of money we need in order to pursue it also has to tend towards endlessness, especially since the relative value of money constantly goes down.

Thus our economic behaviour has to assume a much greater importance, to a point where it may override everything else. Also, since most things we seek in life can be bought, money also serves as the measuring stick of our success and consequently our perception of self-worth. Pursuit of money becomes so important that the morality of virtue is often pushed aside by the morality of utility.

If the danger of punishment can be safely avoided, then – on our scale of values – it would be stupid of us not to do whatever it takes to make our lives more enjoyable, which is to say more fulfilling in our materialistic terms. Thus what is stupid to the second type is intelligent to the first, and vice versa.

The diversion in their ethical protestations is less clear-cut: one would find it hard to say, and impossible to prove, that, if probed, the two types would offer different ideas on what is and what is not moral. Their actions may be something else again, but their pronouncements on morality will be roughly similar. Even if they are unfamiliar with the Ten Commandments, few are the materialists who will regard murder, theft or perjury as acceptable. Even fewer are those who would own up to holding such permissive views.

That is why so many serious thinkers denied any link between morality and religion. Aristotle, Smith and Kant, for example, believed that moral sense is mostly innate and therefore independent of any beliefs. We are born with our morality the way we are born with our gall bladders.

In Christendom, St Thomas Aquinas adapted the Aristotelian doctrine of natural law to the Christian concept of divine law. Actually divine law is easy enough to understand: it is unequivocal because it is explicitly laid down in the Scripture, both proscriptively, as vices to avoid (mainly the Old Testament) and prescriptively, as virtues to seek (both Testaments). That is why divine law is free of any relativity; it is absolute. Natural law, on the other hand, when it is not merely a synonym for divine law, may mean something different to its proponents: it is not so much theological as physio-logical, something innate.

This view is hard to accept on many levels, no matter how much one may venerate those who held it, Kant, to name the most shining example. Here is one objection: it does not explain the cultural, historical and individual differences in concepts of morality. Our gall bladders have been always and everywhere the same, but what is moral to one group of people at one time may be wicked to another group at another time. Divine law does not change; things we regard as natural do.

For example, Plato and Aristotle, both moral philosophers of some note, extolled the virtue of slavery, an institution that their contemporaries considered natural but most of us today find abhorrent. One can come up with endless other examples of this type. Unlike Biblical kings or Muslims, we think polygamy wrong. Unlike most of today's people, most Victorians thought abortion wrong. In the West, the death penalty had been considered moral until the mid-twentieth century, at which point it got to be deemed morally unacceptable in most places.

In other words, if man has an innate moral law within him, this law is oddly flexible: the secular view on what is moral changes from one age to the next, from one society to another and even from one individual to another. Add and multiply all those changes, and Kant's moral law begins to look more like an expedient than an imperative.

As many other such notions, this has to come down to free will: if we believe in God, then it goes without saying that he created morality along with everything else. However, a man's choice of a moral path remains free, and different people exercise this freedom in different ways at different times. Our nature is not a moral guide employed in eternity; only God's nature is. That is why only religion can provide a universal set of immutable moral criteria.

But even taking temporal differences out of the argument, our common sense, all by itself, can lead us towards the view that religion is indispensable to morality. If we feel that every good thing we do is a particle of the absolute good we strive to share in eternity, we are more likely (though of course not guaranteed) to act morally than if we proceed from our own inward conviction only.

Observation suggests that inward convictions based on nothing but our own selves are more likely to break down under pressure. It is hard to escape the conclusion that, if we ride the wave of self-centred morality, at some point we shall have to sail for the safe haven of moral relativism. One has to conclude that morality can conquer on earth only if it comes from heaven.

However, we obviously ought not to separate the two types, the believer and the materialist, into stark extremes. Not everyone who proceeds from the first metaphysical premise is a virtuous, disinterested paragon of goodness. Not everyone who follows the second is a dishonest, money-grubbing hedonist. In fact, many materialists have strong metaphysical passions as well. They may, for example, be avid readers or art lovers. But even for most of such people the fact that their lives will be wholly dedicated to indulging their passions will not change appreciably depending on what those passions are.

Similarly, many believers may want material goods as well, and some will even crave them – at least until they suddenly realise that, though they wanted to go west, they are actually on the northbound M1 somewhere between Nottingham and Sheffield, and driving in a wrong direction fast. If they were serious about their original travel plans, they will have to turn around and go back. In other words, if we follow the first road over a lifetime, we shall usually, though possibly not always, act in one way; if we follow the second, in another.

The same applies to the complex interplay between the state and the individual. The follower of the first metaphysical premise believes his life is eternal. He also knows from history books that the life of a state is not: even extremely successful ones only ever lasted between 1,000 and 1,500 years, and most of the others considerably less time than that.

Compared to eternity, this stretch seems tinier than a speck of dust would appear next to the universe. The individual will therefore perceive himself and others to be more significant than the state and for that reason alone will never accept its tyranny. He is transcendent, the state transient. So he can only regard the state as his servant, not his master. If the state's actions run contrary to this understanding, then the believer may either resist it or pretend to be going along to protect himself from persecution. But inwardly he will never acquiesce.

At the same time, the follower of the materialist premise may well accept tyranny more readily. After all, his lifespan is much shorter than that of the state. The state had existed before his birth and will happily survive his death. That is why when it is communicated to him, overtly or implicitly, that he is but the material out of which the state is built, then, no matter how much he may loathe the idea, he will find it hard to come up with a strong argument against it while at the same time remaining a staunch materialist. Appeals to individual sovereignty ring hollow outside of Judaeo-Christian metaphysics.

That is why John F. Kennedy's most famous entreaty ('Ask not what your country can do for you; ask what you can do for your country!') could only have impressed a modern society that had lost its metaphysical roots. Replace 'country' with 'state', and the exact reversal of this statement would have made more sense to anyone proceeding from the first metaphysical premise. Would you not rather hear something like 'Ask not how you can serve the state; ask how the state can serve you'? Would this not be closer to the principles on which all Western states were constituted?

However, given their metaphysical allegiances, it is natural that the crowd roared with delight at Kennedy's subversive declaration – and also that he had to make it in the first place. For what is true of our two hypothetical individuals is also true of the state. We have already agreed that words like 'the state' are but the shorthand for the people manning the institutions that collectively add up to a larger entity. Therefore the state too follows the metaphysical road these people have embarked on.

Here one is reminded of a Sherlock Holmes story, where the great detective solves his case because he knows that at a moment of danger a woman will always first try to save her most treasured possession. Similarly, no person and certainly no government official will sacrifice a higher end for the sake of a lower one. Plato confirms this: 'No one willingly goes to meet evil or what he thinks to be evil. To make for what one believes to be evil, instead of making for the good, is not, it seems, in human nature, and when faced with the choice of two evils, no one will choose the greater when he might choose the less.'

Thus, when he finds himself in power, a believer is more likely to use it for the benefit of other people. After all, his mission is to serve God by serving the public, and he knows that even if some misdeed may escape the people's judgment, it will not escape God's. On the other hand, a materialist has made a different metaphysical choice: he serves himself and no one else (his family may or may not be regarded as an extension of himself). If in the process of feathering his own nest he also drops a few feathers into other people's, fine. But this could only be a fortuitous outcome of his actions, not the sole intended one.

Since their definitions of intelligence differ, the two gentlemen will apply different types of thinking to their task. And that is precisely what is critical here: the type, not the acuity, of thinking. The self-serving materialist may have a higher IQ than the believer, and some people may mistakenly think this would automatically make him better at his government job. That is not so: the only thing his sharp mind will enable him to do better is using his position in pursuit of self-interest.[11] Getting back to our motorway metaphor, if you are supposed to get to the West Country but drive your Ferrari north on the M1, you will be beaten to your destination by an old Morris Minor chugging along on the westbound M4.

(Towards the end of this essay you will find in Appendix 1 the chapter titled *A Footnote on Plato*. There I expand on the importance of metaphysics by using the example of the Athenian to show how even one of the greatest minds in history can be led astray by a faulty metaphysical premise.)

A high IQ is something people are born with. The type of thinking (and character) that is essential for public service has to be nurtured over a lifetime. Whether this can be achieved by someone not trained accordingly from early childhood is a difficult question, and I shall try to grapple with it later, when talking about the importance of hierarchies. It is the two metaphysical premises that interest us now, and one can make a few observations that again have to do only with historical facts, not faith.

The first and the most important observation is that it was one metaphysical premise that gave birth to the traditional Western world, and the other that gave birth to the modern world. Thus the word 'Western' has lost its erstwhile metaphysical, and therefore cultural, connotation and acquired instead one that is almost purely geographic or, at a stretch, economic. In any other sense it has to be replaced by the word 'modern'.

Nowhere is this distinction clearer than in the relative importance of the economy. The Western states of the past saw their task not in building a strong economy but in creating conditions in which each individual could pursue the salvation of his soul. Economy was understood as a means to that end, and not a

11. I wrote this shortly before the great scandal of British MPs' expenses became public knowledge. That gave me little reason to change my mind – and much reason to bewail my tardiness in publishing this comment.

particularly important one. However, for modern states the economy, to borrow a sports maxim, is not just everything – it is the only thing.

The shift from the first premise to the second was gradual, and for a couple of centuries they overlapped. But such co-existence could not remain peaceful in perpetuity. At some point the human type formed by the second premise had to make its victory absolute – it was too unsure of its own strength to stop halfway, with the adversary still breathing. When this happened, the first metaphysical premise was lost as a social dynamic. It became a matter of antiquarian, or at best minority, interest.

With that in mind, we can now look in greater detail at the metaphysical premise on which the West once rested. The past tense is deliberate here: having built its civilisation on a rock-solid foundation, the West then undermined it. This has had a number of practical consequences that went far beyond metaphysics, religion or philosophy. Unless we come to grips with this process, we shall never understand the present crisis.

THE DIALECTIC OF THE WEST

What then, specifically, is the metaphysical premise that we once had and have since lost? Since we are trying to understand an empirical problem facing us all, the answer to this question has to be factual. Mercifully, the facts are in an easily accessible public domain.

The metaphysical premise that lies at the foundation of the Western world is Christian. Even the rankest atheists, if they are honest and intelligent observers, will concede that our civilisation is rooted in the event that almost passed unnoticed in Palestine two millennia ago but has since shaped the world. Christianity is the cause; our civilisation, the effect.

This is not to imply that there have not been other inputs. Just as it takes more than the foundation to erect a building, so has the Western world always imported some prefabricated components. It could even be argued that the West itself sprang from the fusion of the Hellenic and Jewish souls. In fact, using the fashionable vocabulary, we could describe Christendom as an asset-stripping civilisation. From the very start it was ever ready to accept what it found useful in other religions or philosophies and discard what it deemed inappropriate. But what is critical to us here is that all influential imports reached our civilisation by having been incorporated into Christianity first.

It was through Christianity that the imports had a formative effect on the West, sometimes good, sometimes less so. Primary among such influences was Greek philosophy, first of Plato, later of Aristotle. That, in its turn, acted as a conduit for the wisdom of the East, with which the Hellenic world had been in close contact for quite some time. The appetite of early Christianity for Hellenism is easy to understand. After all, the sacral, and consequently earthly, mission of Christianity was to convert the world. That would have been impossible to do without a thorough understanding of the world, and the Scripture alone could not exhaust everything that went into acquiring such understanding.

A philosophy was needed, it was indispensable, and yet the apostles and their friends were not scholars – most of them were fishermen. Apart from Luke the physician, and possibly John, only Paul among them had a sound, which at that time meant Hellenic, education. That is why both Paul, and especially the erudite Fathers of the Church in the next few centuries, had to work out the theological conundrums of their faith by often adopting not only the methodology but also some conclusions of Platonic philosophy. The task was less than straightforward: the metaphysical essence of Platonism, while sharing some common elements with Christianity at its periphery, was alien to it at its core. Joining it with Christ's passion so that the seams did not show was never going to be easy.

At this point, you may object that we are after all supposed to be discussing the very practical crisis we are facing. Thus what should interest us here is not so much Christian metaphysics as the practical make-up of Christendom. This objection would be valid if the latter had not come from the former. But it did. Or, to phrase more precisely, Christian metaphysics was the lens that refracted the person of Jesus Christ onto the practical world, dramatically changing its shape as a result.

This is an historical fact, and must be recognised as such even by non-believers. It was as if the world had been started anew. The very concept of reality was turned upside down, and with it the morals, laws and social dynamics that had been hitherto taken for granted. Gods were abandoned for God, and the deities of the old cults became the demons of the new faith.

The point cannot be made too strongly that it is the person of Christ, rather than just his teaching that turned our founding creed into a universal religion. Christianity is not so much the teaching *by* Christ as the teaching *about* Christ (when it comes from Jesus himself, it is of course both). Most parts of Christ's teaching, what he actually said, can be found elsewhere, *mutatis mutandis*.[12]

For instance, the essence of his morality is loving others as oneself. But when Jesus spoke those words he was merely developing a theme from the Old Testament. Moreover, long before Christ's incarnation, Buddhism had gone even further by preaching love not only for one's neighbour, and not even one's enemies, but for all living things. Also, most religions referred to the supreme God as Father, and the Persians, like the Christians, attributed a loving and merciful nature to this deity.

In fact, the longer we look at the religious thought that either preceded Christianity or developed concurrently with it, the more similar elements we shall find. In common with Buddhism Christianity accepted that man is sinful (though not originally created that way). In common with Platonism it postulated an ideal world beyond our earthly reach. In common with Judaism it saw the world as the creation of one God. In common with Philo (roughly Jesus's contemporary) and other Hellenised Jews of Alexandria it defined Logos as God's creative force. In fact long before John's gospel, Plato and the Jewish Platonists of Egypt used the word Logos to describe a self-differentiating divine unity, giving Gibbon an opening for one of his many anti-Christian jibes (to the effect that St John's revelation had been taught in Alexandria four hundred years before it was written down).

The only aspect of Christianity that is unquestionably unique to it is the person of Jesus Christ, *Logos* made flesh, and so it was this and this only that Paul revealed to his flock. If you believe the Acts, never once did he as much as mention the Sermon on the Mount.

---

12. Nor do we know much of what Jesus said. Unlike either Moses or Mohammed, he did not leave a written legacy. All we have is recollections of others. And if we were to write down all the words attributed to Jesus in the Gospels, we would find that they could have been uttered in about two hours. Yet the period covered in the Gospels lasted approximately two years. Surely Jesus said many other things as well? This shows yet again that, unlike say Judaism and Islam, Christianity is not a religion of the Book – at least not just of the Book. And if we believe that Christ is the living God, then Christianity is a living and therefore ever-developing religion. That means that today's church is as likely to receive a revelation as were the Galilean fishermen of two thousand years ago.

Following his lead, other founders of Christendom created the most profound and nuanced philosophy the world has ever known, without any close seconds. But it was so much more than just a philosophy – as mentioned earlier, to them theology was like a mirror held up to reflect Christ on the world, illuminating it until he came again. Philosophy in general is never just a way of thinking; it is a way of life.

However, the mirror is only an approximate simile, for the reflected light did not bounce into people's eyes at once. The issues involved were so deep and subtle that it took centuries for their true meaning to sink in. The greatest difficulty was presented by the dual person of Christ whence comes the great synthesis of Christianity, its unique balance. Several Councils of the Church battled with the task,[13] but it was not until the Council of Chalcedon in 451 that the issue was settled once and for all: Jesus Christ is neither just God nor just a man – and nor is he a centaur-like creature, half-man, half-God. He is fully divine and fully human.

But why did this knowledge take so long to dawn on people? The answer will depend on our beliefs or, to rely on the terminology I am using here, our metaphysical premise.

Some Christians may say that the revelation was not given to the people at once; it came gradually and piecemeal. An argument can even be made that the truth was always going to come down to us in three major instalments, corresponding to the three hypostases of the Trinity. The first, the gospel of the Father, was laid down in the Old Testament; the second, the gospel of the Son, in the New; and the third, the gospel of the Holy Spirit, is yet to come in some future, and last, Testament.

Those who proceed from the first, theistic, premise may find it hard to come up with a strong argument against this theory. After all, faith in Christ inexorably leads to belief in the Holy Trinity. The word 'Christ' means 'the anointed one'. Without stepping outside the

12. Some of the battles were not just rhetorical. For example, St Nicholas is reported to have punched Arius in the face during the First Council of Nicaea in 325. But then Arius could try even the patience of a saint.

boundaries of logic, the term thus presupposes the existence of both the anointer (the Father) and the medium of anointment (the Holy Spirit). Since the three hypostases are equal, and since the first two were revealed in two separate Testaments a thousand years apart, while the third one so far has not been confined to a document, logic would suggest that another Testament will come sooner or later. Some might reject this hypothesis, but even they would struggle to dispute the gradual nature of the revelation.

Those who are guided more by the second, materialist, premise may argue that, though Christianity was a purely human construct, it was a complex one. Not only did it have a plethora of indigenous inputs, but it also borrowed freely from other religions and philosophies. Since each little aspect allowed for diverse interpretations, fusing them all into a single cohesive doctrine was bound to take a long time.

One way or the other, it is critical for our purposes to realise that we shall never comprehend a single development of the subsequent millennium and a half unless we come to terms with the nature of the great Christian antinomy and how it is resolved. The only way to understand things we can see is first to understand things we cannot see; on this Christian thinkers agree with Plato.

Whether or not we believe in Christ's godliness, manhood or god-manhood (or indeed his historicity) is a matter of utter irrelevance here. We are not the ones who created our civilisation, and those who did were guided every step of the way by their faith in Christ, as it was revealed to them through the Scripture and church tradition. They set out, consciously and deliberately, to build a world that would make salvation more likely, and damnation less so. In that they did not always succeed but they always tried.

Therefore Christendom, which is to say our civilisation, was neither purely physical nor merely metaphysical. It was the physical embodiment of a metaphysical fact.

THE DIALECTIC OF THE WEST

I have referred to the dual personality of Christ as an antinomy. This term has several meanings, but here I use it in the sense of seeming contradiction. 'Seeming' is the operative word: though many things about Christianity are paradoxical, none is contradictory – regardless of the claims made by those who feel an emotional need to refute the Bible. If they relied more on their minds and less on their emotions, they would see that every apparent contradiction in the Scripture can be resolved. This can be achieved most easily by applying the logical process that later came to be know as Hegelian dialectics, but is in fact rooted, along with all other things Western, in the person of Christ.

The tripartite process can best be represented by the formula of yes – no – yes or, in Hegel's terminology, thesis – antithesis – synthesis. As applied to the person of Christ, it can work in this manner: Yes, Christ is fully God (thesis). No, Christ is fully a man (antithesis). Yes, Christ is God-man (synthesis).

Christendom as conceived by its founders was to be the flesh that grew on the skeleton of this dialectic. But first they had to work out the practical manifestations of the antinomy by matching an earthly equivalent to the theological synthesis. In a shamefully schematic representation, this might run along these lines: Yes, the ultimate aim of our existence is to enter the kingdom of God in Christ (metaphysical thesis). No, we cannot do so straight away; first we have to live out our three-score and ten on earth (physical antithesis). Yes, we can live our physical lives fully while never losing sight of the ultimate goal and moving towards it steadily (synthesis of the two).

By tying the physical needs of man with the metaphysical demands of God, this dialectic provided the only possible basis for the collective morality of the Western world. And it is collective morality that acts as the gravitational force preventing the atoms of individual belief from spinning out of control. A naturally good

62

person does not have to rely on any commonly held ethic to remain good. But a society without such an ethic will not even be weak or evil. It will be nonexistent. Thus the Christian synthesis was in effect to act as a comprehensive how-to guide to mankind. It prescribed, implicitly or explicitly, ways in which people must relate to God and to one another in order to create a worldwide commonwealth.

This sounds simple on paper but in real life our forebears found the synthesis hard to understand, and the how-to guide even harder to implement. The perfect theory clashed with the imperfect nature of man. Here too, we can explain this imperfection using either one of the two metaphysical premises.

The theist will refer to Genesis and point out that the Fall made us all fallible. The materialist will sneer at the idea of original sin but after some gentle persuasion will grudgingly accept that we are indeed a rotten lot. The evidence before his very eyes would be too compelling to deny, unless of course he is a strident social Darwinist for whom progressivist ideology matters more than either facts or logic.

Yet again, regardless of what we believe, we have to agree that in this instance logic is on the side of the theist. Original sin is a straightforward proposition springing from man's relationship with God.

Man was made perfect, but this perfection was contingent on his clear understanding that he was a creature whose Creator was infinitely superior to him and therefore had to be obeyed. Yet mankind committed an act of disobedience and chose to compete with God by trying to be like him – mankind let pride have the better of it. By way of chastisement it was banished from the immediate proximity to God, which for ever branded pride as the gravest of the deadly sins, though it comes seventh on the list.

As a curious aside, this version of man's descent is more scientific than Darwinism and other materialist theories. The Second

Law of Thermodynamics, in broad strokes, states that any system left to itself will tend to entropy, which is to say degeneration into chaos. As a corollary to this, mutations (with only about one exception in a million) are always degenerative. Thus it is consistent with science that man began as something perfect and then degenerated into something sinful. On the other hand, the belief that moral perfection can be achieved by a steady accumulation of evolutionary improvements contradicts the spirit of the Second Law.

It is important to stress that Genesis clearly talks about mankind at large, not just a young couple named Adam and Eve.[14] An unsmiling biblical literalist would insist that the story of the Creation is true in every detail, and the couple were the first, at that time only, people on earth. A more enlightened theist would object that, as the Bible in general and Genesis in particular were written in the language of poetic imagery, Adam and Eve were a symbolic representation of the whole of mankind. But this argument does not matter for our purposes: either way, literally or figuratively, Genesis talks about the human race at large. Whether Adam and Eve made up or merely symbolised mankind has no practical significance.

The story of Adam and Eve proves that pride, being the exact opposite of faith, is the only sin that makes faith impossible. It also shows that good is primary while evil is secondary: evil is merely the absence of good. It was this truth, reaching Augustine by way of Plato's exegesis, that set the young Manichean on the way to becoming a great Christian thinker.

A fall, after all, is an act of tumbling from an original high perch down to a lower one. Any vice is thus the corresponding virtue debauched; it represents a gravity-assisted fall from high to low. Moreover, the greater the height the harder the fall. Witness Satan (whose name, Lucifer, means Enlightener), the embodiment of evil, who started life as an archangel, thus occupying the highest moral berth to which a creature can possibly aspire. His shattering tumble,

14. In one of his books Richard Dawkins shows convincingly, maths in hand, that all of mankind descends from a single female progenitor. The poor chap was not so blinded by his strident atheism that he failed to realise he was vindicating the Genesis story. Yet with his characteristic disdain for logic Dawkins nonetheless managed to claim that, though his calculations were right, the story was wrong.

and that of other fallen angels, confirms the hierarchy of good and evil.

Original sin also acts as a logically irrefutable basis of morality by demonstrating that the criteria of goodness have to lie outside man himself. In any game of morality man can no more be both a player and the referee than a footballer can simultaneously act in both capacities on the field.

On the other hand, any moral theory based on the second, materialist, premise runs head first into a logical brick wall. We may for example, exercise our moral judgment and pronounce that John is a sterling lad while Bill is a sad excuse for a human being. But on what basis do we judge the two gentlemen?

The only criteria we have at our disposal come from our own conviction that we know the true difference between right and wrong. In other words, we assume we can get to the bottom of moral behaviour by using our own faculties only. However, in order to get to the bottom of something we have to start from a level that is higher than the bottom; anything else would be a logical impossibility.

Looking down from the edge of a high plateau we can see the whole valley below, but looking up from a valley we cannot see the whole plateau above. A higher system can understand (and therefore judge) a lower one but not vice versa. Thus in order to pass judgment on the comparative moral fibre of Bill and John we have to presuppose that we possess a personal moral standard that towers not only over Bill's wickedness but also over John's goodness.

That very well may be, although in practice such arrogant presumptions are seldom justified. However, if we are conceited enough to make this assumption, we also have to be logical enough to realise that *ergo* there must exist an hierarchy of moral agents, some sort of pecking order in which we stand above both John and Bill. Now unless we are suffering not only from arrogance but also from delusions of grandeur, the next step would be to admit that in such a hierarchy there has to be someone who stands above us, just as we tower over the hypothetical pair.

If we then imagine ourselves in the shoes of that superior individual and repeat the process, we shall realise that he too will have others who stand higher than him, and so forth – all the way up to the ultimate giver of moral law higher than whom none exists. Thus our materialist faces an unsavoury choice: either he must commit a logical solecism or he has to accept that this variant of the ontological argument (with apologies to St Anselm) invalidates his metaphysical premise either altogether or at least as it is applied to morality.

These are the only sane options. The other kind would be for him to regard himself as the highest moral authority imaginable – but that way madness lies, as a literary character once said.

Collective morality is the most significant factor in social behaviour, this regardless of whether the person in question follows the accepted moral rules or not. If the morality of his group springs from the first metaphysical premise, he will feel ashamed every time he goes against the grain of consensus, even if he cannot help being a miscreant. Similarly, in a society dominated by the second metaphysical premise, any transgressor against it, even if he is certain that God is on his side, may be ever so slightly embarrassed about being a stick in the mud. Peer pressure is a dread term, but it does describe something to which only very few can be immune. Thus, while individual salvation may depend on individual morality, the nature of a society is determined by the moral tenets it holds collectively.

When it came to economic behaviour, Christians always applied the dialectic springing from the person of Jesus Christ – come to think of it, they applied it to everything, though not always consciously. There are many comments on wealth in the Scripture, but we shall focus on just two.

In a well-known incident described in the Gospels of both Mark and Matthew, Jesus stunned his apostles by a bold thesis: 'It is easier for a camel to go through the eye of the needle, than for a rich man to enter into the kingdom of God.' The disciples 'were astonished out of measure', and understandably so. After all, at the onset of their religion Abraham's righteousness had been rewarded with riches, as was Solomon's wisdom.

But then came the antithesis: '... With men it is impossible, but not with God: for with God all things are possible.' The synthesis could not be clearer: as long as we put God first, we are justified in pursuing wealth. Of course, because of the moral implications of sincere Christian faith, and because the Christian attitude to riches has never risen above lukewarm toleration, putting God first would make such a pursuit more difficult. But tolerated it is. It is neither impossible nor proscribed.

In another incident, Luke records Jesus talking about 'mammon', which is the Aramaic for wealth: 'No servant can serve two masters: for either he will hate the one and love the other; or else he will hold to the one and despise the other. Ye cannot serve God and mammon.'

The yes – no – yes dialectic is not explicit here, but it is clearly implied, and in several ways. For we have already seen that to Jesus serving God meant putting God before all else (metaphysical thesis). It did not, however, mean *elimination* of everything else, for life on earth had to be lived (physical antithesis). Therefore, though we cannot serve mammon, which is to say put it first, we may still wish to live comfortably as long as we serve God ('... seek ye first the kingdom of God; and all these things shall be added unto you'), put him first (synthesis). The message in Luke is thus exactly the same as in Mark and Matthew: God is everything, but this does not mean that man has to be nothing.

In fact, whatever the subject, this is the same message that runs through the entire New Testament, from the Gospels to the Acts to the Epistles to the Revelation. Everything is possible with God; nothing is possible without God.

For example, that was the meaning of Jesus's comment on another aspect of life held in inordinate respect by modern people. 'But I say unto you, That whosoever looketh on a woman to lust after her hath committed adultery with her already in his heart.' Before you get red in the face and cast a furtive look at your wife, let us ponder what was really said there.

If any adult male with a palpable pulse, regardless of his religious convictions, looks into his own heart (as Jimmy Carter once did, to such a comic PR effect), he will find that during his daily ride to work he commits that particular brand of adultery every time a good-looking woman gets on the train. And given easy accessibility of flattering clothes, cosmetics, healthy diets and exercise regimens, most women whose locomotion is not boosted by a Zimmer frame can look good enough to consign our commuter to an eternity in hell. That seems to be his only possible destination. After all, the injunction against adultery was chiselled in stone as an immutable part of the Decalogue, which is the law Jesus said he had come to fulfil.

Since no one could possibly observe that commandment as rendered by him, then no one will be saved; everybody is a blasphemous law-breaker to be consumed by the fire of hell. Clearly this could not have been what Jesus meant, for such blanket cruelty would go against God's loving essence.

All he was saying was that, by all means, do try to observe the law (the 'yes' thesis). But without God's help you will never succeed (the 'no' antithesis). Therefore you cannot be saved by your own efforts only. You must seek God's help, which means putting God first (the 'yes' synthesis) – exactly the same message as in the two verses dealing with wealth.

This dialectic was understood by all serious Christian theologians who talked about riches. Thus St Thomas Aquinas: 'The perfection of the Christian life does not consist essentially in voluntary poverty, though that is a tool of perfection in life. There is not necessarily greater perfection where there is greater poverty; and indeed the highest perfection is sometimes wedded to great wealth...'

Note the qualifiers: 'essentially', 'not necessarily', 'sometimes'. St Thomas was not issuing a licence to acquisitiveness. He was not giving the same *'enrichessez-vous'* advice the French statesman François Guizot (d. 1874) offered those who objected to property limitations on franchise. Aquinas was expressing the fundamental Christian view on pursuing wealth: Go on then, if you absolutely must. But do remember what comes first. Jesus, after all, only said man shall not live by bread alone, not that man shall live by no bread at all.

Addressing seven centuries after Aquinas a world that no longer could be automatically presumed to put God first, Pope John Paul II said essentially the same thing as did the Jesus of Mark, Matthew and Luke, and then Aquinas: 'It is necessary to create lifestyles in which the quest for truth, beauty, goodness and communion with others for the sake of common growth are the factors which determine consumer choices, savings and investments.'

The language is modern; the message is two thousand years old. It is based on the Christian balance between the two planes, physical and metaphysical, reflecting the two natures of Christ: God and man.

Of course, during the time our civilisation was being formed, seeking wealth for those who were not heirs to large tracts of land was tantamount to selling the fruits of their labour. The butcher, the baker and the candlestick maker bartered their products for other people's. And, as Adam Smith remarked, they did so in pursuit of self-interest: 'It is not from the benevolence of the butcher, the brewer, or the baker that we expect our dinner, but from their regard to their self-love ' Money was sometimes involved as a means of exchange, and when that was the case it was natural to expect that more money would eventually end up in some hands than in others.

Thus labour implicitly presupposed the possibility of enrichment. Yet in spite of that the New Testament contains direct endorsements of work. These come across in the Lord's Prayer ('give us this day our daily bread'), in Jesus the carpenter talking about 'the labourer worthy of his hire' and in St Paul the tent maker stating categorically that 'if any would not work, neither shall he eat.'

If we look at the Scripture in its entirety, we shall notice that the Old Testament mostly, though not exclusively, focuses on codifying life in this world, while the New Testament mostly, though not exclusively, prepares man for the next. That is why it is to be expected that the Old Testament would pay more attention to material wealth.

Sure enough, in common with the New Testament, the first part of the revelation recognises hard work as an acceptable means of acquiring wealth. The other method, not mentioned in the New Testament, is God rewarding the righteous with riches. Not only Abraham and Solomon but also Jacob, Joseph and many others became wealthy that way, even though the Old Testament also says that wealth can be a curse brought about by the Fall.

However, this endorsement of riches clearly and unequivocally did not extend to what was then called 'usury', and to what we now euphemistically refer as 'financial services'. Though the New Testament ignores the issue of interest on loans, the Christian tradition does not: until Calvin, usury had been roundly condemned, though not without allowing some Florentine exceptions. But the Old Testament proscribes usury in no uncertain terms throughout, starting with *Exodus:* 'If thou lend money *to any* of my people *that is* poor... thou shalt not be to him as a usurer.'[15]

15. Later, in *Deuteronomy*, the Old Testament is more specific: 'Unto a stranger thou mayest lend upon usury; but unto thy brother thou shalt not lend upon usury ' Presumably, this meant that Jews must not charge interest on loans to other Jews. As the essential Christian belief is that all men are brothers, this reaffirms the injunction against usury in general.

Since at first glance this injunction, along with many other similar ones, seems to condemn the entire modern economics, starting with Adam Smith, let us try to see what is really meant here. First, God, speaking through Moses, unequivocally links all economic behaviour, even the kind that escaped the letter of the Decalogue, with morality. Some ways of making money are moral and may be allowed; some are not and must be banned. And according to this passage in *Exodus*, what is immoral is charging interest on any help we give to the needy, which was probably the only group that sought such assistance in Biblical times.

Now let us put this situation in a modern context. If, for example, an unemployed friend asks for a couple of hundred to tide him over until next month, the Bible says you must help willingly and disinterestedly. That is the only righteous thing to do. Similarly, come next month the only righteous thing for your friend to do would be to pay you back, with a word of thanks as the only surcharge. This is as straightforward as it gets: bilateral morality has been served.

But now let us complicate the situation. Suppose another friend has no problems paying his food bills and rent. But he needs cash to play out a hot tip on shares and, let us choose a round number, is ten thousand short. You give him the money, he invests it and makes a 20-percent profit in a year's time (considering the present situation, this sounds like wild conjecture, but surely one can indulge a fantasy every now and then?). Should he still give you back your £10,000 and not a penny more?

First, if you are in the kind of middle-class tax bracket that is these days more or less universal in the West, you would have had to make at least £15,000 gross, and probably £20,000 or even more, to clear £10,000. But forgetting that for a moment, an inflation rate of ten percent (not unheard of over the last thirty years, and likely to come back soon) would by the end of the year reduce the value of your £10,000 to £9,000. Thus, while your friend has made a gross profit of 20 percent (or 10 percent net), you have suffered a net loss of 10 percent, and this does not even include the gross amount you would have had to earn or the investment opportunities you have missed.

That means your friend has not paid you back fully. Whatever your original agreement, he has therefore committed an immoral act, a transgression that you aided and abetted by your misplaced generosity. Would it not have been more moral for you to charge a modest interest on your loan to make sure you break even, or perhaps share in the profit your friend has made? You would still have acted generously, while at the same time preventing an immoral act committed by another.

Now how did your friend make his 20-percent profit on your £10,000? Let us say his hot tip involved subscribing to shares in a manufacturing concern (another fantasy these days, but do let us strain our imagination) that was floating itself on the market because it needed investment to expand and modernise its plant. As a result, it was able to hire more people, previously unemployed, at the same time offering better quality and lower price to consumers. Your loan, though it produced a loss for you, has thus resulted in a social gain.

To put it in Biblical terms, you have loved your neighbour even more than you have loved yourself. Surely there would have been nothing immoral in your behaviour had you charged, say, a 10-percent interest on your loan, especially if you had made it contingent on any subsequent profit?

Perhaps I can answer this question later. Or maybe I have already answered it: everything is possible with God, provided we accept his moral guidance to the problems of everyday life and are prepared to accept his judgement when the time comes. For the time being let us just say that applied metaphysics is a complex science, and when applied to money it often becomes unmanageable.

We can make it simpler by using the dialectic based on the Christian balance of the physical and metaphysical, and for many centuries Christendom tried to do just that, with variable success. Sometimes it worked better, and sometimes worse. But as long as the whole society proceeded from the same metaphysical premise it never was a total failure. Alas, that uniformity did not last.

THE BALANCING ACT

Having established the metaphysical guidelines for the life of a physical world, the founders of Christendom then had to tackle the practical challenge: reconciling the ideal set by an infallible God with the lives led on earth by people who were not only fallible but indeed fallen. Let us put ourselves, for the sake of argument, in their shoes to appreciate the immensity of the task they were facing. While doing so we have to assume for the time being that our metaphysical premise is the same as theirs, even if in reality it is not.

The early Christians were striving to move towards the ultimate goal, the kingdom of God. Yet they knew that this was a metaphysical structure to be built out of the physical material otherwise known as people. The two came together in the person of Christ who established the ontological link between God and his world, between the physical and the metaphysical. Christ revealed the idea of human perfection and realised it through his own life. Son and hypostasis of God, Jesus set an example of the ultimate good made flesh.

But when it comes to us poor mortals, 'ultimate' is the key word. It could not be universally replaced with 'immediate', no matter how much moral absolutists clamoured that this should be possible. More sober heads always knew that human personality would predictably get into the spokes of the wheel of metaphysical progress, which would then slow down or grind to a halt altogether.

The early church knew that a developing individual, the microcosm of a world in flux, must at the end of the road reach the terminal point at which his own personality was no more; it would become dissolved in the collective personality along with all others – above all, in the person of God. And the ideal purpose of any development is the end of the development: having arrived at this end, man would not progress any further. That is another way of saying that man would no longer live, in the sense in which we define living on earth.

The kingdom of God was thus seen as the ultimate goal of human development. Therefore by definition it was the end of human development: having got there, man would no longer travel; he would have arrived. The coming of this kingdom would signify the end of time, for God lives outside that category, as we cannot. And the end of time means the end of life in this world. The church maintained, and the faithful believed, that such an end was to come when God willed it. But until then life had to be lived, if only as a way of edging towards the destination. One had to travel in order to arrive.

This duality of the temporal and the eschatological was the exact mimicry of the antinomian nature of Christ. Scripture clearly stated that mankind would reach the kingdom of God when Christ returned, but not before. That is why the early church had to find ways of reflecting the duality of Christ in order to make it possible for the Christian community not only to survive but indeed to expand until that time, while following an unwavering course towards its sacred destination. Moreover, it had to survive both as Christian and as a community.

On the other hand, our progenitors were aware that this process was not only collective but also individual. However, this awareness introduced a difficulty. Yes, all people walked to the same destination. But each walked at his own pace. That was why postulating asceticism and withdrawal, in the style of Plato or Buddha, could not make sense for everyone. True enough, at the end of the spiritual road people might indeed reach the stage of physical escape from a sinful world, entry point to the kingdom of God. Yet as they all moved at a different speed, they could not arrive at that door all at the same time.

The road leading there was labyrinthine and fraught with numerous pitfalls. It was also sometimes hard to find. That was why mankind needed pathfinders, people able to take the point and raise high the lantern that could light the way for the rest. Such people would reach the kingdom of God before everyone else. They were called 'saints', and they deserved the right to demand moral absolutism because they lived by it. However, the whole mankind could no more be expected to be made up of saints than a whole army can be expected to be made up of heroes. Both sainthood and heroism are the lot of the few.

The rest of us could then and can now only look up to those people, in the hope that one day we may become like them. But the hope is likely to remain forlorn: perfect goals are seldom achieved by imperfect people. Thus since the time of St Paul one, perhaps the main, function of the church has been to find a compromise between the truth as revealed from heaven and life as lived on earth. The static perfection only achievable in the kingdom of God had to be balanced against the dynamic human nature made imperfect by the Fall. The great theological synthesis had to be made to work in everyday life, including the economic aspect of it.

This was not the Eastern synthesis of things similar in nature. It was a balance coaxed out of a clash between opposites: perfection and imperfection, one of them divine and the other human, but both extreme.[16] That is why the balance was so precarious and why it had to be vigilantly observed: one step too far in either direction, towards either the sacred or the profane, and a precipice beckoned. One or the other end of the seesaw will shoot up, tossing either God or man into the abyss.

In other words, the church had to find a compromise between absolute perfection, as reachable only in the kingdom of God, and the relative imperfection of human nature, as precipitated by original

16. Nothing would illustrate this difference better than a comparison between Western and Eastern music. While the latter reflects the serene harmony of a circular world devoid of an eschatology, the former has all the drama of the Christian synthesis. Both the thesis and antithesis are clearly stated and developed in sharply contrasting terms, only to be resolved into a unity in the end. That is the metaphysical essence of the sonata form, or for that matter of any Western music.

sin. This the church achieved during the period roughly demarcated by Paul at one end and Aquinas at the other. In the process it had to fight off numerous heresies, each aimed at destroying the delicate balance.

Here the church had to make sure it was preserving the Revelation to the full, without overstressing any one aspect. Such overstressing is in fact the essence of heresy; for all intents and purposes it might serve as its definition.

Most people assume that a heresy puts forth a wrong proposition, or at least one that contradicts the orthodoxy altogether. That is not quite true. In fact, most heresies are not wrong in their main belief. Where they err is in trying to assign an unduly universal significance to that one idea, passing a part for the whole. This inevitably puts too much weight at one end of the seesaw, destroying the balance.

For example, it is not wrong to assert that Christ is God, as docetism did, and neither is it wrong to say he is a man, as arianism did. It is heretical, however, to deny the balance of the two – the balance without which Christendom would not have come about.

In fact, the Greek word *hairesis* implies a choice, inclination towards one thing, which then forms a distinct view of the world. This can act as the starting point for a political party, religious sect or philosophical school. In other words, the term *hairesis* contains an idea of something unilateral, of an obstinate concentration on just one of all the facets of faith.

While orthodoxy runs across the spectrum, heresy is by definition partisan. The sectarian spirit promoted by a heresy is characterised by egotism and ensuing spiritual isolation. These are unavoidable whenever a partial thesis is proposed as the essence of absolute truth. Such sleight of hand denies the presence of an antithesis to a thesis, making any synthesis impossible. There is nothing to synthesise. The 'yes' and the 'no' are not resolved, they only tear each other apart. The balance no longer works, and religion is divided into aspects that mutually exclude one another.

Thus the business of heretical, sectarian reason is choosing the fragments it finds attractive. On the other hand, the business of orthodox, catholic reason consisted from the very beginning in gathering together all the pieces in their wholeness. (One could argue that the same applies to any walk of life. I may, for example, believe that someone who opposes European federalism is right to do so. But if he turns such opposition into the single issue around which his whole view of the world revolves, he is committing the same blunder a religious heretic commits when putting a small fragment before the large picture.)

However, in trying to achieve this goal universally, the church laid itself open to subsequent attacks launched by critics, from the early heretics to Calvin, from Wycliffe to Hus, from Luther to Jansen. With varying justification, such critics could always find the everyday practices of the church wanting when held up against the absolute ideal put forth in, say, the Sermon on the Mount.

That has been either the nature or at least the tactic of most schisms and all reformations, including the one we spell with a capital 'R'. And even when they were not officially declared to be heretical, they all used the heretic stratagem of placing too much emphasis on one or a few things at the expense of the balance among all.

Once again, the things they stressed may not have been wrong in themselves; they were only wrong in as much as they precluded any workable balance between man and God. However, had the church not found such a balance, Christianity would now be remembered at best as a timid attempt to reform Judaism in the early days of the Roman Empire. It would not have become a world religion, and neither would it have had the chance to civilise the West. Therein lies the strength of the church. But therein also lies its weakness. For, trying to adapt to the relative imperfection of human nature, the church itself had to become relatively imperfect.

Also, trying to fashion a religion that could thrive among peoples of different history, culture and national character, Christianity had to adapt more and more to the local conditions, especially as the monolithic Roman world was dissolving into separate nations. Here the inherent Christian universalism was invaluable: at every critical point, when the world is being put asunder, people need a unifying religion where, in St Paul's words, 'There is neither Jew nor Greek... for ye are all one in Jesus Christ.'

Had the church been able to prevail over the atomising tendencies of individuals and nations, much grief could have been avoided. Yet it was not able to do so entirely, and increasingly it was not people who had to adapt to Christianity, but Christianity that had to adapt to them.

Adapting to the character of each nation meant varying its own character to some extent from one geographical location to the next. As indirect proof of this, the Venerable Bede, England's first historian, testifies that already by his time (d. 735) the barely post-natal English church had already acquired traits peculiar to it, long before the great schism occurred. The underlying faith of, say, an Englishman, a Gaul and a Corinthian was the same. But, when their cultural idiosyncrasies came into play, it was a safe bet that their religions would not stay exactly the same in perpetuity. Thus an institution created to spread the absolute truth had to, by its very nature, overlay its mission with potentially deadly relativities.

That was not just a rhetorical conundrum. It was a disaster waiting to happen. For, trying to be all things to all men, the church had to delve deeper into worldly matters than was good for it. Granted, worldly matters could use the help of a universally civilising spiritual authority, especially during and immediately after the disintegration of the Roman Empire.

In response to that dire need, while still mostly preoccupied with things that were God's, the church had to claim some authority over things that were Caesar's. Somebody had to, for civic order was at the time in real danger of imploding, thereby burying the Christian community under its rubble.

For a while this arrangement worked well. Christendom was seen as the single mystical body of Christ within which the sacred and secular realms worked hand in hand. It was not for nothing that Charlemagne's empire was called Holy Roman. It was indeed both, and not neither, as Voltaire quipped with his usual lightweight wit. But keeping the two in balance was never going to be easy.

Though Christianity and the state may be useful to each other, congenitally they pursue objectives that are not only different but indeed opposite. For the religion, the aim is enabling people to save themselves in the life to come. The only interest the church has in the state's power is subservient to this main function: the state needs to be strong enough to protect the church, thus perpetuating its ability to attract and sustain its communicants.

For the state, the aim is to increase its own political and economic power in the world as it is today. When the church promotes that objective, as it did in the Holy Roman Empire, the state will support it. When the church is at odds with this objective, the state will turn aggressively atheistic, as it did in Soviet Russia and Nazi Germany.

For the church to be seen as useful to the state, it needs to hold sway over people's spiritual lives. When that is the case, the state needs the church more than vice versa. As the demise of the Roman Empire showed, the massive body of a state with its far-reaching coercive arms is helpless against the human spirit stiffened by a sublime idea.

Subsequent states learned their lesson: they had to join the church because they could not beat it. Conversely, had they been able to beat it, they would not have joined it. Thus any flirtation of a state with the church is a tribute to the strength of the Christian sensibility at the grass roots. But if the relationship goes beyond flirtation, the church may be ruined.

Witness the time following the disintegration of the Roman Empire. During that period the church functioned not only within the state but also as part of the state. *Pax Romana* became *Pax Christiana*. Yet an institution that fills the vacuum left by the Caesar inevitably assumes some of his characteristics, including his vulnerability. Caesars can be deposed; they can be cut to pieces.

To a large extent this is what happened to the church. As the remnants of the Roman world went their own way, the church found itself on the receiving end of divisive nationalist (or other secular) pressures that before long adopted sectarian slogans, as a rule mostly for tactical reasons (arguably Catharism and definitely the Hussite movement are examples of this stratagem). The church thus had to fight from a defensive and increasingly vulnerable position.

As a result, it had to forfeit a great deal of its flexibility, its talent for finding various versions of the Pauline or Thomistic compromise. It had to erect an increasingly less permeable wall in order to separate itself from the secular realm it could no longer control. But inside that wall the church still had to balance the human with the divine.

This balance was delicate: an inch here, half an inch there, and it could be upset. This is what happened to the church, more than once. Consequently there always was much to criticise it for, as there still is. Moreover, it is the duty of all good Christians to do so, in the hope that constructive criticism proceeding from love can get the church back on track, help it find a new, workable dispensation.

However, historically not all disagreements with the church have proceeded from the starting point of such benevolence. Many, and increasingly most, were inspired by passions that had more to do with man than with God. Pursuit of money in particular was assuming an ever greater importance, well beyond any the church could countenance.

It is fairly obvious that placing too much emphasis on personal enrichment puts Christian universalism under stress. We have already seen that the church tolerated work and therefore the likely possibility that more money would find its way into some hands than into others. Still, as long as life in general and economic activity in particular were underpinned by faith, social cohesion did not have to be undermined. The church felt strong enough to resist the atomising stress of economic egoism that was a precondition for success, and of economic inequality that was its result.

But only the naïve would have ignored the potential danger: there was indeed a stress to deal with, and the church had to be extremely strong to be able to deal with it. Its resistance to excessive covetousness would always be met with fierce counterforce, which could prevail in certain circumstances. Such circumstances did come about, and at some point the balance was tipped so far towards the physical, human end that it was destroyed.

And here we approach the tragic paradox of modernity. This has to do with the nature of reality, both as a philosophical concept and as the very practical life we see before us. Come to think of it, the two cannot be separated.

That physical reality just may not exist other than in our perception is an unacceptable idea to anyone proceeding from the first metaphysical premise. To such a person our life exists because God created the world and everything in it, including man. Thus it is God who occupies the centre of the universe, with man hugging its periphery. It is not man's idea of his surroundings that has creative power, but God's. It is not man's perception that makes reality real, but God's. The practical organisation of the world is then seen as a reflection of this arrangement, and of the balance it produces.

Conversely, any shift of the metaphysical balance away from God and towards man may well produce a Cartesian mindset where only our own selves are seen as reality. 'I think, therefore I am' is the exact reversal of the theistic perception of 'God is, therefore I am.' Such a shift will inevitably go beyond philosophy, in due course throwing the practicalities of life out of joint. Man's inner world will be bound to assume an inordinate importance. Man's passions, either inward or outward, will then take over, with only the hope that such passions will remain benign standing between us and catastrophe.

And this is the nature of the paradox. The world exists irrespective of our senses, but we cannot survive in it irrespective of our metaphysics. Denying this has led many a thinker towards poor philosophical ideas.

For example, Auguste Comte (d.1851) built his positivism on the assumption that metaphysics is inferior to science. Had he lived to see the present crisis, he might have recanted. And had he considered the implications of Christian dialectics, he would have seen that there is no contradiction between metaphysics and science – they are the thesis and antithesis that can be resolved into a most productive synthesis.

For the reality of the Western world sprang from the metaphysical, and ontological, balance between God and man. Whether or not we believe in the basis of this reality, the fact remains that for at least a millennium and a half there was no other. And once that reality was shattered, people had only two options before them. Either they had to put in place another reality, one based on a different metaphysical premise, or they gradually had to replace the real world with a virtual one. The latter has proved easier.

Step by ever-accelerating step we have effected just such a shift to virtual reality. We have replaced religion with (at best) religionism, Christianity with Christianism, freedom with liberty, wisdom with cleverness, sentiment with sentimentality, justice with legalism, art with pickled animals, music with amplified noise, statecraft with politicking, love with sex, communication with sound bytes, self-confidence with effrontery, equality before God with levelling, respect for others with political correctness, dignity with *amour propre* – in short, everything real with virtual caricatures. We now live in a virtual world – so is it at all surprising that we live on virtual money?

EAST IS EAST, AND WEST IS WEST

So what was it that eventually upset the balance that had taken so much effort to build? An answer to this question will tell us which historical developments can take the credit – or, depending on your point of view, the blame – for setting the scene in which the drama of modernity would be played out. The first three acts are commonly believed to have been the Renaissance, the Reformation and the Enlightenment. There is truth in this belief. But it is not the whole truth.

We have been discussing the efforts the church had to make in order to refine the metaphysical premise on which a successful civilisation could be built. The adversaries were numerous, and they came at the church from every direction, throwing their weight on one end of the balance or the other. To resist them the church had to keep its core together, remembering the prophecy of its founder: every city or house divided against itself shall not stand.

And yet, for reasons too numerous and involved to cover in any detail here, the house did not remain whole. In fact, before the curtain rose on the three acts already mentioned, the house had already been split right down the middle. The axe fell in the eleventh century, and by the beginning of the thirteenth the two halves were no longer together.

G. K. Chesterton regarded the thirteenth century as pivotal in the history of Christendom, more important than even the sixteenth or the eighteenth. He may have been right, though perhaps not quite in the way he intended. The writer concentrated chiefly on matters theological and philosophical, and there his judgment is hard to fault. What mattered to Chesterton was that it was the thirteenth century rather than the eighteenth that was the true age of reason, when Christian scholastics led by Aquinas attempted, after centuries of courtship, to marry the Scripture with Aristotelian rationality.

Thus, by refining a functional blend of faith and reason, the thirteenth century indeed may have advanced Western metaphysical philosophy more than any other age.

However, that was also the time when Christianity was torn asunder, in all likelihood irrevocably. Was there a causal relationship there? Or was this a mere coincidence? One way or the other, the balance began to totter on its fulcrum.

The great East-West schism that reached its climax in 1204 illustrates the point perfectly. As we know, Eastern and Western Christianity originally split in the eleventh century over the organisational issue of papal supremacy and the theological argument over filioque. The dual cleft seems to have cut across the whole spectrum of the physical and metaphysical that makes up Christian theology. Yet neither clash was purely religious; both had a crucial secular subtext. With the benefit of hindsight we know that a shift from God to man in the great balance was under way.

If we look at the first bone of contention, the competition for primacy between the bishoprics of Rome and Constantinople, most historians will agree that doctrinal as well as practical considerations came into play. The claim of Rome was mainly theological and historical, based as it was on the city's two great tombs, those of Peter and Paul. The issue was that of apostolic lineage: Apostle Paul was the founder of Christian theology, Apostle Peter of the Christian church.

On the other hand, the claim of Constantinople was almost purely secular: rather than the sceptre of apostolic succession, the city had picked up the crown of a Second Rome. It was the seat of the emperor and the place where Christianity had become the state religion for the first time. The conflict between the two claims is commonly regarded as the cause of the split. Personal ambitions and wounded pride of the personages involved must have played a role as well, but the essence of the argument was the struggle for ecclesiastical territory.

The second of the two main disagreements seems to be recondite, obscurely theological and, to a non-Christian outsider, trivial. The West, as represented by Rome, had declared unilaterally that the Holy Spirit proceeds equally from the Father and the Son (one can perhaps detect links with Aristotle's logic, based as it was on the syllogism). The Roman bishopric inserted words to that effect into the Latin text of the Nicaean Creed, though not into the Greek version.

In turn the East, as represented by Constantinople, insisted that the procession was not double but single, from the Father *through* the Son. And in either event, the East maintained that the West had had no business deciding such matters on its own, without convening an ecumenical council.

An outsider would perhaps ignore the nuances of the theological disagreement and instead focus on what he would see as the practical subtext. It would probably appear to him that filioque was merely a pretext for the two sides to square off in their fight for territory just as they did on the issue of papal supremacy. They both used the theological cudgel to bust each other's secular heads, and eventually the Roman cudgel proved to be heavier.

Such a view is possible, but it does ignore the never-stopping interplay between the physical and the metaphysical. It is perfectly true that the filioque clash had a practical subtext. But that had to do with much more than just a bare-knuckled fight for territory.

A theologian would concentrate on the singular importance of the dogmatic disagreement and downplay the secular issues at stake. However, he would be at a loss trying to explain the sheer violence of the clash, as coming to the fore both in the 1182 massacre of the Latins (Western Christians) by the Greeks (Eastern Christians) and the 1204 slaughter of the Greeks by the Latins during the Fourth Crusade.

The second is particularly baffling. After all, until then crusaders had not fought other Christians, what with so many infidels offering a more inviting target. The widespread view is that a lucrative sack of Constantinople was the precondition on which the Venetian contingent had agreed to come along for the ride. Yet the carnage of 1204 cannot be ascribed merely to the cupidity of the Venetians, who were supposedly so blinded by greed that they no longer cared about anything else. Let us leave this interpretation for Marxist historians to ponder while we look for the real reason.

We may think whatever we wish about the crusaders, but their driving urge was to serve God, not mammon. Most of them lost more than they gained during the crusades, and many beggared themselves. Of course it scarcely needs mentioning that, people (and wars) being what they are, all sorts of human flotsam drifted towards the crusading hosts. Consequently some wanton murder and looting did occur, often on a large scale, such as the Jewish pogroms in the Rhineland during the First Crusade.

But it takes a lamentable misreading of history to insist that such outrages were either the main animus or the intended aim of any crusades, rather than their tragic by-product. The inspiration for their exploits came from faith, and in that the Fourth Crusade was no different from the previous three.

The violence of 1204 was directly linked to the disagreement over filioque, although not just to the face value of the matter. What the issue of filioque highlighted was the existence of a growing chasm between the West and the East, even though the two shared the same religion. Eastern Christianity had always been under a much greater influence of other Eastern religions, and consequently of the way of life that sprang from Eastern religiosity. For example it was largely for this reason that Eastern (what today we call Orthodox) Christianity tended to gravitate towards mysticism, a direct sensory link with God that at its extreme more or less excluded reason.[17]

---

17. This is not to detract from the critical – and, in the first few centuries, exclusive – contribution Eastern Christianity made to theology. Great minds could of course find a workable balance between the mystical and the rational; their very greatness protected them from intellectual extremism.

Once that faculty is disengaged, God may well appear so remote as to become almost vague. One can see the force of good disappear somewhere in an endless sky, leaving the material world under the sway of dark forces. While a Christian has at his fingertips an immediate link between the absolute grandeur of God and the relativity of earthly life, an exponent of an Eastern religion does not. If for a Christian the absolute is unknowable completely, for, say, a Buddhist the absolute is completely unknowable. What is to him clear-cut is the imprisoning evil of this world, and the need to escape from it to become free.

God being too far away to be reachable, the Eastern road to such freedom is paved with contemplation, meditation and various degrees of asceticism. When one is surrounded with irredeemable filth, inward retreat into the purity of one's own spirit is the only answer.

Eastern (or any other) Christianity obviously could not reject the material world altogether, but at times it came close to such heretical rejection, inspired no doubt by contact with other creeds active in the region. It is not by accident that hermeticism and monasticism began to be practised in the east much earlier than in the west, as were various heresies based on the denial of the physical being of Jesus. The great Christian balance was still maintained in the East, but, if it was ever to be shifted, this would have to be towards the God end and away from the man end.

In the West of the Greco-Roman antiquity it was the other way around. For all their pronouncements along Eastern lines, Plato and other Hellenic philosophers could not detach themselves from worldly affairs, and in Rome it was the organisation of such affairs that was the city's great achievement. Nor was a confluence of man and God such an alien concept there, what with Roman emperors having been deified as a matter of course.

That, incidentally, explains the original violence of a generally tolerant Rome towards the early Christians: by deifying a man other than the emperor they could be seen as direct competition.[18] But it also explains why Rome eventually accepted Christ as fully divine and fully human without being sidetracked all that much by the same heresies that proved to be so pernicious in the east. If the Christian balance was ever to be threatened in the West, the threat was always more likely to come from the man end; and so it has proved.

Inevitably linked to the Eastern view of the physical world was relative indifference to tyranny – after all, hard as people tried, there was no getting away from evil on earth anyway. Introspection offered the only escape route, and that road could be taken in any social and political environment. The world outside was background noise, a distraction to block out.

On the other hand, the West, while obviously accepting that Christ's kingdom was not of this world, still could not be so contemptuously indifferent to this world. Christianity after all sought salvation *of* the world, not *from* the world. Jesus was not only God but also a man, and the Western concept of a sovereign individual is rooted in that fact. Because Christianity sought to become a world religion, it had to meet the physical world halfway.

As a matter of fact, no religion can ever stew in its own juice for long – if it does, it ceases to exist before long. In order to survive as a true religion and not just a sect, it has to excrete and wrap around itself a particular cocoon of ethics, morals, social and political organisation, culture, overall way of life. In time this cocoon may take on an importance all its own, with people ignoring or even forgetting its original source. But even in the absence of such a development, the way of life produced by a religion is often as important to society and its leaders as the religion itself.

18. On the surface Christians were perfect Roman citizens. Willing to render unto Caesar things that were Caesar's, they preached obedience and paid their taxes on time. But what they could under no circumstances accept was the sacral authority of a deified emperor. They thus jeopardised the very idea on which the empire was based – hence the proverbial lions. However, Rome did not persecute Jews, even though they were at religious odds with the empire as well. The reason for this benevolence was purely pragmatical: Judaism has an in-built biological limitation to its spread. Christianity, on the other hand, is by its nature universal. It therefore was perceived as being dangerous to Rome.

In this instance, it is to a large extent the seemingly inconsequential differences in Western and Eastern theology that explain why political (and economic) liberty found its natural home in the west, and tyranny in the east. One may suggest that what seems to an outsider to be an arcane point, *filioque*, hinted at something vital to the Christians of the time. What to us is a matter of academic interest, to them might have been a matter of life or death. It may even have been more important than that.

After all, expressed geometrically, double procession would look like an equilateral triangle. The Father and the Son have true equality underpinned by the Holy Spirit. The three hypostases thus possess what today we call equal rights. Translated to a civilisation based on this concept, the triangular Trinity is likely to be reflected in pluralism.

Conversely, single procession from the Father through the Son implies a straight line, an immutable vertical hierarchy, with the Father sitting at the top. The implications of this went beyond theology. What was at stake at the time was the overall path Christendom was to follow, the kind of commonwealth Christians wished to build while still living their physical lives. In that way Kipling's idea of the split between the West and the East had been vindicated long before Britain became an empire.

The fundamental difference between West and East would later work its way into the economic sphere too. It was natural that, given the contrasting doctrinal tenets and resultant ethos, Western Christianity would tolerate a greater emphasis on economic activity than the East could ever stomach. A gradual shift towards the man end of the balance was always fraught with the danger of excessive covetousness, whereas a shift in the opposite direction was likely to result in a cavalier attitude towards material possessions (widespread in much of the non-Christian East as well).

Today, if a casual traveller were to compare the way in which, say, the average Swiss and the average Russian organise their financial affairs, he would notice a marked difference, without necessarily identifying its historical roots straight away. And even if he were to consider them at all, the issue of filioque would not come up quickly, if ever. Yet it lies behind the divergence as one of its causes.

The story of Russia's conversion to Christianity in 988 is a useful illustration of the complex ways in which religion is intertwined with the way of life. Faced with a choice between the Eastern and Western confessions, Prince Vladimir, the ruler of Kievan Rus, chose the former. And in the fifteenth century, after Constantinople became Muslim, Russia assumed the mantle of the torch bearer for Eastern Christianity, what the Russian monk Philoteus called the 'Third Rome' ('and there will not be a Fourth').

Yet the real reason for the original conversion had to do not so much with fine theological points as with the whole ethos of Western Christianity. For already, less than fifty years after the split with Byzantium, the West was acquiring a character that was distinctly different from what the East was ready to welcome.

At that time Western Christianity was already spawning the kind of statehood in which the relationship between the sovereign and the people was based on inchoate liberties. That was something that princes from further east were finding hard to countenance, and largely for the reasons I have outlined. Vladimir was no exception. The prince knew that, given some breathing space, the people he ruled could well begin to get ideas above their station. But he wanted them to remain abject slaves, not to become mere subjects.

However, Western Christians were already showing signs that they would never agree to act as malleable putty in their rulers' hands. That was the nature of the problems Vladimir had with the Western confession and, by extension, with the West itself. In time hostility towards the West became an essential fibre in the fabric of the Russian psyche, though not always in a clear-cut way.

For instance, Vladimir's thirteenth-century descendant Alexander Nevsky (recently voted by the Russians as their greatest compatriot ever) fought those celebrated battles[19] against the West, one of which gave him his nickname. He would accept no compromise with Catholicism spearheaded by the militant monastic orders.

However, Alexander was more than willing to accept a compromise with the Mongol invaders from the east. In fact, rather than fighting them, he fraternised with Sartak, the son of the Mongol chieftain Batu, thus becoming the Khan's foster son. And though he had never heard of Quisling, Alexander acted in a similar capacity by busily collecting tribute for the Mongols from his fellow Russians, and ruthlessly punishing those who would not pay.

(Describing the several revolts Alexander put down, the chronicles of the time specify such tax-collection practices as gouging people's eyes out and cutting their tongues off. We must be thankful that our own Inland Revenue is so much more civilised, if no less determined.)

But even before Nevsky, feuding Russian princes from the eastern provinces had tended to fight their equally Russian rivals to the west of them much more ruthlessly than they ever battled their eastern neighbours. Obviously, such contaminating proximity to the West no longer qualified the western principalities as strictly Russian. It could just be that the Russians were the first to recognise that the West and the East had already gone their separate ways, with each dragging half of Christendom along.

The split between the West and the East was the first blow that Christianity could not slip. However, it was not to be the last. Christianity was to be knocked from pillar to post – and as a result it

---

19. Eisenstein's 1938 film greatly exaggerated the scale of those battles, which are now believed to have been no more than skirmishes. For the record, Pyotr Stolypin, Prime Minister to Nicholas II, came in second in the same poll, and Stalin third. None of the three was the most cordial friend the West has ever had.

was to loosen its hold on the souls of men, allowing their bodies to pursue 'happiness' unimpeded.

HUMANISM: WHAT'S IN A NAME?

1

The semantic larceny so characteristic of our virtual world has expanded the meaning of the word 'humanism' to make it synonymous with 'kindness', 'compassion' and 'empathy'. One wonders why those other words were found to have become so enfeebled as to need help from an impostor. In fact, they were quite capable of doing the job by themselves. With the benefit of our terminology, all humanism really meant was the shifting of the metaphysical balance from God to man.

The word 'Renaissance', which is used either on its own or as a modifier to 'humanism', is another such misnomer. It means 'revival', 'rebirth'. Yet, considering that the phenomenon hiding behind the term was definitely a reflection and possibly a cause of Christendom's decline, 'decadence' would perhaps be a more apt way to describe it.

Actually, the word *renascita*, better known this side of Italy by its French equivalent, was first used by Petrarch in reference to Dante's poetry, which owed much of its formal perfection to Virgil. Leaving aside the question of what, other than its form, Dante's sublime Christian poetry did to deserve that soubriquet, let us instead ask something else: So what was it exactly that was being reborn?

A quick answer straight out of school textbooks would focus on the revival of curiosity about the pre-Christian world of Greco-Roman antiquity. Almost a millennium after the 410 sacking of Rome by the ancestors of today's Germans, that event assumed the scale of a Euripides tragedy. As a result of that outrage, claimed the Renaissance men, the classical heritage had been either lost or at least damaged. And it was self-evident to them that no civilisation would be possible until those treasures were restored to their erstwhile primacy. Was Hellenic culture not the sky-bound summit of human achievement? Well, then there could be no higher aspiration than climbing back up to that shining peak.

But most quick answers only elicit more, equally quick, questions. Such as, why was it that in the second half of the fourteenth century Europeans suddenly felt the burning need to get back in touch not only with classical languages but also with pagan art, literature and philosophy? After all, widespread interest in other cultures, past or present, usually reaches its fervour pitch when people find their own culture wanting. (Whether or not such feelings are justified is immaterial.) So why did our ancestors decide in the fourteenth century that there was a vacuum to fill? How had Christian culture failed them?

This development represented a confluence of so many streams that analysing them exhaustively would be a difficult, if not impossible, task even for a panel made up of experts in various disciplines: theology, philosophy, history, economics, psychology, aesthetics – and even epidemiology. All that a single writer can attempt to do is look at the more obvious factors and try to make some sense of them, relying on plausible conjecture where facts are scarce.

Paradoxically, one such factor could have been the predominance of scholasticism in the intellectual run-up to the Renaissance. This is indeed a paradox because Aquinas and other scholastics used Aristotle's rational methodology to reach, and teach, impeccably orthodox Christian conclusions. But in the process they presaged the Renaissance by bringing pagan philosophers to the forefront of people's attention, and also by showing the awesome power of human reason.

If St Anselm in the eleventh century and St Thomas in the thirteenth could use sequential logic to prove the existence of God, then lesser mortals felt justified in thinking that they too could use their minds to gnaw at the outer edges of the truth. As to the orthodox conclusions reached by the scholastics, most people either resented their uncompromising rigour or misunderstood their relentless logic. In fact, it would be fair, if not impeccably consonant with our aggressively polite times, to say that most people were ill-equipped to grasp the subtleties involved.

This is hardly surprising, for the requisite training was not widely available. Until then religion had been mostly esoteric, with the education in applying reason to faith limited to a handful of savants. In the first millennium of Christianity its universal spread was owed mostly to the emotional power of its message, with its emphasis on charity.[20] Reason was kept in the background, wielded with power by the theologians but more or less kept out of reach for the lay masses. The Neoplatonist and Aristotelian infusions of the early Middle Ages partly rehabilitated the popular appeal of reason, but that affected an average Christian only indirectly, through almost imperceptible changes in liturgical rhetoric.

During the Middle Ages, the Scripture was inaccessible to most Christians, if for no other than linguistic reasons, what with the teaching of Hebrew, Greek and Latin being controlled by the very priests who had a vested interest in particularism. The linguistic problem deepened after the break-up first of the Roman and then of the Holy Roman empires. Even the liturgical language varied from Latin in the west to Old Greek in the east, while the onslaught of numerous vernaculars had taken both languages out of everyday circulation.

Thus most denizens of Christendom were excluded from any deep study of their religion. That could only mean that they were also excluded from the culture produced by religion: cultural exclusion follows the linguistic kind with the certainty of night following day.

---

20. Julian the Apostate (d. 363), while rejecting Christianity in favour of paganism, still lamented that the Christians were so much better than the pagans at caring for the sick and destitute – not only their own but also the pagans'.

A moat was dug around the clerical estate with its subtle mysteries, and trespassers were prosecuted with relentless firmness, though the pace of such oppression quickened with the advent of early modernity. Vernacular Gospels would pop up in tiny numbers here and there, but a serious attempt to produce and disseminate a vernacular Bible was a burning offence in England and elsewhere as recently as the sixteenth century. This shows that the church had no intention of engaging people's minds and removing its own mediation between man and God. In view of later events, this attitude was nothing short of prescient, and its failure nothing short of lamentable.

For humanists proved in short order that Aristotle and Plato could be used not only to support Christian orthodoxy but also to kick the legs from under it. More and more people were growing unhappy with intellectual exclusion, and they welcomed any invitation to think for themselves. And if they were unable to read the Scripture in the original, vernacular translations had been steadily drip-fed into the intellectual bloodstream even before the Reformation, thanks to the death-defying efforts of such humanists as Erasmus and Lefèvre d'Etaples.

More and more people found themselves in a position to analyse the Scripture without relying on any ecclesiastical exegesis. But an invitation to analyse is an invitation to doubt, and religious scepticism had begun to spread long before the Reformation made it commonplace.

This is not to imply that reason ought to play no role in a religious quest. On the contrary, it is a valuable cognitive tool in Judaeo-Christianity – as long as it is used in equilibrium with piety. The trouble is that for most people this equilibrium is hard to find on their own, and impossible to maintain. Qualified help is always desirable and at times essential, for the interplay between faith and reason is not straightforward.

Unless one is careful, reason can become egotistical, while faith is an attempt to go back to the Creator by humbly placing one's individuality at his feet. It is an act of submission, the self-effacing acknowledgement that our sins are so grave that we cannot save ourselves without God's help, and our minds so small that only by dissolving them in God's endless mind can we hope to use them for the purpose of salvation. We can be blessed only if we are meek.

If faith is an act of self-sacrifice at God's altar, then the mind is perhaps the greatest offering, especially for people with the greatest minds. But giving one's mind to God does not mean that the believer becomes mindless as a result. Quite the contrary: God accepts the sacrifice and rewards the donor by giving him his mind back, having first cleansed it of everything extraneous, scoured it of everything dreary. Thus purified, the mind acquires the freedom it never had before, because, just as no content is possible without its form, no freedom is possible without discipline. The greater the mind, and the more sincere its original sacrifice, the greater God's reward, the higher the mind can soar.

In the absence of such a sacrifice, the mind remains for ever shackled to the earth with its mundane concerns; the mind itself remains mundane. Thus prideful refusal to submit one's reason to God's is punished by a diminished power of the reason. For, when looking at the world, the mind can see so much more by rising above quotidian problems than by staying mired in their midst.

How does one arrive at faith? Many roads lead to Rome, and even more to God. But, whatever the route, it takes intuitive predisposition to embark on the journey. In Pascal's view, 'You wouldn't be searching for Me if you hadn't already found Me.' This is a brilliant aphorism, as Pascal's sayings tend to be. But in a less epigrammatic format one ought to add that the search must be conducted in good faith. The seeker must not set off determined to look only where God is sure not to be found: the traveller's own ego.

Once this condition is met, every seeker will find his own way and his own level. But by assigning undue importance to unaided reason, the humanists encouraged people to use their minds before other faculties, which produced mixed results. Humanist reasoning found itself in conflict with God's reason.

We are born with the power of reason, but faith needs to be acquired either by our own efforts (assisted by instruction) or by God's grace or, most likely, by a combination of the two. But the motivation to make such efforts may be understated in many people. That is why it is faith and not the mind that needs stimulating first and above all: once it has received some most rudimentary education, the mind will eventually go as far as it can anyway by relying on its own resources.

Moreover, faith is more likely to lead to rational understanding than the other way around. As Anselm wrote (echoing a similar thought by Augustine), 'I do not seek to understand in order to believe, but I believe in order to understand.' When reason is placed before faith, the latter, and possibly also the former, will tend to diminish as a likely result.

From the onset of the Renaissance this tendency was bolstered by various secular developments, such as the bloody clashes between the supporters of papal and imperial authority. The two factions, called respectively the Guelphs and the Ghibellines, turned Central and Northern Italy into an intermittent battleground throughout the twelfth and thirteenth centuries. That cast further doubt on religion, and not without justification.

After all, Christ's kingdom is not of this world, which is to say it is higher than this world. The Guelphs, though ostensibly propping up ecclesiastical authority, in effect brought it into disrepute first by fighting the Ghibellines, their fellow Christians, on a secular battleground and then, having won their victory, by turning against one another. In doing so, the papal party brought the heavenly kingdom down to the earthly level, thus laying it open to the kind of mockery that had become common currency in the secular world. (It was not only Virgil and Horace but also Aristophanes who had made a comeback.)

From the fourteenth century onwards the personage of a corrupt, lustful, crooked monk, priest or nun was ever-present in Southern European literature. And while such writers as Boccaccio and later Aretino, Rabelais, Molière, Diderot and Voltaire lent their considerable talents to the task of mocking the church, few satirists of similar attainment came forth to take on the opposite task. When Rabelais, for example, lampooned scholastic theologians with devastating effect, there was no literary counterbalance of equal weight, subjecting, say, Erasmus to similar scorn. The church must have felt that resorting to cutting satire was beneath it, which was probably a mistake – wit is too powerful a weapon of mass instruction to ignore.

The secular, humanist cause was advanced no end by the Black Death, the murderous pandemic that struck Europe in 1348-1349. Epidemiologists still argue about the exact nature of that disease (bubonic plague and haemorrhagic fever being the frontrunners among the candidates), but there is no arguing about its far-reaching effects. Up to a third of Europe's population perished, which tragedy went beyond the simple death statistics.

For one thing the church could no longer administer the full burial rites, one of the key sacraments, to all the deceased. With millions of deaths on their hands, and with many priests themselves catching the lethal infection from the dead and the dying, the church simply could not cope. Yet the bereaved families did not care about its problems – sacraments were a serious matter to them, and the thought of their loved ones being denied salvation was unbearable. Thus, through no fault of its own, the church laid itself open to the charges of indifference and lack of sympathy.

Also, when everyone had to suspect that everyone else might be a likely carrier of deadly contagion, the social cohesion of society was bound to be undermined. Treating every stranger as a potential killer could hardly have promoted cordial community relations. People tended to keep themselves to themselves, which was illustrated by Boccaccio's *Decameron* whose ten protagonists come up with their (mostly ribald and anticlerical) stories in isolation from the outside world. It is conceivable that the atomising nature of modern society can be traced back to that time.

Also theodicy, the defence of God, was put under a great strain. People were asking all the usual, and quite superficial, questions, later reiterated by Hume: If God is merciful and good, then how did he allow such a catastrophe? If that was beyond his control, then how omnipotent is he? And if he did not know what was going on, is he really omniscient? The church did not always field such queries with sufficiently persuasive power, and the embers of humanism began to glow redder. One way or the other, the world that emerged after the watershed of the Black Death was not the same as it had been before the calamity.

2

It was during the Renaissance that the foundation was laid for the triumph of the second metaphysical premise. The soulless materialism of modernity was erected on the layered slab of humanistic rationalism and neo-Gnosticism, poured down during the period signposted by Aquinas at one end and Luther at the other. And once the slab hardened, there was no going back.

In due course humanist thinkers like Niccolò Machiavelli, Michel Montaigne and Francis Bacon would preach, each in his own way, the agnostic scepticism that is so familiar to us today. It was during the high noon of humanism that the founding political ideas of Western modernity were developed. Machiavelli, ably assisted by Aristotle, described in dispassionate, not to say cynical, terms the best ways of running a secular state, with religion not assigned any significant role to play. If religion to Machiavelli had any value at all, it was not as a divine institution but as a power tool, a way of keeping the masses in check. In *The Prince* he became perhaps the first thinker to describe Christianity as being useful only to rule people, not to save them.

However, he was not the last: this is exactly how religion is treated in modern Marxist textbooks. And in between Machiavelli and Marx, Voltaire and his like-minded contemporaries kindly accepted that Christianity was a perfect religion for ensuring the servants did not get ideas above their station. That was all it was good for; clever people obviously knew better.

This sort of Christianism is echoed by many contemporary thinkers who seem to believe that clericalism can happily unite with atheism for the secular good of all. We can, they seem to be saying, jettison God while keeping the church. This is of course a gross fallacy: common good can only ever be based on truth. The view that society can thrive on an idea they regard as false is self-refuting.

Machiavelli not so much postulated humanism as showed how it could be applied to running secular affairs. Since in the following few centuries most states did become secular, his seminal contribution to political theory cannot be gainsaid. In particular, following Aristotle and presaging Montesquieu, the Florentine showed that no political arrangement can exist in its pure form without degenerating into something unsavoury.

Machiavelli argued in his *Discourses* that, when their purity is intransigently maintained, a principality turns into a tyranny, an aristocracy into an oligarchy and a democracy into anarchy. For a political arrangement to last, and for liberty to endure, a state must combine the elements of all three known forms of government. That is why, explained the writer, the synthetic constitution of Lycurgus in Sparta lasted longer than the purely democratic constitution of Solon in Athens. A division of power, in which none of the estates feels the need to usurp the total power, is thus a proven guarantor of social longevity.

This thought later became the cornerstone of political liberalism, a natural extension of humanistic agnosticism into public affairs. In that sense, the current prevalence of single-estate democracy in the West, to the exclusion (more or less) of other parallel forms of government, paradoxically runs against the grain of traditional liberalism. Now, describing Machiavelli as a proto-liberal and modern democracy as illiberal may seem far-fetched, but in fact is not. It is but a hint at the virtual reality of modernity – but I am running ahead of myself.

It was also during the Renaissance that various precursors of New Age philosophising became essential parts of intellectual discourse. Not only Aristotle but also Plato was taken off the mothballs for that purpose – the West could no longer do without him.[21] People had to believe that ultimate reality lay beyond what the eye could see, and yet they could no longer accept the Christian version of that reality, at least not without reservations. Neo-Gnosticism, championed by the likes of Giordano Bruno and Tommaso Campanella, reinforced the humanistic belief in the infinite reach of the human mind – provided it sought, and was granted, access to special knowledge.

It was not just home-grown Gnosticism that became fashionable, but also foreign borrowings, such as Cabbala and Sufism. However, with a reductionism so characteristic of modern intellectual history, eventually the demand for secret knowledge was no longer seen as ironclad. The human mind was deemed capable of arriving at the truth unassisted, by applying logic to empirical evidence.

---

21. The two thinkers are often bracketed together, and there are indeed many ideas they share. Yet in methodology their philosophies are more opposite than alike. Aristotle's stock in trade (in his science, not logic) was induction – empirical observation of physical fact as the starting point of thought. He was the first great, if often misguided, scientist. On the other hand, Plato mostly operated deductively – he explained visible life by applying to it his concept of a higher invisible reality. He was the first great, if often misguided, metaphysician.

Humanists maintained that any attempt to jump-start reason by reference to revelation or church tradition would be at best unnecessary and at worst harmful. This punched gaping holes in people's perception of reality, and those had to be plugged for humanism to hold sway. One such hole was morality, which until then had been seen, and taught by the church, as a derivative of God's truth.

By way of an alternative, humanists suggested a cold-blooded calculation of self-interest based on reason. In a way this was a revival of Socratic (and Platonic) ethics: people, if properly taught, can learn to tell right from wrong simply by using rational thought. Everyone was supposed to be intelligent enough to be moral enough.

Selfishness, for example, would have to be moderated because it did not pay, not because the church said so. If in pursuing self-interest we trampled over the interests of others, they would then put obstacles in our way. As there are more of them than of us, we would come off the poor second.[22] It scarcely needs pointing out that nineteenth-century utilitarianism, with its concept of arithmetical morality, descends from Renaissance humanism in a direct line, boosted along the way by the two good friends Adam Smith and David Hume.

3

It was during the Renaissance that the church put its objections to usury on hold, or at least mitigated them. Granted, such objections had often been ignored during the crusades, as the urgent need for financing could not have been met by papal or princely war chests all by themselves. But the church blessed such temporary concessions to secularism as they were seen to serve a higher purpose in the long run.

---

22. Leo Tolstoy preached this type of rationalist morality *ad nauseam* in his philosophical works. I can refer interested readers to my book *God and Man According to Tolstoy* (Palgrave-Macmillan, 2009) in which I enlarge on this subject in quite some detail.

Alas, the church was to find out the hard way that secularism never relinquishes what it has claimed. No concession to it can ever be temporary; not only do today's compromises become tomorrow's entitlements, but they also open the sluice gates to an on-rushing flood of new and greater compromises. The process worked the way of mathematical reduction to the common denominator: the crusades could only roll along if their wheels were greased by usury; people's passions could only be satisfied if indulged by usury. Eventually the crusades ended and the passions changed. Usury was the common element that had to survive – and indeed get a life of its own, outside the womb that had begotten it.

As humanism became the new orthodoxy, religion began to cede its positions even in its core business, never mind in secular affairs. Thus it could offer only feeble resistance to the spread of usury. The banking industry was born, and its growth was only ever so slightly slowed down by the church; it was never really stemmed.

Usually the banking and tax-collection functions were at that time combined in the same institutions, as a rule Guelph, especially after Philip IV expelled the Jews from France in 1306. His subsequent 1311 expulsion of Italian bankers back whence they had come effectively turned Northern Italy into the banking centre of Europe. In France only Avignon, home to the Holy See from 1305 to 1378, remained active in finance. In a critical development, one of the Avignon Popes, John XXII, rejected (heretically, in Occam's view) the Franciscan insistence on the absolute poverty of Jesus and his apostles, thus setting the stage for the ecclesiastical endorsement of wealth.

For about a century it was touch and go, with the church still retaining enough vestigial power to wage its limited war on usury. Therefore the traffic was not exactly one way, with victories and defeats following one another with reliable regularity. Early in the fifteenth century Italian bankers were expelled from England,

Flanders, Aragon and Paris – score one for the church. Yet at the same time new banks were founded in Genoa and Barcelona – score one for the humanists. The most important development came in 1403 when charging interest on loans was ruled legal in Florence, which was the first time neonatal capitalism managed to sweep aside the *de jure* resistance of the church in a Christian society.

When we add all those developments together, we shall see that Renaissance humanism marked the time when secularism began to make inroads on the metaphysical premise lying at the foundation of Western reality. The period left a large body of evidence to that effect, and this came across not only in the written but also in the pictorial documents of the epoch. For example, it is instructive to observe how the depiction of sacral subjects changed as the Renaissance gathered momentum.

Comparing Giotto and Piero della Francesca at one aesthetic end of it to Raphael and Michelangelo at the other, we see not only the development of technique but also the gradual secularisation of scriptural protagonists. As we travel north to Florence from the Assisi of Giotto and the Sansepolcro of Piero, in front of our eyes iconic images, with the genius behind them harnessed and driven by church canon, transform into paintings of buxom ladies with their rosy-cheeked breasts being sucked by well-fed babies. Brilliant artistry is very much in evidence, but God is beginning to recede into the background.

We have already seen that the more deeply the church got into the secular world, the more its mission suffered and the less capable it was of combating humanism effectively. Taught that their own minds could lead them to the truth, with no outside help necessary, people began to feel sceptical not only about religious institutions but also about the faith behind them. They still paid lip service to God but they could no longer be automatically presumed to serve him in any meaningful way. In ever-increasing numbers they began to serve themselves first.

With the benefit of hindsight we can see what the people lost at that time: the sacred and secular realms were no longer complementary. Increasingly, they were at loggerheads, which affected both in many ways, few of them positive. This was also the time when the embryo of the virtual world began to kick inside the belly of Europe.

'Virtual' in this sense means illusory, and so naturally it was an illusion that had to give rise to it. For the idea of a DIY religion, of reason able to reach the ultimate truth all on its own, is a fanciful fallacy, and one on which our virtual world would be based.

Moreover, the falsehood of this idea must have been evident even to those who preached it most fervently. As we are now, people at that time must have been made aware of their own limitations in every walk of life. In common with us, they must have found out that every new mystery they uncovered revealed a multitude of other mysteries of which they had hitherto been unaware. Just as we do, they must have barged through many an intellectual door only to bang their heads against the brick wall hiding behind it. And yet they persisted in their folly, stepping further and further away from things as they were and towards what they felt things ought to be. They put their souls up for sale, and a mess of virtual reality was the asking price.

Renaissance humanism paved the road to the Reformation, another service, or rather disservice, it did for the West. As an anonymous wit once quipped, 'Erasmus laid the egg that Luther hatched.' Paradoxically, the link between Erasmus and Luther was strong even though at first glance the two men held diametrically opposite views of the world.

Erasmus, along with other humanists, was an incurable optimist. He believed that, though the Fall may have damaged mankind, it certainly did not corrupt it irredeemably. There was no room for determinism in his philosophy; neither salvation nor damnation was predestined. Critically, Erasmus stressed free will, and in this he probably came closer to the truth than Luther ever did, with his staunch belief in arbitrary predestination.

This belief sprang from a profoundly pessimistic view of mankind which, according to Luther, was so corrupted by original sin that nothing an individual could do would ever have the slightest bearing on his salvation or damnation. Only God's grace, bestowed for reasons known to God only, could act as the agent of salvation.

Where the optimist and the pessimist converged was in shifting, each in his own way, the great Christian balance from God to man. While Erasmus did so more comprehensively, with his optimistic view of human nature extending to every aspect of life, Luther busied himself mostly with theological matters. However, the humanists and the reformers joined forces in reasserting the sovereignty of the individual, for which they are to be thanked.

Yet there was negation in their assertion, for they ascribed to the individual certain powers that went against the grain of Christian tradition and indeed observable evidence. In doing so, they – though usually sincere believers themselves – pushed the West away from actual reality and towards the virtual kind.

THE BLESSING OF ACQUISITIVENESS

1

'Man is dominated by the making of money, by acquisition as the ultimate purpose of his life,' writes Max Weber in his canonical work *The Protestant Ethic and the Spirit of Capitalism*, first published in 1904-1905. Even before him, Dostoyevsky remarked that modernity is characterised by 'materialism, the blind, insatiable desire for personal accumulation of money at any cost.'

To Desiderius Erasmus, Martin Luther, Huldrych Zwingli, John Calvin or any other sixteenth-century thinker (either humanist or Protestant or both) this line of thought would have sounded not just wrong but downright daft. Yet Dostoyevsky's and Weber's readers nodded their collective understanding. As far as they were concerned, that observation went without saying.

Something must have happened in the intervening four centuries to account for this tectonic shift. On the basis of what we have discussed so far, we know exactly what it was: the first metaphysical premise had been thoroughly and irrevocably ousted by the second, which alone could have made it possible for a deep thinker to define man in such narrow terms. But 'what' has to be followed by 'why', and also possibly by 'when'. And it is the answers to these questions that tend to cause much disagreement.

Weber's brilliant, if debatable, analysis hinges on the causal link between the Reformation and capitalism, both its rise and spread. Yet we have already seen that capitalism, narrowly defined as the free use of one's own or borrowed capital to achieve economic ends, had been spreading steadily throughout the Middle Ages – in spite of the variously vigorous resistance on the part of the church. Granted, there is no denying that capitalism benefited from the Reformation, but was it caused by it?

The answer is probably no, and Weber tacitly acknowledged as much. But neither is this a case of a simple coincidence in time. Witness the fact that even in our time, Protestant countries boast a per capita GDP that is 1.5 times higher than in Catholic countries, three times higher than in Orthodox ones, and five times higher than in Muslim lands – this despite an ocean of petrodollars sloshing underfoot in the largest Orthodox country and quite a few Muslim ones.

An understanding, however schematic, of what really went on is essential. After all, if all the Protestant thinkers mentioned above would have confirmed without stopping to think about it that man does not live by bread alone, then something seismic must have occurred for Weber to be able to get away with his observation on what dominates man. So let us accept as a working hypothesis that the Reformation had something to do with it and see if the picture becomes any clearer.

But before we attempt to answer the 'why' question already posed, let us ask another one similar to it. Why did the Reformation become so successful at that particular time? After all, attempts to reform the day-to-day running of the Catholic church were made both before and after the advent of Protestantism. The Englishman John Wycliff and the Czech John Hus before Luther, along with the Fleming Cornelius Jansen (or rather his followers) immediately after him tried to correct all those iniquities that so excited the sixteenth-century Protestants. Yet their efforts neither destroyed the traditional church nor created a new one. Whatever their original intent, those reformers achieved just that: some reform, not much.

Conversely, first Luther and then Calvin succeeded in breaking away from the Catholic church altogether, starting worldwide confessions of their own. In many areas of dogma, liturgy, everyday practices and the whole tenor of religion, these confessions veered as far away from orthodox Christianity as was possible while still remaining Christian. Yet, though the original animus of the Protestants was indeed directed at dogma, liturgy, and clerical abuses of God's law, their success had little to do with correcting any of those. At the risk of sounding materialist, one has to come to the conclusion that the contributing factors were almost all secular.

In a way, these show that the 'why' had much to do with the 'where'. The Holy Roman Empire of the German Nation, to give it its full name, was a feudal network of various principalities, mostly though not exclusively Germanic, that acted as vassalages to the supreme feudal lord, the Emperor. Some of the potentates were desperate to assert their independence from the papacy, sensing correctly that the Emperor's power over them would diminish if denied its ecclesiastical underpinnings.

The most effective way of breaking away from the Pope would have been to break away from Catholicism altogether. However, for reasons I mentioned in an earlier chapter, by that time the only alternative to it, the Eastern confession, had become no alternative at all. Thus, when Luther came up with his sweeping reforms, his audience was captive, and the seeds of his dissent fell on a fertile soil already softened up by the Renaissance.

The feudal aristocrats of the Holy Roman Empire did not take long to realise that what was under way was the birth of a new religion, not just a reform of the old one. A new religion meant a new social arrangement, this they could see clearly. And, following two centuries of humanist scepticism, that was probably all they needed to know. Their secular aspirations came first. Fine points of theology and liturgy were strictly of secondary importance.

But the power of the feudal aristocracy was being curbed not only by the Pope but also by the emergence of the bourgeoisie, a new, mostly urban, class. The economic, and consequently political, power of that class derived neither from inheritance nor from arable land. Mostly the bourgeois relied on labour, their own or hired, to get ahead in life. And their economic success was measured not in acres but in money – the more of it, the better. This put them on a collision course with the Catholic church in more ways than one.

First, though the traditional church opposition to usury had by then weakened, it had by no means disappeared. Even if some secular authorities had made the charging of interest legal, the general attitude of the church was that of half-hearted toleration, barely masking the tacit disapproval underneath. Yet credit was the bloodline of the urban middle classes, as without it they could never take advantage of the numerous business opportunities arising in the rapidly growing towns. Therefore the bourgeoisie of the Holy Roman Empire would have felt uncomfortable with the Catholic church for that reason alone.

But there were many other reasons as well. For one thing, humanist education notwithstanding, the bourgeois were sincere, and often ardent, believers. As they wanted to stay on the right side of their religion, its disapproval of their activities mattered. Nor were they particularly happy with the Jewish domination of financial services that would inevitably ensue if Christians were banned, or at best discouraged, from lending money at interest.

Whatever latent anti-Semitism the bourgeois possessed to begin with became more virulent because they felt that their own church was pushing them into the hands of the Jewish money lenders, a traditional resentment well described in English literature, both approvingly (by William Shakespeare in *The Merchant of Venice*) and disapprovingly (by Sir Walter Scott in *Ivanhoe*).

People tend to dislike their creditors, usually in proportion to the amount owed. In the sixteenth century this tendency was hardly mitigated by the fact that, because of stringently enforced restrictions, the Jews really had few other ways of making a living. It was due to such constraints that they had to go against their own religion: we have already seen that, contrary to centuries of anti-

Semitic propaganda, opposition to usury was even stricter in Judaism than in Christianity.

Incidentally, it was not only the growing middle classes but also many of the traditional feudal aristocrats who were often indebted to the Jews, and those gentlemen were conditioned to solve financial problems by violence. After all, their original fortunes had been made that way. This was the nature of many anti-Jewish massacres, including the 1190 pogrom in York (the last such event to take place in England), where the mob led by local noblemen first broke into the Minster to destroy the promissory notes kept there, and only then went after the Jews.

The difficulty of obtaining credit was not the sole problem the urban middle classes had with the church. Their wealth, and indeed survival, depended on hard work – not only around the clock but also around the calendar. Yet both the clock and the calendar were affected by the traditional practices of the church: it was not just the Sabbath day that was supposed to be kept holy.

The 'days of obligation' set aside for religious worship numbered at least 100 in many dioceses, which meant that a third of the year was to be taken out of wealth-generating toil. This paled by comparison to the 200 such days demanded by the Eastern church at its most orthodox, but that was little consolation for the upwardly mobile Germans.

It was not just the sheer number of days devoted to worship; it was also its whole style in the Catholic church that clashed with bourgeois sensibilities. Upwardly mobile classes are innately opposed to any traditional hierarchies, and this held true for the Germanic bourgeois of the sixteenth century. That is not to say they were intuitively egalitarian, far from it. It is just that, for their aspirations to be pursued unimpeded, they needed to replace the old hierarchy of status derived from birth by the new hierarchy of status derived from money, with a concomitant change of style.

Yet the church was constituted along feudal lines, and even ecclesiastical titles resembled those of the secular aristocracy. Addressing the Pope as Your Holiness, a cardinal as Your Eminence and an archbishop as Your Grace was not a far cry from Your Majesty, Your Highness (Serene or otherwise), Your Excellency and other titles of nobility. Nor were the clerical vestments stylistically different from the royal and aristocratic garb symbolising traditional hierarchical power.

As it always does, the church's style betokened a certain substance, and both were alien to the new class. Its wealth came not only from back-breaking work but also from penny-pinching thrift. This was usually reflected in an attitude to life that later came to be called puritan.

'The style is the man', remarked Georges de Buffon (d. 1788), and few German townsmen of two centuries earlier would have disagreed. Their own style of dress, for example, was the exact opposite of the gilded and brocaded opulence favoured by the clergy. Simple in cut and sombre in colour, it reflected their dour commitment to unsmiling frugality in finance and unflinching austerity in life: in short, they had been puritan even before the term was coined.

Throughout the Middle Ages the emerging class of urban bourgeoisie had been fighting for political independence from the aristocracy. Municipal government and other local institutions, such as courts and law-enforcement bodies, had been wrenching bits of sovereignty away from the feudal noblemen, including ecclesiastical ones.

The wealthier the bourgeoisie became, the more political power it could wield – and the more prepared it would be to break away from the church. Yet, pious as most of the townsmen were, they were not quite ready to part ways with their faith even if they had problems with their church. And in those days they tended to use the words 'faith' and 'church' almost interchangeably.

When the reformers came along to tell them that the former was not necessarily tantamount to the latter, the bourgeois heaved a sigh of relief. They no longer had to be good Catholics in order to be good Christians. Thus it stands to reason that they welcomed with open arms the original reformer, Martin Luther, and especially Calvin who reformed the Reformation by pushing it even closer to the middle class.

Luther stayed within the confines of the German principalities, and his success was largely owed to his appeal to the secular aspirations of the German princes, however carefully they tried to mask such aspirations with pious verbiage. Calvin, on the other hand, escaped, one step ahead of an Inquisition pyre, from his native aristocratic France to settle in Geneva, which at that time was an independent city state in all but name, rather than part of the Swiss Federation. And since, unlike Germany, or for that matter France, Geneva was a bourgeois state already, Calvin's egalitarian animadversions were music to its denizens' ears.

However, the music was soon to become rather discordant. For Calvin shortly went on to prove what to us today hardly needs proving: egalitarians do not eliminate hierarchies. They merely replace the old ones with new ones. This Calvin demonstrated by effectively turning Geneva into a theocracy, with an ironclad line of descent running from God (more or less as interpreted by Calvin) to the church (more or less Calvin himself) to the state (more or less an extension of Calvin) to the people (more or less dominated by Calvin).

But before we consider the economic implications of Protestantism, Lutheran, Calvinist or any other, we must have a quick look at the nature of Protestant theology. For it was rather obscure doctrinal points that produced what the Catholic church could never deliver: ecclesiastical blessing of cupidity.

2

Luther was an Augustinian monk, and it is only natural that he would have been strongly influenced by the spiritual teacher of his order. But St Augustine left hundreds of treatises, sermons, letters. As these added up to millions of words produced over a lifetime of spiritual quest, predictably some of those words contradicted one another. Anything else would have been unthinkable and indeed unnatural.

Thus it was possible to cite Augustine in order to justify a broad range of belief, and Luther took full advantage of the possibilities. In the time-proven manner of a politicised exegete, he focused on those teachings that supported his own thoughts and ignored those that did not (such as unquestioning obedience to the church, which was one of the mainstays of Augustine's legacy).

Obviously, I cannot analyse Augustinian theology in any great detail here. However, it is essential that we look at those aspects of it that are critical to the theme of this essay. One such aspect stands out: vital to Augustinian beliefs was the doctrine of predestination, which was closely linked to original sin.

The Fall, according to Augustine – and, following him, both Luther and Calvin – stigmatised man for ever. Original sin was so grave that it could under no circumstances be redeemed by anything an individual would do in his lifetime. Only God, the transcendent, omnipotent and omniscient deity, could determine who would be saved and who would be damned (Augustine did not stress the second very much; in his works, predestination usually was neither quite single nor truly double, but rather in between).

God to Augustine was so far removed from man that his reasons for deciding the issue were both unknown and unknowable to us. As far as we were concerned, they might as well be arbitrary.

Thus no one but God could either know a person's final destination or affect it in any way.

All an individual could do even to hope for salvation was believe in Christ. In this both Augustine and the Reformers had scriptural support, most lucidly enunciated by St Paul: 'Therefore we conclude that a man is justified by faith without the deeds of the law' (Rom. 3: 28). Justification, which in the language of the Scripture meant achieving righteousness, is thus supposed to depend on faith alone, irrespective of any works. What are we to make of this?

First, the New Testament authors were not only saints but also polemicists. Trying to convert a world weaned on Greek rationalism, they had to be. The success of their mission hinged on their ability to build a strong enough case to win a debate. Jesus himself argued vehemently against the Hellenised Sadducees and fundamentalist scribes, and the evangelists never shied away from an intellectual scrap either. For example, when writing his Gospel, St John clearly had in his sights the widespread Gnostic creeds of the time.

And of course every epistle of St Paul was an argument for Christianity and against whatever opposing beliefs his recalcitrant audience held. Now, being human, Paul of Tarsus was in some ways like the rest of us. Therefore he would occasionally overstress an idea to make a polemical point – it is hard even for a saint to maintain a fair balance in the heat of debate. In that particular instance, Paul was arguing that no ritual postulated by the Law, and specifically not circumcision, would ever justify a man; only faith in Jesus Christ would.

It is of course possible to draw from this passage the uncompromising conclusion that therefore any works (other than faith itself, which is a work too) are irrelevant to salvation. But then it is also possible not to, especially if we consider the contradicting pronouncements made by other New Testament writers, and also by Paul himself. Here is a brief random selection:

'For the Son of man... shall reward every man according to his works.' (Mat. 16:27)

'... every man shall receive his own reward according to his own labour.' (1 Cor. 3:8)

'... your labour is not in vain in the Lord.' (1 Cor. 15:58)

'What *doth it profit*, my brethren, though a man say he hath faith, and have not works?' (James 2:14)

Perhaps the best way to make sense of this would be to remind ourselves yet again that no scriptural contradictions are truly contradictory. They can all be resolved using the dialectic based on the Christian synthesis. In this instance, the tripartite process will lead us along this kind of path: yes, we can only be saved by divine grace – no, that does not mean there is nothing we can do for our own salvation – yes, though faith must come first, works are essential too; our salvation depends on both.

An important point to remember is that Augustine was a polemicist too. As his most influential adversaries were followers of the Celtic heretic Pelagius who belittled justification by faith (and consequently predestination), so Augustine overemphasised it. Had he known that eleven centuries later Luther would use his polemic to tear the church asunder, Augustine probably would have phrased it in a more nuanced way.

The greatest philosophical problem arising from predestination is its seeming contradiction with free will. If the two doctrines are allowed to fight each other, neither will come out the winner; they will both lose. It is absolutely essential that they be reconciled. After all, if choices we make using our free will are irrelevant to our salvation, what makes our will free in the first place? And why do we need it at all?

Augustine's attempt to find such reconciliation is one of the few parts of his legacy that, to me, sound less than completely persuasive. To begin with he confirms his commitment to predestination. God, he says, is omnipotent, and he uses his power to predestine our lives in eternity. But as he is also omniscient, he allows us to make our free choices whenever they are called for: he knows in advance which way we would go, but he does not force us to choose one way or the other. This is all beyond dispute.

However, what Augustine refuses to grant is that choices made by our free will have any bearing on our salvation or damnation, which essentially makes them an exercise in futility. We can infer from this any kind of counterintuitive possibility we wish, such as that a mass torturer who on his deathbed accepts Christ may well be saved, while a good Christian who devotes his whole righteous life to serving others may be damned.

Interestingly, this theory implies a relationship between God and man that is more characteristic of the Old Testament than of the New. Though early in life Augustine denied the significance of the Old Testament altogether, he later softened his position and came to see it as the first part of the revelation, typologically presaging the second.

True enough, Christ fulfilled more than 300 Old Testament prophesies. But critically he also bridged the gap between heaven and earth, which is the essence of the great Christian synthesis. And one can even suggest, at the risk of upsetting our fundamentalist friends, that in doing so he changed, or ought to have changed, our understanding of original sin.

By definition, Christianity is founded on the belief that Christ sacrificed himself to redeem the sins of the world. But which sins? Surely not just a little boy telling his mother to shut up, or a fair maiden turning out not to be quite so maidenly? Anyway, according to another basic tenet, all individual sins derive from the original collective one. So, in the conviction of any Christian regardless of his confession, it was that sin that Christ redeemed by accepting an awful death.

This means that his sacrifice wiped man's slate clean of the Fall and therefore of wholesale guilt. Yet as the evidence before our very eyes shows that man did not become impeccably pristine as a result, a second sin, Mark II as it were, must have replaced the first one, and chronologically this substitution could only have occurred after original sin had been redeemed.

Logically, this must have been the sin of rejecting Christ. That offence is not identical to original sin, though neither is it dissimilar to it. Both, after all, represent rejection of God: the first by disobeying and the second by failing to recognise him. If Original Sin Mark I was disobedience and therefore rejection, then Mark II is rejection and therefore disobedience. The opposite of the second rejection is the kind of faith to which Augustine and, following him, Luther ascribed the sole justifying power.

But whereas man in general was implicated in original sin, mankind in its entirety never rejected Christ. Some – arguably most – people did so, yet some – arguably few – did not. However small the second group may have been, it was made up of people who of their own accord chose to belong to it, thereby, if we follow this logic one step further, cleansing themselves of the new version of original sin. Therefore the choice between acceptance and rejection cannot be collective. It has to be individual and it has to be free.

This can only mean that after Christ's sacrifice each individual can establish a personal account with God, and, even if we start out that way, we do not have to stay tarred with the brush of original sin for ever, be that Mark I or Mark II. It stands to reason that a man could do nothing to redeem the collective Mark I; Christ's sacrifice was necessary to achieve that. But it is equally clear that a man can do something to redeem the individual Mark II.

This understanding, incidentally, precludes any blanket theory that denies individual choice. For example, Jews can neither be collectively loved because some of them brought Christ to the world nor collectively hated because some of them screamed, 'Crucify him!' Nor can all Germans be held responsible for the Holocaust or all Russians for the GULAG – they must be judged individually on the basis of the free choices they made.

In fact, whenever we demonise some people for presumably belonging to a diabolical corporate entity, without any proof that they indeed belong to it, we dehumanise not only them but, by denying free will, all of mankind. To pursue the same example, a German who belonged to the SS was complicit in its atrocities, by association at least. But if one accuses an ordinary person who lived in Germany at the time, the accuser must bear the burden of concrete proof. The same goes for Russia and her KGB. Neither nations nor religions do murder; it is people who do that.

It can still be argued that, as the world at large demonstrably did not accept Christ, we may be slated for collective perdition. But what is undeniable, at least for any Christian, is that Christ showed a clear path to individual salvation, and we are free to take that path or not.

Free will thus becomes the most important possession of man, and it can only remain so if we stand to gain from a correct choice or suffer the consequences of a wrong one. In fact, if our will were not free, if we were but puppets on God's string, one would struggle to see why God would have bothered to make us so different from animals, or to create us at all.

Moreover, if we accept as a given that God loves us, that indeed God is love, then we must find it hard to explain how such love could have been expressed by turning us into puppets, or else pre-programmed robots. God's is the absolute freedom, but if we are truly created in his image, ours has to be at least a relative one. Only God can be totally free, but that does not mean man has to be totally enslaved.

What does that do to predestination then? Jesus is the Word, transcendental God, the creative force of the Trinity. During his finite life on earth he was in our midst; but in infinity his human and divine natures are conjoined. God is as immeasurably above us as the Old Testament says. And if we proceed from the first metaphysical premise, then we have to believe that God has far-reaching plans for the world in general and man in particular. Otherwise we would fall into deism, which is as unsound in theory as it is unlikely in practice: it is hard to believe on the one hand that God lovingly created the world, while believing on the other hand that he then lost all interest in it.

Does this mean we are predestined after all? And if so, provided we are not entirely happy with Augustine's explanation of it, how do we reconcile predestination with free will? If the former subsumes the latter, how can there be any perceptible justice in the world?

Luther struggled with this problem, resorting to paradoxes such as, 'If it were in any way possible to understand how God who is so wrathful and unjust can be merciful and just, there would be no need for faith.' Such meek intellectual surrender is odd, considering Luther's character and his insistence on the self-sufficiency of every Christian in dealing with God.

One can sense that Luther's convictions were close to those of the second-century heretic Marcion who believed that the two Testaments showed two different Gods: the wrathful, jealous God of the Old Testament and the loving, merciful God of the Gospels. Though for Luther (if not indisputably for Calvin) the New Testament God eventually won a victory, it was a close-run thing.

One can detect some wavering on Luther's part, and one can sympathise with his problem. Nonetheless, we must still try to come to terms with it. After all, if we believe that it was God who gave us reason, we might as well explore this faculty to its maximum, which cannot be just the ability to calculate compounded interest.

The whole issue of predestination is rooted in the timelessness of God's life, as opposed to the temporal existence of man. This juxtaposition gave rise to the most elegant solution to our problem, that by the Spanish Counter-Reformation thinker Luis de Molina.

In effect, though he himself did not use this terminology, Molina linked the philosophical category of time with the grammatical category of tense. Our lives unfold within three basic tenses: past, present and future. But God, being timeless, has only one tense: the Present Perfect. Thus, what is 'will be' for us is 'has been' for God. This means that when he predestines each individual for salvation or damnation, God does so not arbitrarily but on the basis of the free choices he knows the individual will have made during his life – before he has actually made them within earthly time.

In a way, this line of thought makes free will trump predestination as a philosophical notion. Predestination, as defined by Molina, is hardly worth talking about; it may be simply taken for granted. If, just as God's omniscience, the concept is based on God's timelessness, then it resides in the very definition of God. Using our God-granted free will, we may choose to believe in God or not. But if we accept him, then we have to take the whole package, including predestination. Basing, as Luther and especially Calvin did, a complex theology on predestination means assigning to it undue importance. An attribute resident in a synthetic *a priori* definition hardly rates such distinction, and insisting that it does may in some quarters be regarded as heresy.

Free will, and freedom in general, on the other hand, becomes part of the definition of man, and possibly the most important part. The freer we are, the more human and the more godly we are; the further we are removed from animals.

3

I have devoted much time to discussing predestination, but it is time well spent. For the Protestant interpretation of this doctrine either affected or, if we take Weber's view, even determined our economic behaviour from the time of the Reformation onwards.

Actually, it is only for the sake of brevity that it is possible to talk about the Reformation as a homogeneous phenomenon. In fact, there are significant differences between Luther and Calvin, and certainly between either of them and ensuing Protestant sectarianism. Perhaps one can go so far as to say that, all things considered, there was not one Reformation but two, or possibly even several. But for our purposes the common elements matter more than the differences.

When he declared that every man was his own priest, Luther essentially extended humanism to religion by assigning to man the kind of power that hitherto had been thought beyond his reach. No clerical mediation between man and God was any longer needed; no one could claim apostolic succession; a priest was only a *primus inter pares*, merely another communicant elected to officiate church services. In one fell swoop this made the church hierarchy, from the Pope down, redundant and therefore useless.

But it could not have been made completely useless for as long as the church hierarchy was considered essential to the task of preserving Christian tradition. Showing laudable consistency, Luther chopped through that Gordian knot with Alexander's élan: if it takes a useless church hierarchy to preserve tradition, then tradition is useless too. Who needs it anyway if the Scripture contains the whole truth of Christianity?

This explains why 300 years later John Henry Newman felt justified to write that 'To be deep in history is to cease to be a

Protestant.' For Luther's denial of equal rights to tradition ignores both the history and the nature of Christianity.

To begin with, as is generally believed, the first Gospel was not written until at least twenty years after Jesus's death, and possibly quite a bit later, with St John's Gospel usually dated between 90 and 100 AD.[23] Yet the church had survived in the intervening period by subsisting on tradition, mostly oral, though probably not exclusively so. (The Aramaic texts on which the Greek-language Gospels are thought to have been based did not survive, but extensive, though hardly undisputed, scholarship backed up by linguistic analysis points at their existence.)

Moreover, as Christ is a living God, Christianity is a living religion whose communicants have to believe that its truth did not come down chiselled in stone, once and for all. If they adopt Christianity, they have to accept as a given that the church today is as likely to receive parts of the revelation as were the Galilean fishers of souls. Unlike Judaism and Islam, Christianity is not a religion wholly contained in a written document, and nor can it ever be regarded as such this side of heresy. The Scripture may be the first, second and tenth most important parts of the religion. But it is not the only part.

In general, as I suggested earlier, one senses that Luther's (and even more so Calvin's) concept of God was in some ways closer to the first part of the Scripture than to the second. For instance, his exclusive stress on a personal, unmediated search for God relegates the priest to a status similar to that of a rabbi, a religious teacher and prayer leader, but not the conduit between man and God that a Catholic, Orthodox or High Anglican priest is.

In common with Augustine in his later life, Luther actively encouraged the study of the Old Testament, drawing people's attention to its numerous prophesies that Christ went on to fulfil. However, while venerating the Old Testament, Luther somewhat illogically loathed those to whom it had been revealed, which was yet another glaring contradiction of his personality.

---

23. Some scholars take issue with this commonly accepted chronology. For example in his *Redating the New Testament* J.A.T. Robinson argues that the first Gospel was written as early as 40 AD. One way or the other, the church had to depend on oral tradition for quite some time.

Or perhaps there was no real contradiction there: where in the past the Jews had been so far removed from Christianity that they could merely be despised as aliens, now they found themselves close enough to be hated as apostates. In an odd sort of way, Luther claimed that he had shown the Jews how they could become better Jews by renouncing their Jewishness, but they would have none of it. And of course, in common with most charismatic leaders pursuing a viscerally felt destiny, Luther could not just let something like that go without at least delivering himself of some mighty invective.

Towards the end of his life he vented his pent-up feelings in a ranting tract *On the Jews and Their Lies*. Jews, explained Luther, were 'devil's children' whose synagogue was a 'defiled bride... an incorrigible whore and an evil slut'. Jews were full of the 'devil's faeces... in which they wallow like swine.'

Luther's remedy for rectifying such hygienic disasters would be these days considered somewhat radical if hardly unfamiliar. He advocated burning synagogues to cinders, destroying Jewish scrolls and prayer books, banning rabbis from preaching, seizing Jews' money and property, smashing up their houses and forcing these 'poisonous envenomed worms' into hard labour or else banishing them 'for all time.'

Having thus presaged the *Kristallnacht*, the first stage of the Nazi massacre of the Jews, Luther swiftly moved on to a longing for the final solution. With praiseworthy self-deprecation he admitted an oversight committed by himself and his contemporaries: 'We are at fault in not slaying them.' Four centuries later his compatriots tried to correct that fault, with well-known results. In fact, one can say that Nazi Germany effectively married Plato's totalitarian idea of a state with Luther's anti-Semitic passion.

As I shall do with Plato (see Appendix 1), perhaps one may suggest that this sort of thing casts doubt on Luther's metaphysics. Metaphysical or any other philosophy is worthless unless it uses things we cannot see to explain things we can see. For such an explanation to have any other than academic value, it must suggest or at least hint at a certain way of life. If realised in practice, this can then be used as a litmus test of the philosophical starting point.

Obviously, there was more to Luther than a longing for mass murder, as there was more to Plato than a yearning for a totalitarian state. But the presence of such elements in their thought means they failed an important part of the test.

4

Luther effectively eliminated any clerical hierarchy, thus leaving the aristocratic hierarchy of German principalities to run free, or at least freer. The aristocrats expressed their gratitude by shielding Luther from charges of heresy, using their swords as a hedge.

Possibly to spare their traditional sensibilities, Luther in turn did not push his reform to a fanatically radical extreme. For example, in his doctrine he did not renounce the real presence of Jesus Christ at the Eucharist[24] (as Calvin did), while in his liturgy he retained much of the Latin mass (considerably more than Vatican II did) and some of the Latin opulence.

Himself an artist, Luther did not dispense with church music, encouraging his followers to express their faith and innate talent through musical composition. This may partly explain why he had such a strong influence on J.S. Bach and why music went on to become an essentially German art, at least if one considers the proportion of German composers among those who have made music what it is.

(*Encyclopaedia Britannica* once compiled a list of the twenty most influential composers of all time. Seventeen of them were German or Austrian, which meant the same thing at the time the bulk of great music was being written.)

24. However, his concept of the real presence was different, Catholics will say heretically so, from the traditional one: Luther believed in consubstantiation, which is that Christ's body and blood are present in parallel with the Eucharistic bread and wine. Catholics and some Anglicans believe in transubstantiation: the substance of bread and wine is wholly replaced by Christ's body and blood. This is largely based on Aristotle's ideas on substance and accidents absorbed into Christianity by the scholastics.

Calvin, on the other hand, went much further, possibly because he did not have to cater to aristocratic tradition. He operated in what for all practical purposes was a middle-class city-state, with no feudal hierarchy in place. Having escaped to Geneva from an aristocratic France, Calvin had a rich field in which to sow the seeds of his reform.

This was not to be limited to purely godly matters – Calvin had sweeping ideas that went beyond clerical rectitude. Geneva, he felt, had to be shored up by a theocratic hierarchy, with himself at the top. The kingdom of God had thus found its earthly viceroy. However, one could argue that such an arrangement was not only undemocratic but also un-Christian, if only because it contradicted Christ's words about rendering unto Caesar the things which are Caesar's.

A theocracy, or for that matter any other state, cannot be included in the kingdom of God. That realm has to remain stateless, for the state is by definition coercive. However, faith, the ticket to the heavenly kingdom, is a free union between two entities. A man born to a faith usually has the option of not espousing it; the same man born within the domain of a state has no option but to follow its laws on pain of punishment. A theocracy by its very nature cannot accept freedom of conscience to the same extent as Christianity and most other faiths must. But logic mattered no more to Calvin than it ever did to any other charismatic leader in history.

In common with Luther he also took from Augustine things he needed and discarded those he did not, downgrading for example the importance of sacraments, which Augustine extolled as 'the visible form of an invisible grace.' At the same time, Calvin pushed the idea of predestination to an absurd extreme. In that, he acted in the manner of an heretic who attaches undue significance to one single aspect of faith, however correct it may be.

We are predestined for salvation or damnation, pronounced Calvin, and, as we live in 'total depravity',[25] we can do nothing whatsoever to affect the outcome. The idea of good works as restitution for sin is dangerous Catholic nonsense, a way of keeping the masses in check. Some will be saved and others damned, regardless of their works.

Frequently asked to put a number on the lucky winners of this divine lottery, Calvin tended to change his mind, presumably depending on his mood. The range varied from a miserly one in 100 (dark mood) to a generous one in five (a brighter one). In any case we were talking about a small minority, but out of curiosity, how would we know which of us had drawn the lucky ticket?

It is Calvin's answer to this question that led Weber to regard capitalism as a predominantly Protestant phenomenon. God, according to Calvin, gave those to be saved a sign of his benevolence by making them rich.

Their wealth would be acquired not the Old Testament way, as God's gift; not the aristocratic way, through inheritance, martial valour and pillage; but the bourgeois way, through hard work and thrift. That is why God would not just rain gold on the elect. Rather he would guide them to a way of life that would deliver wealth as a reward. Hard work would be an important part of it, but piety, frugality and austerity also had a role to play, if only as a way of thanking God for the lucre he had allowed the righteous to make. Virtuous conduct was thus an equivalent of a thank-you note to God.

This was nothing short of a revolution, a crucible of class war. For the first time since Christ had made his appearance, a major religious figure upgraded wealth from an object of bare toleration to a sign of divine benevolence. Grace became quantifiable in pieces of gold.

In common with most other successful revolutionaries, Calvin sensed the mood of the masses and told them exactly what they

25. This is an example of the intellectual dead end awaiting any uncritical follower of Augustinian 'prevenient grace' theology.

craved to hear. For the good burghers of Geneva had already come to believe what Calvin so clearly enunciated. Money for them was a tool of self-assertion and a road to political power. And the only way for them to make money was by offering sweat in return. So they worked their fingers to the bone, resenting any church restrictions on hard work.

Secretly they had always known that God continued to reward righteousness with money, just as he did in the Old Testament; now they no longer had to be secretive about it. And they were already frugal, spending money only on necessities and never on whims. Austerity too was in their nature, and the burghers eschewed opulence both out of inner conviction and also to emphasise the difference between themselves and the idle, degenerate aristocracy.

On second thoughts, perhaps describing the people to whom Calvin appealed first as 'the masses' is imprecise. The way of life based on toil and thrift was really the prerogative of the urban upper and middle classes. Those they employed as labourers, apprentices or assistants did not necessarily subscribe either to the practice or the theory of a physically joyless life. They liked their wine, women and song. Given half the chance they would spend their time indulging in those frivolous delights rather than putting in dawn-to-sunset shifts.

Potentially this represented a threat to the burghers, if only because the ungodly layabouts were so much more numerous that they could have a puncher's chance in any physical showdown. Thus the middle class found its ethos sandwiched between those of the aristocracy and the lower classes, who converged in their sybaritic tendencies.

By allowing the bourgeoisie to strike out against both, Calvin provided a much needed tool of social control. He married remunerative work and religion, thus making indolence a sin, only matched by the sin of pleasure-seeking. Now if hoi-polloi were to rebel against the rich, they would be rebelling against God – not something they were prepared to do. Not yet anyway.

In some important ways Calvin pushed Christianity even further towards its Judaic antecedents than Luther did. For one thing, material reward for virtue had until then been a feature of the Old Testament only. Followers of Christ were supposed to leave their possessions behind, not try to multiply them. Unlike Abraham whose faith was rewarded by riches, theirs was rewarded by a lifetime of penury. St Francis, shedding his clothes and walking out of his father's house naked, was closer to Christ than a successful merchant could ever be.

Also, the Jews were chosen to receive the Law, obeying which over a lifetime was a precondition for remaining in that select group. Likewise, those who according to Calvin were predestined for salvation had to show their gratitude by pursuing puritanical self-denial not just during some festivals, such as Lent, but every minute of their lives. Though he attacked Catholic monasticism among all other church institutions, Calvin effectively took his own version out of the monastery, extending denial of the world to the world at large.

In theory, there is something attractive about the ideal of pursuing virtue one's whole life, not just a hundred or so days a year. And it is easy to poke fun at an hypothetical Catholic who divides his week between debauchery and double-dealing only to go to confession on Sunday and be forgiven. In practice, however, there is a serious obstacle to turning such an ideal into reality. It is called human nature.

Perfect life can only be achieved by perfect people, and few of us fit this description. The rest welcome any excuse to practise what they do not preach. As a result, many Protestants used their religious freedom to steer clear of the more taxing demands on their lives. In heeding Calvin's simple explanations, they slit their own religious throats with Occam's razor.

Gradually many of them, along with much of what used to be called Christendom, moved away from the religion itself. This is not what Calvin envisaged, and it is something both he and Luther would have abhorred. They themselves believed in God with sincere passion. What they did not seem to believe in was consequences.

One detects some muddle in Calvin's theology, and indeed he lacked not only Luther's literary talent but also his consistency. This included his attitude to the Jews. While Luther was rabidly and constantly anti-Semitic, Calvin would alternate philo-Semitic pronouncements with such diatribes as '[The Jews'] rotten and unbending intransigence deserves that they be oppressed unendingly and without limit, and that they die in their misery without the pity of anyone.'

Calvin's anti-Semitic moods were brought on not only by his innermost feelings but also by his assessment of the economic picture that emerged from his teaching. Since money-lending was now regarded not as a sin but rather as a facilitator of divine grace, Christians could indulge in it to their hearts' content. Therefore, rather than being despised as usurers, Jews could now be loathed as business competitors. Calvin was thus enunciating the resentment already felt at the grass roots, and in this he used the stratagem of every successful rabble-rouser.

5

Understanding other people's motives is an ungrateful task – coming to grips with our own is hard enough. Thus we cannot know whether the aims Luther and Calvin inscribed on their banners were the same as those written in their hearts. It is the practical results of their activities that interest us here, and one can safely say that those may not have been foreseen by either man.

It can never be otherwise: every sweeping reform produces at least some results that are different from those desired. The likelihood of those results being not just different but opposite are directly proportionate to the reformers' zeal. And few reformers in history have been as zealous as Luther, Calvin and Zwingli. So even if we assume for the sake of argument that they pursued nothing but noble aims, we should still not be deterred from disparaging their results, or at least pondering them in isolation from their slogans.

One immediate consequence was psychological: people's acquisitive instincts had been freed from any religious constraints. When overlaid upon the humanistic tendencies growing in influence during and after the Renaissance, such freedom could be confidently expected to take people away from the religion whence it had come. When a child is allowed to stay up late provided he has no homework to do in the morning, he will remember only the first part and stay up late regardless. And if a grown-up is told that the third deadly sin does not have to be a sin, provided he kept his faith, his hearing just may be more acute when listening to the statement than to the qualifier.

The seven cardinal sins (lust, gluttony, greed, sloth, wrath, envy, pride) were singled out by the church specifically because they are deeply rooted in man's nature. It is the task of any civilisation, and certainly of any religion, to leaven the innate vices with the opposite virtues. Eternal vigilance is a must: any slackening in the hand keeping vices down, and they will wrestle themselves free. If a religion sends mixed signals, it will produce mixed results. And there is no doubt that any blessing of cupidity, no matter how extensively qualified, sent a mixed message.

In fact, both Luther and Calvin had an element of self-refutation in their teaching. On the one hand, they believed that original sin was so grave that nothing people did could ever absolve them of it. This made most people, apart from the few chosen by God for reasons known to him only, inveterate sinners slated for perdition. And, as every little sin came from the big one they could not expiate, they sinned consistently throughout their lives.

On the other hand, those same people were deemed good enough to be fully autonomous in religious matters. They had the freedom to decide which, if any, parts of Christianity were acceptable to them, and which were not.[26] And they were all supposed to have the subtlety of mind to study the Scripture on their own, resolving for themselves any possible conundrums as they arose and interpreting every word as they saw fit. Now, if we accept the sinful part, we shall have to believe that, so encouraged, most people would take out of the Scripture precisely the bits that justified their sinfulness and egotism.

Protestantism was custom-tailored to make it easier for people to hear only what they wanted to hear. And what they wanted to hear most was that, contrary to what Paul wrote to Timothy, neither money nor even love of it was the root of all evil. For the growing middle classes, money was not just a medium of exchange; it was their way to political power, social prominence and ultimately self-respect. Initially, they doubtless wished to honour the preconditions that Calvin had imposed on acquisitiveness, and some still do.

But the resolve of the majority could not have lasted century after century, especially since it was under attack from a predominantly humanist education and indeed the whole Zeitgeist. Sooner or later, pursuit of money had to be elevated to an independently high perch. It is no coincidence that the founding document of a predominantly Protestant United States of America canonised acquisitiveness (coyly referred to as 'pursuit of happiness') as an inalienable human right.

Another immediate effect of the Reformation was geopolitical. Overnight, the nature of geopolitics changed for, until the Reformation, Europe had been in effect a loose federation. Nation states in our meaning of the term did not exist, and different Christian princes had more things uniting them than those setting them apart. Military conflicts did happen – clashes of interests were

26. Thomas Jefferson took this tendency to its logical conclusion by clipping the passages he liked out of the Bible and pasting them into a notebook, thus creating his own Scripture.

unavoidable. But, even when protracted and bloody, they were more in the nature of local feuds than the all-out wars of extermination that are routine in modern times. If the princes got on with each other, there was peace. Otherwise, there was the occasional bloodletting, ferocious though it may have been. One way or the other, the rifts were never too deep.

The Reformation changed all that. Suddenly, France and Holland or England and Spain acquired a divisive difference, one that could not easily be settled by nuptial arrangements or by bartering territory. From then on, European countries were no longer just Christian. They became either Catholic or Protestant, and their respective churches had to take political sides.[27]

God, having first been privatised by the Reformation, was now nationalised by it. Thus one instant effect of the Reformation was the ever-growing politicising of religion, a development that had to be harmful to that institution. The commandment of loving one's neighbour had to be qualified by 'provided his brand of Christianity is the same as yours.'

Christianity was brought into further disrepute by the ensuing religious wars that raged throughout the sixteenth century, reaching the murderous peak of the Thirty Years' War in the first half of the seventeenth. To be fair, those wars mostly used religion as a pretext: their real reasons were to a large extent secular. Witness the fact that a Protestant England happily sided with a Catholic France against a Protestant Holland at the very beginning of the eighteenth century. Nevertheless, it was under religious banners that hundreds of thousands of young men were wiped out and whole provinces were devastated by armies living off the fat of the land.

In such wars there could only have been one metaphysical winner: scepticism (at best) and atheism (more likely). If Luther and Calvin had been told that their zeal would be a contributing factor in the triumph of atheism, they would no doubt have been appalled. But the law of unintended consequences worked against them.

---

27. In due course, the politics of religion transcended the religion of politics, as illustrated by this story. One Irishman asked another whether he was a Catholic or a Protestant. 'I'm an atheist,' was the reply. 'Yes, but are you a Catholic atheist or a Protestant atheist?' As they often do, funny stories reflect serious truth.

Another effect of the Reformation was purely monetary. As the burghers' innate urge to better themselves by hard work had been blessed by God, they redoubled their efforts. In those days hard work was the only reliable way of striking it rich, so their incomes had to increase. Yet the demands of their new religion meant that for the time being their outgoings remained low: thrift was still seen as an essential virtue.

This dual tendency led to a great accumulation of capital, and this was no longer spent on acquiring the rolling acres adjacent to one's original holdings: the burghers' wealth was in their heads and hands, not in their land. The only way they could invest their money was to finance the heads and hands of others. This was bound to produce a dynamic economy driven by capital, which is as useful a definition of capitalism as any.

Nor could this process be confined to Protestant countries only. Their Catholic neighbours had to follow suit not to find themselves at a competitive disadvantage militarily, as well as economically. The church had to go along, for any resistance to economic expansion in Catholic countries could have spelled a fatal weakening of its own position. As a result, the lines between secular and ecclesiastical authority were becoming increasingly blurred. In fact, such blurring was a direct, if unintended, result of the Reformation, and one that was of the greatest detriment to Christianity.

It was not by accident that from 1624 (the heyday of the Thirty Years' War) to 1661 the French state and therefore economy was run by two consecutive cardinals of the Catholic church (Richelieu and Mazarin). These were the years in which France became a major economic player in an increasingly capitalist Europe. If Paris, which is to say secular power, had been worth a mass, which is to say religion, to Henri of Navarre, then the two political cardinals could have dispensed with God altogether if politics had demanded it. Indifference to religion was becoming a religion in its own right.

We can conclude that, wittingly or unwittingly, the sixteenth century reformers changed the nature of the world by replacing, or at least beginning to replace, one reality with another. They may or may not have been aiming simply at improving the church, but the practical result of their activities was that they weakened it. The church was no longer strong enough to resist the advent of the virtual world, which is an immediate consequence of any destruction of a traditional culture, understood here in the broadest possible sense. Destroying it was easy, but replacing it with another has proved impossible. T.S. Eliot diagnosed the condition accurately:

'If Christianity goes, the whole of our culture goes. Then you must start painfully again, and you cannot put on a new culture ready-made. You must wait for the grass to grow to feed the sheep to give the wool out of which your new coat will be made. You must pass through many centuries of barbarism. We should not live to see the new culture, nor would our great-great-great grandchildren: and if we did, not one of us would be happy in it.'

Eliot had the benefit of hindsight in his observation: long before the time of his writing barbarism had indeed arrived. Incongruously, it was called the Enlightenment.

THE ENLIGHTENMENT AND OTHER MISNOMERS

1

By the eighteenth century 'the privatisation of the spirit' (I have borrowed this precise term from the German-American philosopher Eric Voegelin) had been more or less complete. Religion, be that Catholicism or Protestantism, could no longer curb the free flow of secular passions.

But a century and a half before those passions splashed out in the scarlet dye of 1789, the philosophical basis for the Enlightenment had already been laid by a thinker who called himself a Catholic. For it was René Descartes who effectively took God out of philosophy, thus claiming the laurels of laying a scientific basis for atheism.

'I cannot forgive Descartes; in all his philosophy he did his best to dispense with God. But he couldn't avoid making Him set the world in motion with a flip of His thumb; after that he had no more use for God.' This comment came from Blaise Pascal as he forlornly watched Descartes steer the ship of philosophy away from theology. The course thus charted presupposed no return. Rather than liberating philosophy, Descartes was casting it adrift.

Whenever likeminded thinkers have tried to sail back ever since, the ship would either get stuck in the sandbank of deism or else shatter against the rocks of rationalism. Eschewing what they called 'blind faith', they found themselves in philosophical blind alleys. Failing to make sense of God, they stopped making philosophical sense.

This was the outcome Pascal foresaw when he spoke of 'the God of Abraham, the God of Isaac, the God of Jacob, not of philosophers and scholars.' Shakespeare had said a similar thing first: 'There are more things in heaven and earth, Horatio, // Than are dreamt of in your philosophy.'[28] 'The heart,' confirmed Pascal, 'has its reasons which reason knows nothing of.'

Descartes established the only unassailable starting point possible for a proud thinker who wishes for philosophy to go it alone, leaving theology in its wake. 'I think, therefore I am' is a neat summation of the solipsistic epistemology flowing out of man himself. I am certain that I exist because I think. *What* I think is irrelevant; *that* I think passes every possible test, for such tests too have to come from thought. For all I know, everything else may or may not exist; in any event, everything must be doubted, including God.

However, Descartes did not get around to explaining the origin of thought (nor did he explain the nature of language, which is by definition public property). Presumably he believed it was eternal. If so, and if in all likelihood he himself had not existed before he was born, then thinking cannot be self-contained. It can only be regarded as an extension and indirect proof of a greater whole, but Descartes did not wish to go there: his solipsism was too dear to his heart.

Having thus rubbished the first metaphysical premise, Descartes did not even have the courage to adopt the second, atheist one. Actually, he need not have bothered. Such a solipsistic epistemology, if logically developed to a point where it replaces metaphysics, will surely lead to deism, at best relegating God to the lowly status of a clock-winding aforethought. Atheism is the next, almost redundant, step, even though Descartes himself never got around to making it. In fact, he illogically maintained that it was God who guarantees the veracity of 'clear and distinct' ideas.

Nonetheless, Descartes could have signed his own name under the aphorism attributed to the pre-Socratic philosopher Protagoras: 'Concerning the gods, I have no means of knowing whether they

28. Shakespeare is generally regarded as a proto-Cartesian, an agnostic existentialist before his time, with 'to be or not to be' cited as evidence. But the same play can be read differently. Hamlet confronts the spirit of his father, the physical meeting the metaphysical. The spirit then charges Hamlet with a mission. That, coming as it did from a metaphysical entity, had to be metaphysical at least partly. To fulfill that mission, Hamlet had to dissolve himself in it, deny his physical life, accept the loss of everyone he loved on earth, be betrayed by friends, then sacrifice his physical being altogether. Were these conscious Christological parallels or an artistic response to a vague echo resounding in a far recess of Shakespeare's mind?

exist or not or of what sort they may be, because of the obscurity of the subject, and the brevity of human life.'

The Greek did not know better; the Frenchman ought to have done. And of course for his followers 'I think; therefore I am' was to become a reliable proof of God's existence. If God is doubted, the doubter is on the way to becoming his own God. He thinks; he is God; therefore God exists. One yearns for the time of yore, when such syllogisms represented a shortcut to a lunatic asylum.

After Descartes the first, theistic, premise was no longer presumed by any thinker of serious influence (which is of course not at all the same as any serious thinker). Secularism ran first primary and then supreme, and the only service to God philosophers ever offered was thenceforth of the lip variety. This, however, was marginally better than no service at all. To paraphrase de la Rochefoucauld, frequent, if insincere, references to God are a tax one pays on atheism in an essentially theist country. That a non-believer feels called upon to make such references is testimony to the prevailing intellectual standards of the time (or place). They are proof that the authority empowered to collect such a tax is still in business.

Thus both major books of Adam Smith are strewn with bows towards God in whom, by all accounts, the author did not believe any more than his friend David Hume did. It is a safe assumption that had Smith been writing not in Scotland, where making overtly atheist statements was still dangerous in the eighteenth century, but in a more permissive England, not to mention France, the deity would have fallen by the wayside.

But following the victory of the Enlightenment, there would no longer exist any need for such subterfuge. Whereas before it had been socially unacceptable not to mention God now and then, it had now become decidedly outré to do so. The old reality was no longer seen as real.

As Eliot argued in the passage quoted at the end of the previous chapter, destroying a real world is relatively easy. But replacing one reality with another, if it is at all possible, can take centuries. Meanwhile, people may have to make do with a virtual world, covering their denuded culture with the emperor's clothes of make-believe.

2

However, no virtual world will ever be accepted even on its own limited terms unless it bears some resemblance to the real one. It must look like a duck, walk like a duck and quack like a duck – even if it is not a duck.

The Enlightenment, in order to be indeed seen by the credulous as a source of light, had no other choice but to shoplift the traditional culture and adapt its terms to the virtual reality that had taken its place. Otherwise people would have realised that this was the kind of fire that could only scorch, not illuminate.

This can best be illustrated using the example of the French revolutionary slogan *liberté, egalité, fraternité*. In the early stages of the revolution this triple lie of a motto did not run unopposed: other desiderata, such as unity and justice, were occasionally proposed as replacements for the brotherhood element. The ultimate winner was probably determined by its Christian overtones purloined from the original owner for PR purposes.

To start with, let us consider its tripartite form. We shall notice that many revolutionary slogans of post-Christian modernity are constructed of three elements, either words or phrases. Apart from the French one, we could cite the American 'life, liberty and pursuit of happiness', the Russian *'vsia vlast sovetam'* (all power to the Soviets) or the German *'ein Volk, ein Reich, ein Führer'* (one people, one nation, one leader). And even a somewhat less significant twentieth-century revolution had to chip in with a vapid *'Work harder, produce more, build Grenada!'*

What we are witnessing here is the first stage of shoplifting larceny: the revolutionaries sensed that the world around them was alive with Trinitarian music. As people's ears were attuned to it, they were predisposed to respond to similar sounds even if they conveyed a different meaning. In this instance, however, it was not just the music.

Also hidden in the French slogan was another mock-Christian allusion. For, according to the Enlighteners, 'fraternity' flowed out of 'liberty' and 'equality'. Philosophers of the time argued that no brotherhood was possible without liberty and equality, which is to say that the third part of the triad *proceeded* from the first two. One does not have to be a theologian to see how the deep and subtle Christian doctrine of the Trinity had been vulgarised for a very un-Christian purpose by adding the faked echoes of the Nicaean and Athanasian Creeds.

Each element of the French triad was stolen property. To the original owner, freedom came from – and led to – the truth, which is to say God; equality was a natural consequence of jointly loving, and being loved by, a supreme being, which is to say God; brotherhood implied a spiritual kinship bestowed by a common father, which is to say God.

The intellectual cardsharps of the Enlightenment deftly pulled the ace of God out of the pack, leaving people with a hand of cards that were not only low but also marked.

In a similarly devious way the linear nature of Judaeo-Christian eschatology was transformed into the secular doctrine of progress.[29] Unlike the Eastern mind trained to respond to circular, static philosophies, the Western mind had been conditioned by its philosophy to expect a vertical, upward movement. With an enviable sleight of hand, the *philosophes* replaced the kingdom of God as the

---

29. Christological mimicry also lies at the base of sociology, a wholly modern and therefore aggressively materialist science. From Comte (d. 1857) and Durkheim (d. 1917), sociologists have viewed man as a duality of the mortal individual and immortal collective. Durkheim even spoke of a 'collective soul'. By way of apology for having resorted to such archaic terminology, he attacked metaphysics every chance he got.

final destination of linear development with the eudemonic idea of happiness as the ultimate goal of life – which, courtesy of St Anselm, had been known since the eleventh century as a sure recipe for amorality. And as I have already mentioned, in the United States, the first country constituted along Enlightenment lines, the word 'happiness', as used by the Founding Fathers, became interchangeable with money.

Almost the exact wording as in the Declaration of Independence can be found in John Locke, the shining light for both American and French Enlighteners. In an often quoted statement Locke mentioned 'life, liberty and estate' in the context of 'natural rights', a concept of his that can only charitably be described as dubious, especially when used widely and indiscriminately.

A natural right is an entitlement that presupposes no ensuing obligation on anyone else's part. Estate ownership clearly does not qualify for this lofty designation: my natural right to own an estate would presuppose your natural obligation to provide one, something you may or may not agree to honour. Therefore, rather than being natural, this right is a matter of consensus.

However, in that particular context Locke's full statement was unobjectionable. What he talked about was *preserving* a man's 'life, liberty and estate against the injuries and attempts of other men', the rule of law in other words. But this was not how it came out in the Declaration of Independence. Its statement was snappy, a quality essential to slogans but sometimes detrimental to truth. The Founding Fathers chose a less precise term 'happiness', preceded by 'the pursuit of', a combination they declared to be a natural (inalienable) right.

This was more than a matter of semantics only: the underlying idea was turned around. Pursuit of property, rather than the Lockean legal protection of property already amassed, was a *de facto* declaration of dependence on money. The teleological nature of wealth, beatified by the Reformation, was thus canonised by the Enlightenment. Now it was time to turn economics into a science.

3

Unlike philosophy, which until then had been in Europe mainly a method used by theology, economics had never had any theological links. Perhaps because of that, until acquisition of wealth suddenly gained a spiritual dimension, economics had never existed as an independent discipline.

Christian states saw their principal task not in building a strong economy but in creating conditions in which each individual soul could be saved, or at least conditions in which such salvation would not be hampered. An economy producing comfort and therefore 'happiness' was understood as a minor means to that end. For most people the ultimate economic desideratum was not comfort but survival, an aspiration whose fulfilment did not necessarily involve the Faustian barter.

Predictably, the modern state, forged by the Enlightenment and annealed by the fire of two revolutions, American and French,[30] had to find its own eschatology – the memory of Christendom was still too vivid in people's minds for them to have settled for anything less. Again the techniques of a virtual world came in handy: people weaned on the expectation of the kingdom in heaven were now fed the illusion of one on earth.

Since God had been removed as the central figure of any realm, man himself had to fill the vacancy thus formed. The philosophes hoped that the new reality would effortlessly slot into the groove of the old one. But the fit turned out to be imperfect.

30. I find it hard to accept as immediately persuasive the commonly drawn distinction between the 'left-wing', i.e. French, and 'right-wing', i.e. Anglo-American, Enlightenment. Though in effect championed by the wonderful Burke, this is yet another example of a distinction without a difference. Philosophically the two variants were identical, with only their pronouncements differing somewhat. Their methods did differ, but only quantitatively, rather than qualitatively. Both after all resulted in bloody revolutions. The volume of bloodshed was not quite the same (although not far apart, if we justifiably regard the American Civil War as the second act of the Revolution), but this pales compared to their joint contribution to the triumph of modernity or, in our terminology, the second metaphysical premise.

Alas, from the very start of this project, man proved his unsuitability for such an exalted role. For a while the perpetrators of the French Revolution managed to convince the world that martial law was liberty, a cull of the upper classes (and anyone else the revolutionaries did not like very much) was equality, and dressing most of the eligible population in uniforms of the same design was brotherhood. But the ruse could not last indefinitely; people may be gullible enough to fall for short cons, but given time they can usually figure out the long ones for what they are. Pointed questions began to be asked: What is it all for? What comes in the end? *Quo vadis*, you poor man?

In common with most secular revolutionaries in history, the Enlightenment brigade realised that the threadbare fabric of empty phrases would soon be torn to shreds. Violence could only keep it stitched together for so long. And in any case, for old times' sake the thesis of a stick had to be counterbalanced with the antithesis of a carrot, hoping that a successful synthesis would somehow emerge.

A tangible promise was urgently needed, some material, palpable replacement for the reward people had been taught to expect in heaven. The self-appointed Enlighteners took stock of their puny bag of tricks and found only one item that could possibly qualify in any meaningful sense: money. Economics was bound to assume new significance as a result.

By then the scientific advances of the previous century had produced a certain concept of the world that the new 'science' of economics could adapt to its use. Galileo, Newton and Leibniz had changed the way people viewed life and the universe. And in an odd sort of way the heliocentric notion of the cosmos catered to the egocentric view of man.

The earth was no longer seen as a unique stage chosen by God for the drama of man to be played out. The universe was now perceived as a mechanical entity wholly describable in mathematical terms. It took another three centuries of scientific progress for mystery to make a comeback, but for the time being all seemed to be crystal-clear: the divine clock-winder did his bit at the beginning, and then Copernicus and Newton took over. The world was no longer a stage. It was a machine, with people as its cogs.

But as the cogs were sentient and sapient, they decided they could do more than just turn within the machine. They thought they could run it by the simple expedient of learning more about the mechanism and seeing how different parts of it fit together, so as to be able to predict and consequently affect its behaviour in eternity. Since the only tangible workings of the machine, those that had a direct impact on people's lives, were economic, the square peg of the economy had to be forced into the round hole previously occupied by religion.

The economy became central to human existence, and it gradually began to be seen as a complex system of interacting mathematical equations, rather than just so many people scrambling to put food on the table. But it could not just be a self-contained circular system: like any other system of the post-Christian world it had to have its own eschatology. The newly enlightened people were now ready to express this eschatology in numerical terms – after all, if Galileo had told them that the whole universe spoke the language of mathematics, then surely an economy could speak no other.

And in that language the only word for economic eschatology is growth, a linear teleological progression to ... where exactly? Good question. In the actual reality of Christendom, eschatological aspirations had a clearly defined end. Man in general had a beginning, adequately described in *Genesis*, and every man in particular directed his development towards an end, otherwise known as the kingdom of God. And so any development towards a specific goal has to come to an end. A perpetuum mobile is no more possible in life than it is in physics.

This is simple enough, yet in a virtual world such simplicity goes the way of all flesh. Replace a clearly defined metaphysical goal with year-on-year growth in most economic indicators, and the goal becomes a desert mirage; it moves further away when we feel we have reached it. Logically, there is no limit to economic growth: you can never be too rich, as an American socialite once put it so tersely.

And what is true of an individual also applies to society. If an economy had some final figure towards which to strive, say exactly ten times its current per capita volume, then the long eschatological con might have enough credibility to fool all but the least gullible. Every year could then be assessed in terms of getting closer (or not, as the case may be) to the figure people could see emblazoned in the sky. But such a figure does not, and cannot, exist. Therefore 'still bigger' can be the only answer to 'how big?'.

Thus the orderly house created by Christendom was replaced by a structure without a roof. People living inside such a structure could be reasonably happy when the sun shone, but they would be despondent every time it rained.

4

The upsurge in the science of economics was remarkably different from other sciences that also went through a veritable revolution during and around the time of the Enlightenment. There things that had been unknown became known. Discoveries were made, which in turn led to other, greater discoveries. People gained a better understanding of electricity and optics, astronomy and mechanics, chemistry and biology – and the names of those who spearheaded such understanding are still inevitably mentioned whenever the subject of human greatness comes up.

By contrast, the celebrated economists of the Enlightenment did not really discover anything new. The scholastics of the late Middle

Ages knew all about supply-demand determining prices. The Florentine bankers Amatino Manucci in the thirteenth century and Giovanni di Bicci de' Medici in the fourteenth already used a double-entry book-keeping system that was no different from ours (except perhaps with less reliance on a second set of books). Small manufacturing concerns had practised division of labour long before it was a twinkle in Adam Smith's eye, and Cistercian monks carried hydraulic technology to the outskirts of towns all over Europe.

Their expertise in marshalling water power turned them into leading metal producers, and in fact Europe's first foundry was built at the Cistercian abbey in the Burgundian village of Fontenay. Just like modern multinationals, if on a smaller scale, Cistercians diversified into all sorts of areas: from the wine industry, which they pioneered, to wool exports from England, which they monopolised.

Share ownership in some simple corporations was already practised widely at the same time, even though the system of limited liability did not exist. And the concept of property rights, much touted by Enlightenment economists as the bedrock of stable society, goes back even further: to Leviticus, Numbers and Samuel. Modern business law, specifically the practice of contracts and arbitrage without which a modern economy would be unimaginable, also has Old Testament antecedents.

What Adam Smith and his colleagues did was not so much develop new ideas or make new discoveries as provide an eloquent account of the old practices they observed. They obviously sensed a need for such efforts as they realised that a new type of society was emerging, one in which the economy would act as a virtual substitute for real metaphysics. In that they were indeed scientists, but as philosophers, not economists.

And their philosophy had to be atheistic: it was after all in the service of a nascent atheist modernity. The fact that, unlike Cistercian traders and Florentine bankers, most of the prominent Enlightenment economists were non-believers is telling: from that time on the economic sphere was no longer accountable to an authority infinitely higher than itself.

Nor was it just the economic sphere: from the time of the Enlightenment onwards religion has been seen as variously important but definitely separate from everyday life. Life was one thing, religion another. The USA, the first Enlightenment country and therefore the first modern country, proudly declared separation of religion and state.

When pressed on the subject, the framers of the Constitution usually suggested that the purpose of that clause was to protect religious freedom from encroachments by secular authority. Some of them probably believed that explanation; some did not. But irrespective of their beliefs, it became instantly clear that the only outcome was separation of every sphere of life, above all economic, from any constraints imposed by the Judaeo-Christian view of the world. To use our terminology, this represented the *de facto* triumph of the second metaphysical premise.

Freedom of religious worship, when married to Enlightenment principles, became freedom of manifest religious indifference. In a real world, there is no need to guarantee spiritual freedom; in every meaningful sense it is already guaranteed by God. At times and in places one may not be free to follow or ignore religious conventions, but one is never coerced by God.

We are free either to accept or to reject him, and no authority, secular or divine, can restrict this inner existential freedom. The outer liberty of behaviour towards religion is a different matter. This can indeed be inhibited for believer and infidel alike. Even those who despise religion can be made (or self-made) to profess respect for it. But is it necessarily a bad thing?

Observing elementary religious rituals and offering lip service to religion without actually believing in God may sound hypocritical.

But it is the kind of hypocrisy we can do without no more than we can dispense with the hypocrisy of civility and good manners. We may be insincere when wishing a good morning to someone we dislike. We may be two-faced when saying 'never mind' to someone who has just stepped on our foot. We may be disingenuous when wishing many happy returns to someone we would joyously see go straight to hell. But without such petty hypocrisies no civil society would be possible. As Augustine said, we ought to pretend to be good until we become good.

After the Enlightenment it became socially acceptable in most Western countries to be openly derisory towards God. In fact, it almost became socially *infra dig* not to be. One might be tempted to think that, for people other than believers, whose relative numbers have been steadily diminishing ever since, this represented a victory of honesty. In fact, it was not honesty but the virtual world that vanquished, at first tentatively and soon decisively.

For honesty is not among the founding virtues of post-Enlightenment modernity, quite the opposite. It is only in its atheism that modernity is candid. Its other founding beliefs are mostly false, which is another reason money became so inordinately important: just like in wine, there is truth in it. And people weaned on falsehoods yearn to get intoxicated on any tangible truth, no matter how lowly.

5

In fact, lies are the ever-present telltale sign by which we can know a virtual world when we see it. Of these there are many, but an insistent use of words like 'equality' and 'democracy' should top the list. These words never thrived in the reality perceived on the basis of the first metaphysical premise. Take equality, for example. Though it cannot be gainsaid that Christendom's goal was the ultimate equality of all, the kingdom of God, there was never much doubt that it took an hierarchical society to get there. Earthly hierarchy was seen as a vertical structure enabling man to climb to heavenly equality.

This may sound paradoxical, but in fact is not. For true equality can only exist in heaven; in earth, the belief that all men are created equal is wishful thinking at its most fanciful. In fact, if we believe what we see everywhere around us, men are demonstrably created very much unequal in size, physical strength, intelligence, talent, character, will power, industry, perseverance, appearance, sexuality – in fact, in everything.

Most of these qualities are instrumental in achieving greater success in various fields of endeavour, those requiring either muscular prowess or intellectual subtlety. Thus earthly inequality is a natural order of things, and it can only be distorted by unnatural means. Even then it will not disappear; it will either be replaced by a worse type of inequality or else camouflaged by demagoguery.

For example, all egalitarians other than militant socialists acknowledge that equality of result is an indigestible pie in the sky. However, they insist that equality of opportunity is a goal that is both laudable and achievable. In fact, it is more or less the other way around.

Equality of result can indeed be achieved by enforced levelling downwards (the only direction in which it is ever possible to level). All we have to do is follow most of Marx's prescriptions, and some of Plato's. It is possible to confiscate all property and pay citizens barely enough to keep them alive (this was more or less achieved in the country where I grew up). It is possible to put in place the kind of dumbed-down schools that will make everybody equally ignorant (this has been more or less achieved in the country where I grew old). It is possible to provide the kind of equal healthcare for all that has little to do with either caring for most citizens or keeping them healthy (both countries have achieved this).

What is absolutely impossible is to guarantee equality of opportunity. A child with two parents will have better opportunities to get on in life than a child raised by one parent. A boy who grew up surrounded by books will have a greater opportunity to get ahead intellectually than his coeval who grew up surrounded by discarded syringes and crushed beer cans. A British middle-class girl who goes to a good private school will have greater opportunities in life than one who attends a local comprehensive (closing private schools down, an idea so dear to many on the left of the political spectrum, would not redress this imbalance: middle-class parents will find a way of supplementing their daughter's education either abroad or at home). A child of two professional tennis players will have a better chance of becoming good at the game than a child of two chartered accountants. A young businessman who inherits a fortune will have a better opportunity of earning a greater fortune than someone who has to start from scratch (again, confiscatory inheritance laws will fail: as with all unjust regulations, people will either find a way around them or flee).

Yet equality has become such a shibboleth for the post-Christian classes that they are prepared to deny obvious facts in its name. Take IQ for example. Whoever dares to observe that different groups, be that class or race, have different median IQ scores will be immediately accused of (or even charged with) racism, fascism, elitism or any other ism that happens to be the faddish bogeyman at the time. The accusers are undoubtedly entitled to their own opinions, but they are not entitled to their own facts. And these show that a) IQ scores do differ from one group to the next and b) they are the most reliable predictor of practical success in any occupation (except perhaps, on current evidence, public service).

For example, in spite of being discriminated against, the Malayan Chinese are heavily overrepresented in professional and managerial positions. All sorts of spurious explanations are offered for this, but never the real one: the median IQ of the Chinese is a huge 16 points higher than that of the ethnic Malays. In the US, the descending scale of median IQ scores goes from the Asians (refuting the usual Eurocentricity argument against IQ tests) to the Jews to the other whites to the blacks, and this happens to correspond to the relative scale of these groups' success in life. No matter. Actual reality is no longer allowed to interfere with the virtual kind. If the facts do not support the egalitarian bias, then so much the worse for the facts – and for whomever as much as mentions them.

Material success is the real desideratum of the virtual world, with the real and the virtual clashing yet again on the issue of IQ. When the first metaphysical premise still affected social mores, intelligence testing, had it existed, would have been dismissed as a quaint irrelevance. The ability to get ahead in life was then not regarded as the indicator of human worth. It went without saying that some groups of people tended to be more intelligent, on average, than others. But this did not matter. Because it came from a sphere that was infinitely higher, the true equality shared by all people towered over the inequality of worldly success.

The bogus equality of the modern world, however, has to presuppose parity where none exists: practical ability. Lies and deception are the only way out of this conundrum: as empirical evidence destroys this presupposition everywhere we look, the evidence must either be falsified or, better still, hushed up. In this the virtual world displays more ruthless consistency than the real world ever did in opposing, say, the heliocentric theory.

As a curious aside, committed egalitarians often direct their attentions towards spelling (another fruit by which we shall know them). The traditional version formed over centuries, they claim, is by its nature discriminatory because the broad masses find it hard to master. Thus the ostensibly different egalitarian regimes in America, Russia and China all set out to reform spelling after they grabbed power. In America this process took a few decades, in China a few years and in Russia a few months, but the ultimate outcome is similar in all three: a spread of real ignorance masked by the extension of virtual literacy. This is the only possible result of any attempt at enforcing equality, not only in education but anywhere else.

An important thing to remember about egalitarianism is that levelling downwards is not just the only possible direction but, for the champions of this virtual-world idea, the only desirable one. To Burke 'compulsory equalisations,' could only mean, 'equal want, equal wretchedness, equal beggary.' To modern egalitarians they are the shining beacon. But any *true* equality is anathema to them, and it is amusing to watch them tie themselves in knots trying to pretend it is not, against both empirical evidence and sound common sense.

Progressive income taxation highlights this by setting up a conflict between two pieties. On the one hand, redistributive taxes strike a blow for the virtual world inasmuch as they represent an egalitarian attempt to push high earners down to the level of the low ones. On the other hand, they are a flagrant violation of the principle of equality under the law.

True enough, it goes without saying that someone who makes twice as much as someone else must pay twice as much tax in absolute terms. But making him pay twice (or, increasingly, three or four times) the *proportion* of his income makes all believers in justice and true equality cry havoc and let slip... well, they have no one to let slip. Their cause is not supported by anyone, save for a few eccentrics who are not received in polite society.

But for egalitarians the choice is clear: they are prepared to sacrifice justice, fairness and even utility (flat tax rates would make the economy healthier) at the altar of the virtual world. The results of such urges, however, are real-world, as shown by the example of the USA: 50 percent of all Americans pay no income tax at all; over 50 percent of all taxes are paid by the wealthiest three percent of households; 90 percent are paid by the wealthiest 10 percent. In Western Europe the situation is even worse. Thus in any reasonable sense the word 'equality' is a clear misnomer when applied to this levelling run riot.

Yet it would be wrong to say that equality, in whatever sense of the word, is a pipedream. In fact, every country in the world has achieved it in small enclaves where people's clothes, food, lodgings and indeed rights are not merely equal but identical. The people may or may not work, but their way of life is not affected either way. Their medical care and education are free, and things like TV sets and sports facilities are equally available (or sometimes not) to all. These perfectly egalitarian places are called gaols, and indeed prison is the epitome of egalitarian aspirations, the ideal towards which they strive.

This may sound facetious, but in fact it is just an illustration of an immutable truth: the relationship between earthly freedom and equality can only ever be inverse. The more of one, the less of the other. Total tyranny is a precondition for total equality (that is, below the level of the tyrant, who stands above the equal masses the same way the unequal prison warder stands above the equal inmates).

What is more, vociferous champions of equality for all know this, as they are aware of the virtual-world provenance of their animadversions. They know that any other than a half-hearted attempt to equalise people will only succeed in impoverishing them. In that event the modern state would renege on the only real promise on which its legitimacy rests: money.

People's minds, normally numbed to accept make-believe as real, will wake up with a jolt when the physical trappings of their lives are threatened. They may have been brainwashed to sing hosannas to equality, but the songs will turn to screams of rage the moment people are made to move from their cute suburban houses to the kind of stinking communal flat in which I grew up. That would be an inevitable result of any shifting of equality from the virtual to the real world.

For it is extreme inequality that is the ultimate end of a lifelong pursuit of 'happiness'. It could not be otherwise: The road to infinite growth has to be infinitely long, but our earthly lives are not. Different people will come to their final rest at different points along the way.

What is telling is that even the church, an institution created to promote the equality of all before God, was from the very beginning organised along hierarchical lines. It acted as a vertical fulcrum on which rested the fine balance between God and man. Though the church has always used elements of democracy to arrange its leaders in sequential order, it has never been wholly democratic in the one-man-one-vote sense in which the word is used these days. Nor, in any real sense, has any secular society.

6

That not only individuals within small groups but also societies at large are always organised hierarchically is no accident either. A society cannot function in any other way. What distinguishes one type of society from another is not the presence or absence of a hierarchy, but who rises to the top, and by what means.

It may be philosophers, though such a society only ever existed in Plato's imagination. It may be the valorous, the paladins who come to power by doing battle outside city walls while the townsmen cower inside – this used to happen, but has not for centuries. It could be the rich, although traditionally wealth prefers to exercise its power as a ventriloquist puppet-master hiding behind the screen: anything more overt could make it vulnerable to expropriation driven by envy. It could be party bureaucrats, which is the unfortunate state of affairs in the West today. What a society absolutely cannot be under any circumstances is an out-and-out democracy, and whenever the word is used in earnest we must be alert to the presence of a virtual world.

Let us qualify this statement. Unadulterated democracy can, indeed must, exist in a small community, for it is not only a just but also the most efficient way of running one. Plato set the upper limit beyond which no real democracy is possible at a population of 5,000. He may have been too generous, but undoubtedly those living in a village of a few hundred inhabitants can get together and by a simple show of hands elect the best possible mayor.

The choice is easy. They know that White is a fool, Gray is a knave, Green never gets out of bed before noon, and Brown drinks whisky at breakfast. On the other hand, Black, you know, the bloke who lives next door to the bakery, is bright, honest, hardworking, teetotal and gets things done. Do let's elect Black, he won't let us down. The villagers have thus exercised their informed choice because they had one.

Such a choice cannot exist even in a small country of a few million inhabitants, never mind the leading Western nations of today. There most people are supposed to elect one of the candidates they do not know from Adam. All they know is what those candidates, ably prompted by their publicists, say about themselves.

Jones is supposed to represent the future, while Smith stands for change. Jones thinks it unfair that some people make so much more money than others. Smith thinks it disgraceful that some people make so much less than others. Both promise to do something about that, though they are hazy about the specifics. Unless an economic disaster is upon them, they stand for higher government spending and lower taxes, though they are reticent about how such mutually exclusive ends can be achieved at the same time. They would never penalise hard work (as far as they are concerned, prising, on pain of imprisonment, half of people's income out of their wallets does not constitute such a penalty). At the same time, they would not let down the less fortunate (this means increasing taxes on the more fortunate, which is to say the majority, even further, though this is seldom stressed).

The voters thus do not have a real choice between two men. They have a virtual choice between two waffles. When that is the case, we know we live in a virtual world.

The word 'democracy' in both Greece and Rome had no one-man-one-vote implications, and Plato usually used it in the meaning of 'mob rule'. The American Founding Fathers never used it at all, and neither did Lincoln. But towards the end of the nineteenth century the word gained a little currency, as the more ambitious denizens of the virtual world had found it a useful smokescreen, while the more gullible among them actually believed the implicit promise, that of the *demos* calling the shots in reality.

Yet it is absolutely impossible for the people to govern themselves, if for no other than purely technical reasons. Citizens cannot delve into the nitty-gritty of government; they cannot ponder the very details in which the devil resides. A small department of just one ministry has to make hundreds of supposedly informed decisions every day, a process that takes many officials much time and specialised knowledge. Multiply that by the number of departments, and then by the number of ministries, and we realise that self-government can never be what the word suggests. The only promise a government could ever make is that at the next election it would be accountable to the people for the decisions it takes.

But even this promise becomes larcenous when democracy is unchecked by the power of other estates. By atomising the vote into millions of particles, democracy renders each individual vote meaningless. What has any weight at all is an aggregate of votes, a faceless, impersonal bloc voting for faceless, impersonal characters. Consequently, political success in democracies depends not on any talent for government, but on the ability to put such blocs together.

This has little to do with statesmanship. Coming to the fore instead are such qualities as disloyalty, a knack for demagoguery, photogenic appearance, absence of any constraining principles, ability to tell lies with convincing ease, cold disregard for *bono publico*, selfishness and an unquenchable quest for power at any cost – all typically, though not exclusively, modern, post-Christian traits. That modern democracy throws up mostly politicians of that ilk inevitably follows the triumph of the second metaphysical premise.[31]

Democracy, as it is practised in the West today, manifestly fails on the most vital criterion on which any political system must be judged: it does not elevate to government the fittest to govern. When democracy was merely a part of the political mix, England had Disraeli and Gladstone or, if you prefer, Canning and Pitt. Now that democracy has become the only part of the political mix, we have Major and Blair, or, if you prefer, Cameron and Miliband. (Readers living in other countries will easily come up with examples closer to home.) This goes to show that the candidates' ability to run a country is neither tested by modern elections nor sought by modern electorates.

This is not surprising: statesmanship is a real quality and as such belongs in the real world. But the game is now played by the rules of the virtual world, and what matters there is not reality but appearance of reality. How a candidate looks and sounds is not just more important than anything else – it is the only thing that matters. The electorate is prepared to accept at face value the kind of promises that a politician has no way, or indeed intention, of keeping.[32] People know, and do not mind, that a game is being played, like children pointing their index fingers at one another and shouting, 'Bang! You're dead!'

Virtual reality is being created, and it is the only kind that can subsist on falsehoods known to everyone for what they are. It never occurs to most people that a system in which lies are a congenital

---

31. We may be able to come up with a few rare exceptions, but they are unlikely to be numerous enough to act as anything other than the kind that prove the rule.

32. To cite a current example, in the last election the Tories explicitly promised a referendum on Europe. Neither they nor most voters seriously thought this would happen once they got into power.

disease, rather than a lamentable side effect, is as corrupt as it is corrupting. Both the liars who get elected and those who elect them knowing, and not caring, that they are liars, suffer from the kind of moral deficit that cannot be reduced within the dictates of the second metaphysical premise.

In the past, the princes who ruled countries were usually trained for the job from the day they were born. The most accomplished minds of the time were their tutors; the most prominent clergymen their moral guides. The system did not always succeed: even the best teachers will have stupid and indolent pupils who are either unwilling or unable to learn. But at least it was *designed* to succeed, a claim that can under no circumstances be made for our modern perversion of democracy.

In fact, the position of, say, a US president has to be the only white-collar job in the country for which neither appropriate credentials nor related experience is required. Thus the current holder of the top government job in the world had never held any other administrative position before being elected. He had never managed anything, not even a small company or its department.

Now, anyone who has ever written 'none' in the job-application rubric dealing with 'management experience' will know that the chance of securing employment in any other than the lowliest position equals, in round numbers, zero. And yet the same man who on the basis of his CV would not be regarded as qualified to manage a furniture warehouse with half a dozen employees, is deemed fit to run the biggest economy in the world, command a potent military force and offer rather imperative advice to other countries on how they ought to run their affairs. In that (and, one hopes, only in that) sense Mr Obama resembles Stalin who started his military career at the rank of marshal, rising to generalissimo two years later. The consequences of such a career path were quite disastrous for a 1941 Russia, and one can only hope, fingers crossed, that Mr Obama's tenure will result in less misery.

When they ascend to power, such newly elected 'leaders' justifiably fear that they will be found out. So they strive to put some clear blue water between themselves and the people who have elected them, thus reversing a truly (as opposed to virtually) democratic process. They seek to remove every remaining bit of power from the local, truly democratic bodies, which stay close to the voters, and to transfer it to the centralised Leviathan, claiming all the time that the people are governing themselves.

Thus unchecked democracy inevitably leads to ever-increasing centralisation, and for that reason it is wrong to complain, as today's conservatives often do, that growing centralisation undermines democracy. This is like saying that pregnancy undermines sex or bankruptcy undermines fiscal irresponsibility.

This explains the unstoppable march of the European Union, a corrupt setup designed to absolve the ruling elite of even vestigial accountability to the people they govern. There is not a single rational argument in favour of this abomination that cannot be destroyed in ten seconds flat by an averagely educated person. But rational arguments need not apply when the virtual world puts its foot down. We must, say the champions of European federalism, counteract the economic power of the United States, and dissolving the sovereignty of every European country into a giant, and gigantically corrupt, entity is the only way of doing it.

Leaving aside the question of why there is such an urgent need to oppose America, especially in the face of her dwindling power, one may instead ask another question: If that is the case, then why has every US administration in the twentieth and twenty-first centuries been firmly on the side of European federalism? Are they all bent on self-destruction? Cutting off their noses to spite their economic faces?

The answer is that modern governments no longer act in the interests of their countries or, God forbid, our civilisation, what is left of it. They are out to make sure that the real world cannot break through the fog of virtual reality, and the EU suits this purpose perfectly by thickening the fog and thinning out reality. Denationalised centralisation is the epitome of the virtual world.

If we personalise the governments involved, we shall see that the people who man them cannot help loving the EU. They know that this superstate will provide a nice little earner for them after their own fickle electorates have thrown them out. And their own good is all that matters to individuals worshipping at the altar of the second metaphysical premise, which is to say materialism. Also let us not forget power. Not only is it a glittering prize in itself, but it can also provide a natural transition to all sorts of other prizes, such as money, to name the most obvious one. (Tony Blair made millions in the first months after moving from Downing Street.)

While perpetrating centralisation run riot, the ostensibly democratic, but in fact neo-tyrannical, state acquires more power over the individual than any monarch who ruled by divine right ever saw in his dreams. French subjects, for example, were shielded from the absolutist Louis XIV by several layers of local government, and the Sun King wielded more power over his loftiest courtiers than over the lowliest peasants. The King was aware of this, and his famous pronouncement on the nature of the state fell more into the realm of wishful thinking than reportage.

By contrast, a freely voting French citizen or British subject of today has every aspect of his life controlled, or at least monitored, by a central government in whose actions he has little say. He meekly hands over half of his income (or more), knowing that the only result of this transfer will be an increase in the state's power to extort even more. Clutching the few remaining notes, he hopes that Leviathan, no longer athirst, will let him keep them for his family. He opens his papers to find yet again that the 'democratic' state has dealt him a blow, be that destroying his children's education, raising his taxes, wiping out his pension fund, devastating the army that protects him, closing his local hospital or letting murderers go free. In short, the word 'democracy', whether used to denote the perfect system for countries already considered democratic or – even worse – as the desired end for countries that still fall short of that ideal, is an unfailing indicator of virtual reality.

Liberal democracy, so beloved of American neoconservatives that they are prepared to lay about them like Macduff to spread it over every tribal society on earth, is in fact neither truly democratic nor particularly liberal. As it presupposes the *ad infinitum* expansion of a centralised state's ability to acquire ever-growing powers over the individual, it is not liberal in any other than the virtual sense of the word. And as the state has dictatorial powers (in spite of putting people through the charade of virtual elections every few years to make them believe they govern themselves), it is not democratic. In other words, 'liberal democracy' has become nothing but a mendacious slogan of a virtual world.

Therefore a 'democratic' government's claim to legitimacy is rather tenuous this side of its own propaganda. Consent of the governed has not been given freely and fairly. It has been tricked out of them by false pretences. Yet people are sometimes, though increasingly more seldom, capable of peeking through the fog of virtual reality to see the falsehood hiding behind. As they usually find what they see quite revolting, they indeed may very well revolt. When this happens, a 'democratic' government responds with the violence that would do most totalitarians proud.

This is best exemplified by the American Civil War, in which the country suffered heavier casualties than in all her previous and subsequent wars combined. Such extravagant bloodshed was to be expected: this was a clash between the real, decentralised democracy of small local governments and the virtual democracy of a giant centralised state.

THE ENLIGHTENMENT AND OTHER MISNOMERS

What was at stake was the distance between people and government, which the North wished to lengthen and the South to shorten. The issue of slavery used as a pretext for the war was never its real cause.[33]

Both sides displayed an all-out commitment to the Civil War, sensing that no conflict between a real and virtual world could ever end without a decisive victory for one side. Hence the unrestrained savagery displayed by the victorious Yankees in the closing months of the war; and hence the gallant effort of the Confederates who stood to the last man.

The North realised that nothing short of a 'scorched earth' policy would do. The South knew that the North did not just desire the end of slavery – it sought to impose on the South the dictates of a centralised state, riding roughshod over the real democracy of state rights.

In the process, certain iconic personages behaved in a way that belied their subsequent reputation. Abraham Lincoln, for example, closed down 300 pro-Southern newspapers (and had their presses smashed), suppressed the writ of habeas corpus and, according to the Commissary General of Prisoners, had 13,535 Northern citizens arrested for political crimes from February 1862 to April 1865. Comparing his record with that of the hideous Mussolini, who only managed 1,624 political convictions in 20 years and yet is universally and justly reviled, one begins to see modern hagiography in a different light.

33. It may, however, have been a factor in the defeat of the Confederacy. The Southerners never received the support they expected from England partly because the English regarded slavery as abhorrent. Though the slave trade was only formally outlawed in 1807, this attitude goes back much further. For example, a report of a case from 1569, in the reign of Elizabeth I, states that: '... one Cartwright brought a slave from Russia and would scourge him; for which he was questioned; and it was resolved, that England was too pure an air for a slave to breathe, and so everyone who breathes it becomes free. Everyone who comes to this island is entitled to the protection of English law, whatever oppression he may have suffered and whatever may be the colour of his skin.' Incidentally, the practice of slavery in America was also an important reason for England's intransigence during the American Revolution, though this is seldom mentioned. But at the time Enlightenment demagogues like Jefferson saw no incongruity between their liberal rhetoric and owning hundreds of slaves. Dr Johnson did: 'How is it that we hear the loudest yelps for liberty among the drivers of negroes?'

7

One consequence of the war is not much commented upon, though it is very serious. For the Civil War was the first time income tax was introduced in America: the North could not finance the war in any other way. Though standing at a reasonable three percent, the income tax was duly abolished after the war. But the precedent was set: the ends of a virtual world had to be paid for in real money.

However, by and large people in the West have been brainwashed not to peek through the emperor's clothes of a virtual world. They are prepared to have the wool pulled over their eyes for as long as the state does not renege on its underlying real claim to legitimacy: money. Therefore, in a virtual world hatched by the Enlightenment the economy had to assume an inordinate importance: no virtual government could survive a real economic collapse.

Politicians know this, at least the successful ones do. Hence the phrase 'it's the economy, stupid', coined by the Clinton strategist James Carville during the 1992 campaign for the presidency. The US economy, still reeling from a recent recession, was not doing well, and yet in his own campaign President Bush was carrying on about his (virtual) achievements in foreign policy. He was on a guaranteed loser there.

For underneath it all the *raison d'être* of a modern government has nothing to do with foreign policy – especially in America where most people have only a vague idea about the map of the world, routinely confusing Austria with Australia or Sweden with Switzerland (the British are rapidly catching up with them in that respect). The government has to promise, nay guarantee, prosperity. If it keeps its word, it will be allowed to indulge in any amount of virtual-reality shenanigans, even including the odd war with ill-defined objectives and a dubious moral justification.

People do not mind this any longer: money is the only thing that matters. That is why it is so cringe-making to see US dollar bills displaying the slogan 'In God we trust'. It is the green-backed medium, not the message it carries, that has any real meaning in the virtual world.

8

The virtual and manifestly unenlightened world emerging out of the Enlightenment was ready to pursue happiness to the exclusion of everything else. Most moral, and all religious, considerations no longer mattered: they were either discarded or shifted into the virtual world and thereby perverted.

The case of Goethe, widely regarded as the greatest man of his time, is characteristic. A key figure of the Enlightenment, Goethe admired Napoleon so much that he publicly vindicated the latter's order to slaughter 2,000 Turkish POWs, which had caused some mild stir even in the Enlightenment-happy circles. That was the clearest signal of a moral retrenchment: what used to be objectionable was now permissible, if not actually laudable, provided it was perpetrated for the benefit of the virtual world.

People, even those of Goethe's stature, had lost the knowledge held by the real world: most secular causes are relative, while the value of a single human life is absolute. What was the massacre of a couple of thousand Turks after the murder of hundreds of thousands in, say, the Vendée? After France herself had been decapitated by the guillotine? Whatever it was, the post-Enlightenment man did not want to know. He had other priorities.

'We only live once' had become the underlying notion of modernity, though it took another century or so for it to be enunciated clearly and universally. The formula based on the victorious second metaphysical premise was attractively simple: 1) our three-score and ten is all there is, 2) therefore we must derive as much comfort and pleasure as we possibly can, 3) as both comfort and pleasure cost money, we must make as much of it as possible. This formula was always in the background of the state's handling of its affairs. Whatever else it was striving to achieve, the state simply could not afford to neglect or, worse still, stand in the way of its subjects' economic aspirations.

Therefore, since empirical evidence, supported by much recent and current scholarship, had demonstrated that economic success was directly proportionate to economic liberty, the newly hatched modern state had to curb its tyrannical, centralising instincts enough not to make 'happiness' as illusory as, say, equality. However, the best the state could hope to achieve was not to get into the spoke of the economic wheel. No government could set the wheel in motion, not yet anyway. It took another revolution to do that.

9

The Industrial Revolution exploded onto Europe concurrently with the halcyon days of the Enlightenment, starting with Britain in the second half of the eighteenth century. Britain led the way for a variety of reasons. The national character undoubtedly had a role to play: the pragmatic Brits were always more likely than, say, the Italians to process Enlightenment rhetoric into remunerative practicalities. But that aside, in broad outlines the reasons fell into four major groups: political, geopolitical, social and religious.

Politically, after the Glorious Revolution of 1688 Britain was the only major European country that enjoyed a stable government, based on a constitutional monarchy. Though Louis XIV's famous pronouncement on the nature of the state was mostly wishful thinking, his rule was still too absolutist to be conducive to a full-blown economic explosion.

But in England power was becoming more and more balanced among various estates, providing the institutional skeleton on which the flesh of a dynamic economy could then grow. Real democracy had not yet been ousted by the virtual kind.

Unlike the rest of Europe, the Kingdom was truly United under the crown. All other key European states, even if they formally could be described as such (which, say, Germany and Italy could not), were divided into more or less autonomous provinces that did not perceive much kinship between themselves and their neighbours.[34]

Even linguistic commonality could not be taken for granted: it is characteristic that as late as the mid-nineteenth century, most French citizens did not regard French as their first language. Internal, to say nothing of foreign, trade in those countries was difficult, what with some provinces imposing duties on others. Britain, on the other hand, had been a united country since the 1707 Acts of Union (and England for centuries before that), which made not only trade but also free exchange of technological and scientific innovations much easier.

Geopolitically, Britain was a maritime nation with by far the largest merchant marine in the world, and the strongest navy able to protect her commercial fleet while it went about its business. Thus Britain was able to benefit from her colonial expansion more than, for instance, France or Holland could benefit from theirs. And during the second phase of the Industrial Revolution in the nineteenth century, Britain's rule of the seas became absolute as during the Napoleonic wars the Royal Navy had wiped out every continental merchant fleet. One effect of naval domination was the country's ability to control her borders, thus limiting the spread of resource-sapping epidemics and so increasing the available labour force.

The early stages of the Industrial Revolution also produced an agricultural revolution, when food production became more efficient and less labour-intensive. That released even more people into

34. Russia, to the extent to which it could be considered a European power, was of course united. But it was held together by a tyrannical absolute monarchy, too rigid to allow the kind of flexibility that is a precondition for a thriving economy.

manufacturing while, at the same time, the middle class grew in both size and power. Socially, Britain was becoming a mixed society that was for the next century able to maintain a balance between a mostly aristocratic culture and a mostly bourgeois economy. None of the estates felt hostility towards any of the others, not much anyway, and whatever social conflicts did arise could be solved without the gushing bloodshed that was such an endearing feature of the French Revolution.

And religiously, Britain was not only a Protestant country, but also one in which numerous Protestant sects were sprouting up. Though, as we have seen, capitalism had begun to raise its head long before the Reformation, there is no denying that Protestantism generally and Protestant sectarianism in particular were instrumental in removing all stops in capitalism's way. Most British sects had Calvinist antecedents, and therefore saw personal enrichment as a sign of God's benevolence. They could thus direct their energy into commercial channels self-righteously, without feeling the slightest remorse.

Moreover, as membership in the established Anglican Church was an ironclad requirement for entering public service, few non-commercial channels were available to communicants of other confessions. Nor could they necessarily receive the classical education provided by English universities, of which at the time there were, all told, two. Non-Anglicans could still be educated in Scotland, and some took advantage of that opportunity, though most chose a commercial bird in the English hand rather than two educational birds in the Scottish bush.[35]

At the same time, religious fervour, only rarely an overriding factor of English life to the extent it had been on the continent, was on the wane. The violent clashes during the Stuart reign were never

35. It is interesting to compare their situation with that of Russian Jews at the time. They too had to go into commerce, for most other venues were statutorily blocked. They too could not enter Russian universities in numbers exceeding small quotas. Those who still sought higher education had to go abroad, mostly to Germany. Even in the early twentieth century Boris Pasternak had to be educated at Magburg, rather than Moscow, University. Another Russian parallel would be with the Old Believers who were persecuted with various (though steadily diminishing) degrees of savagery. Just like British sectarians, they too sought their revenge in the business arena, which they more or less dominated in the nineteenth century.

wholly, or indeed largely, animated by religion, though it did have a role to play. In general, the English incline towards moderation, or at least they did at that time. This trait is reflected in the Anglican theology and the inclusive makeup of the country's national church ('a Catholic liturgy with Calvinist Articles').

Characteristically, arguments about the true nature of the Anglican church are still on-going. Some claim it is Calvinist, others object that its Protestant body houses a Catholic soul, and most see it as an amalgam. Only moderate (or else slightly indifferent) people could have produced a creed under whose aegis near-Catholics can coexist with near-Calvinists for centuries. In any case, at the time of the Industrial Revolution, religion did not hold a strong enough sway to inhibit people's acquisitiveness in any way.

It has to be said that, though the Industrial Revolution began in Britain, it did not remain confined to those shores for long. Far and away the world's biggest manufacturer throughout the nineteenth century, by 1910 Britain had been overtaken by both America and Germany. That was to be expected: as Britain had shown the way to riches, and therefore power, other countries had to jump on the bandwagon of the Industrial Revolution willy-nilly. They simply could not afford to let Britain pull so far ahead that she could dominate European affairs. This is the more obvious explanation of the rapid and seemingly coordinated spread of industrialisation throughout the Western world. There is also another one, lying slightly underneath the surface.

As most things, this has to do with the vagaries of the human soul, which Tertullian wrongly claimed was by nature Christian. Just a few pages later in the same book he corrected himself: 'Christians are made, not born.' If people have to be made to be something, they were not that way to begin with. If we attempt to resolve the contradiction between the two statements by applying his test of empirical evidence, surely we shall see that Tertullian's first statement is wishful thinking, while his second is true to life.

As amply demonstrated by the entire history of man, the human soul is not by nature Christian. It would be closer to the truth to say that by nature it is pagan. If we look at Christian ethics, for example, who among us will claim that loving not only our neighbour but also our enemy comes naturally? Who will suggest that putting God before all else, including oneself and one's family, is an innate impulse?

It would not be a gross exaggeration to suggest that even within Christendom such saintly individuals would have been hugely outnumbered by others, those who had turned themselves into Christians by overcoming the pagan temptation. As such people would have readily testified, this involved not only the original effort, but also a life-long exertion of willpower, required to make sure they did not fall from the perch they had reached.

This is consistent not only with empirical observation but also with the doctrine of original sin: we are all fallen to begin with and only by divine grace (aided or not, depending on whether one follows Catholic or Protestant doctrine, by our good works) can we be saved.

Now, neglecting our own material wellbeing while making life-long efforts for the sake of other people is not something that most of us find easy. We are at heart a selfish bunch. But in order to maintain a modicum of self-respect we tend to seek an inner justification for egotism, an excuse not to do those things that do not come naturally. The Industrial Revolution, coming as it did in the wake (and partly as a result) of the historical triumph of the second metaphysical premise, provided such an excuse.

It dangled the temptation of enrichment before people's eyes, and this was much more subtle than the old diabolical entreaty. The implicit message was not just 'all this can be yours', but 'you can have all this without in any way violating any covenants or moral principles – on the contrary, by pursuing wealth in any other than an illegal way you can strike a blow for religious rectitude.' The Protestant countries led the way, but the others applauded when no skies had opened and no lightning had come down. Following suit with maximum speed and efficacy came to them as naturally as a smile comes on to a baby's face.

The Industrial Revolution put the last brick into the edifice of economism. Economic growth in the Western world became so rapid and all-conquering that it created a powerful magnet drawing everyone in. Economy had become the only real world then, and for a while it managed to step out of the shadow cast by virtual reality.

There was nothing virtual about the economy during the Industrial Revolution: it was heavily slanted towards manufacturing, which is to say actually making things people needed and wanted to buy. And they could afford to do so in ever-increasing numbers because the nature of a vibrant economy is such that riches have to be spread widely, though never evenly. Happiness, if not quite achieved yet, now seemed achievable.

People knew what they wanted (money and the physical comfort it could buy), what they did not want (religion and the spiritual solace it promised as a result of life-long exertion) and what they saw in their future (bliss in this world, for there is no other). The second metaphysical premise had conquered: economy, reflecting the creative power of the individual, had ousted religion, reflecting the creative power of God.

As a result of the complex interplay between Renaissance humanism, Protestantism, the Enlightenment and the Industrial Revolution, man had placed himself and his passions at the fulcrum of the universe. And he had found in the economy the ultimate lever that could move the world.

We have already seen that, economy apart, there was little that was real about the new reality. Yet even when it comes to the economy, the post-Enlightenment, post-Christian world of virtual reality was not without some congenital contradictions. And unlike Christian antinomies, these could not be resolved by a successful synthesis. Not easily and not indefinitely at any rate.

VIRTUAL SCIENCE IN THE SERVICE OF TOTALITARIAN ECONOMISM

1

Towards the end of the nineteenth century, the West found itself in an odd situation. The real world of frantic economic activity was being packed in the cotton wool of virtual reality. Moreover, the packaging did not always fit the content, with sharp corners sticking out all over the place.

The illusory world was made up of many apparently disparate elements that were nonetheless linked together by a chain of unreality. It was this chain that bound together social and natural sciences, politics, art and even economics, though not yet the economy itself. And people, locked in their increasingly narrow-minded pursuit of 'happiness', were too busy to notice the growing gap between how things were and how they were depicted to be. Nor did they recognise the totalitarian elements in their ostensibly democratic society.

In fact, the word 'totalitarian' deserves to have its application widened. It is normally used to describe the Soviet Union, Nazi Germany, China and other states that resemble these more or less closely. Such states are considered to be totalitarian because they strive for absolute control over every aspect of society in general and each individual life in particular. One has to acknowledge that this definition makes sense on a superficial level. It tags adequately the mechanics of running a country in that particular way. But do let us keep in mind that at a deeper level the glittering ideal that totalitarians see in their minds' eye is not merely, or even primarily, the creating of a certain type of state. It is the creating of a certain type of man.

As we always must, let us listen to the experts, in this case such an eminent authority on the subject as Dr Goebbels: 'The revolution we have made is a total one. It has encompassed every area of public life and fundamentally restructured them all. It has completely changed and restructured people's relationships to one another, to the state, to questions of existence.'

If we were to single out this 'restructuring' aspiration as perhaps the most salient aspect of a totalitarian society, we would find out that red, brown or black are not its only possible colours. Red, white and blue can work just as well. For the seismic change brought about by the universal shift from the first metaphysical premise to the second produced a new type of man more sweepingly, and perhaps irreversibly, than any other development in Western history, including Bolshevik and Nazi revolutions.

The phenomena I have described so far, Renaissance humanism, the Reformation, the Enlightenment and the Industrial Revolution, for all their obvious differences, pulled towards the same goal. What emerged at the other end was a new type of man and a new type of reality. A new world, in other words.

Political differences, when measured against the defining character-forming aspect of this world, matter relatively little – and certainly much less than is commonly believed. That a commissar or a gauleiter is politically different from an MP or a senator is obvious enough. But what brings them all close together is their shared dependence on the new man, and their commitment to either creating or perpetuating him.

In this they rely on a full armoury of weapons forged in both worlds, virtual (propaganda, sloganeering, pseudoscience) and real (economy). I have already commented upon the striking resemblance between the economies of the liberal-democratic USA and the totalitarian Nazi Germany in the nineteen-thirties. Underlying both was a clash of the two worlds, with virtual reality breaking into areas that had hitherto been beyond its reach. But a totalitarian society will allow nothing to stay out of its reach for long.

The core of the new society was economic, as it had to be with people conditioned to pursue happiness rather than virtue. So it was that core that had to be shifted into the virtual world for its triumph to be complete. The science of economics could be converted to virtuality easily enough; all it took was a quick divorce between the science itself and its object of study. The actual economic life was a tougher nut to crack, but modernity is never short of a sledgehammer or two. In this case it was science that acted as one such blunt instrument.

Science, both social and natural, had a foot in each world. On the one hand, its very essence would suggest that its stock in trade was dealing with facts. And so it largely was, with its core business thriving throughout the nineteenth century. But on the other hand, as the virtual world is by its very nature totalitarian, it cannot accept that some of its domains would be able to deal with reality only. If real science came up with facts that contradicted the assumptions of the virtual world, then virtual science had to step in either to destroy reality or to distort it beyond recognition.[36]

Thus it fell upon the first post-Enlightenment century, the nineteenth, to create a virtual science that, contrary to every available fact and indeed plain common sense, would then explain the world in a way that would justify the basest instincts of man.

2

It is only in those conditions that something as manifestly false as Marxism could gain prominence and eventually, in some parts of the world, dominance. Even when rejecting the revolutionary content of Marxism, more and more people were ready to welcome some of its assumptions, for the primacy of matter and the all-conquering significance of the economy vindicated the virtual basis of modernity. Marx's portrayal of social life as a product of struggle

36. Studying physics at a Soviet school of the late fifties, we were told that the atom was 'the smallest and further indivisible particle of matter'. Even as eleven-year-olds who had never heard of Rutherford but had heard of nuclear weapons, we knew this was not so, and the teachers knew that we knew. But it was tacitly understood that reality was one thing and the virtual world another. Nor was there any doubt as to which of them came first.

among hostile classes also struck a chord with the masses who had been encouraged over the previous three centuries to perceive themselves, somewhat oxymoronically, as both the hub of the universe and also as victims of social, economic or religious oppression.

Now their deep-seated resentments had found an updated intellectual base. They had been shown a clear path to social advancement that did not require a dedicated effort to improve themselves in any spiritual or cultural sense. A class structure based upon people's relation to the 'means of production' made it easy for them to achieve social elevation by simply being good at making a living. And victory in the class war could at the same time remove any meaningful competition, both economic and cultural. That was really all they wanted to know, and hearsay was good enough. Few were prepared to peruse Marx's barely readable tracts, but, what with a small army of exegetes ever busy, there was no need.

However, had people read Marx, instead of relying on apostolic mouthpieces, they would have known that the central doctrines of Marxism were false even at the time of writing. Marx wrote for political, not intellectual, ends, and he was ever ready to suppress the data that contradicted his theories. For example, the first edition of Das Kapital gives most statistics up to 1865 or 1866, except those for changes in wages that stop in 1850. The second edition brings all other statistics up to date, but the movement of wages again stops in 1850 not to show an upward curve.

Any serious study will demonstrate that Marx based his theories on industrial conditions that either were already obsolete at the time or were on the way out – or had never existed in the first place. That is no wonder, for Marx never saw the inside of a plant or a farm. He could have done so easily enough (his accomplice Engels owned a factory), but no prophet of the virtual world would allow reality to puncture holes in his tissue of lies.

Actually, the point about Marx's selective treatment of facts is only worth making because of all the numerous claims to scientific truth made by and for him in the virtual world. Yet it ought to be clear enough that, whatever else he was, Marx was not a scientist. He did not pursue truth, and all his writings were designed for one purpose: to justify the burgeoning virtual world, make it feel good about itself and hostile towards reality.

Marx gave the denizens of that world something they had been sorely missing: a secular eschatology to fit their instincts. While the kingdom in heaven had been debunked beyond a comeback even before Marx, the kingdom in earth was at last described in detail. Marx went the likes of Campanella, Saint-Simon, Fourier and Owen one better by creating a utopia that did not look utopian. His ideal society appeared to be there for the taking, however long that took to achieve. It was a utopia nonetheless, but one put together with more thoroughness than any of his predecessors had been able to bring to the task.

Since for 70-odd years the most formidable propaganda machine in history was dedicated to spreading Marxism, many feel they know what Marx is all about without having to resort to the primary source. That is a pity for, if more people had actually read *The Communist Manifesto*, one hopes there would be fewer innocents who echo virtual-world propaganda by saying that Marx's ideals were wonderful but regrettably unachievable; or else that Marx's theory was perverted by Soviet practice. In fact, Marx's ideals are unachievable precisely because they are so monstrous that even the Bolsheviks never quite managed to realise them fully, and not for any lack of trying.

For example, the Manifesto (along with other writings by both Marx and Engels), prescribes the nationalisation of all private property without exception. Even Stalin's Russia in the thirties fell short of that ideal. In fact, a good chunk of the Soviet economy was

179

then in private hands (small agricultural holdings, repair shops, construction and other co-ops, some medical care, etc.). And people were allowed to own cottages, flats, clothes on their backs, radio sets, dovecotes, tools – really, compared with Marx, Stalin begins to look like a humanitarian trying to get in touch with his feminine side.

Echoing Plato's ideals, Marx also insisted that family should be abolished, with women becoming communal property and their children being taken away from them, pooled together and raised by the state as its wards. That too remained a dream for the Bolsheviks who tried to make it a reality by forcing both parents to work, and leaving no place for children to go but the state-owned crèches, kindergartens and young pioneers' camps. But that was as far as it went: kindergartens and young pioneers' camps were not compulsory, and those fortunate women who could get by without full-time employment were still free to raise their children more or less as they saw fit. Nor did they put themselves into communal ownership, unless they wanted to.

Post-Plato slave labour, such an arresting feature of both Soviet Russia and Nazi Germany, also derives from Marx – and again Messrs Lenin, Stalin and Hitler displayed a great deal of weak-kneed liberalism in bringing his ideas to fruition. Marx, after all, wrote about *total* militarisation of the workforce to be achieved by organising it into 'labour armies'. Yet no more than 10 percent of the Soviet citizens were ever in enforced labour at the same time. The rest could still more or less choose their professions, and for some it was even possible to choose their place of employment. The more recalcitrant elements (kindly described by Lenin as 'especially noxious insects', these included everyone who was a bit slow in seeing the light) were kept in what Engels envisaged as 'special guarded places', but even in Soviet Russia no more than 15 million people were ever in concentration camps at any one time (unless of course one regards, with justification, the whole country as a giant concentration camp).

The Nazis did not even manage to come close to that figure, although, to be fair, they were too involved in their external wars to devote proper attention to fighting their own people, Soviet style. Nor was it as necessary, considering the overwhelming support the Nazi regime enjoyed within Germany – something denied the Bolsheviks in their country.

That Marx, for all his monstrosity, was able to set the semantic terms not only in his time but also in ours testifies to the width of the inroads the virtual world has made into any coherent reality. And set the terms he did, for even economists who worship at a different theoretical altar have accepted the Marxist view of the economy as the be-all and end-all of society.

For example, such distinguished Austrian scholars as Ludwig von Mises and Friedrich Hayek, along with their Chicago followers, such as Milton Friedman, flew the flag of conservative economics. Their ideas were rooted in those theories of Adam Smith that had not been hijacked by Marx. But underlying their so-called conservative, but in fact classical liberal, thought is the same belief in the centrality of economics as one finds in *Das Kapital*.

For Hayek, for example, civilisation (and civility) began with industrial expansion, which is to say Renaissance humanism – the period that proper conservative thinkers usually see as the beginning of the end. And Hayek is well disposed towards the Enlightenment, though not in every particular. One has to infer that he equated civilisation with the rapid liberation of economic activity and its ensuing growth. That view is no less materialistic than Marxism, and ultimately as perilous to the survival of actual reality, especially since economism has taken such a strong hold in the USA.

Free up the economy and everything else will follow is a notion as false as its opposite. We have seen that making an economy free enough to be highly productive does not necessarily make the state any less totalitarian than before. Today's China proves that our tendency to judge societies on the basis of their economies leads us into intellectual dead ends. Libertarians and Keynesians argue themselves hoarse, but they both miss the point. What is at fault in modern economics is not that some of it is libertarian and some Keynesian, but that all of it comes from a materialist view of the world. As such, it represents, and deepens, the victory of the second metaphysical premise and the attendant triumph of the virtual world.

Godless capitalism is more palatable than godless communism, but ultimately as much of a menace to what is left of Western civilisation. It may even be more dangerous for being more durable and infinitely more seductive, for serpentine temptations are harder to resist than sheer violence. When asked to become a KGB informer, a decent Russian often found variously tactful ways of saying no[37] – anything else would have led to a lifelong loss of self-respect, and most people find such self-abasement hard to accept.

But our Western serpent would be able to ask many seductive questions to which we would have to nod our assent. Would you like to have two chickens in your pot and two cars in your garage? Yes. Would you like to own a large house? Yes. With a swimming pool? Yes. In a nice suburb? Yes. And so on, *ad infinitum*. By the time the 64-thousand-dollar question is sprung (Would you sell your soul to get all those things?), we are so used to saying yes that it seems churlish to say no. Our appetites have been whetted, and if that is what it takes to satisfy them, well...

Social alienation is one inexorable effect of creating a society that is but an extension of the economy. Deprived of any reason to regard one another as brothers, people acquire every reason to see one another as competitors. Some recognise the falsehood of zero-sum economics and realise there is enough to go around for everyone, but even such people feel they have to stay on guard against greedy neighbours with an eye on the main chance. Let us

---

37. This was easier when I was growing up after the war than during the more carnivorous reign of Stalin. Then such refusal, no matter how tactful, represented an instant ticket to a concentration camp, or worse. Consequently there were few refusals.

stay cordial to them by all means, but without losing sight of our wallet.

In a way, the situation has become reminiscent of the medieval Black Death: then social cohesion suffered from fear of contagion; today it suffers from fear of competition. A few generations of this, and social links, either among friends or families, begin to weaken. Social molecules can no longer keep their atoms together and they spin out into nothingness. In the absence of God, money can only be divisive.

The Unites States provides a vivid illustration of this atomising tendency. Friendships among Americans tend to be more superficial than even among the English, never mind the more emotional southern Europeans. Shoulder-slapping conviviality and easy first-name familiarity mask this problem, but never quite succeed in hiding it. The word 'friend' loses its erstwhile implication of lifelong self-sacrificial loyalty and gains one of someone I know, occasionally see socially and who has done me no harm yet. It is as if a friendship is only ever allowed to reach the shallow depth at which a steel gate clanks down: thus far, but no farther.

Attachments are mostly short-lived anyway, what with most Americans regarding the whole country as a vast job market. They tend to lead nomadic lives, especially during their younger years, which traditionally used to be the time when friendships for life were forged. When young Americans are offered a marginally better job two thousand miles away from their present set of friends, few hesitate. 'Follow the bread' are words to live by. Friends are left behind as easily as junk in the attic: there is more where this came from.

Even more destructive is the extension of the same general attitude to family life. In America it is considered decidedly 'uncool' for a youngster to go to university in his hometown, thus staying with his parents for a few years longer. This is regarded as too heavy a sacrifice: who would want to miss those four ecstatic years in a campus dorm? Fledglings have to fly the coop, and henceforth most will see their parents once a year, usually at Christmas, when they feel it is their duty to pay a flying visit to the place they incongruously still call 'home'.

Granted, it is physically uncomfortable to have three generations of the same family living in the same house, the way things often used to be before economism ousted religion as the principal dynamic of life. But then it is spiritually degrading to have all connective tissue among generations eaten away. This is not to say that no happy medium can be found, only that totalitarian economism costs, and it can be dear at the price.

3

What Marx was in social sciences, Darwin was in biology. Both made a seminal contribution to virtual-world economics, the first directly, the second at one remove but in some ways even more significantly. To his credit, the Englishman was somewhat less politicised than the German, and rather more honest. In fact, the worst, though by no means all, excesses of Darwinism are attributable more to the Darwinists than to their guiding light. But such excesses apart, even the original core of Darwinism is firmly planted in the virtual world.

The cardsharps operating there point at the well-documented ability of living organisms to adapt to their environment as proof of Darwinism. True enough, there is plenty of irrefutable evidence of microevolution, which is the proper term for such adaptability. But when it comes to macroevolution, which is one species turning into another, not a shred of proof exists. That Darwinists have managed to build an all-encompassing theory of life on this groundless conjecture points at its provenance in the virtual world. It is this, rather than any groundbreaking discoveries, that sets Darwinism apart from other natural sciences.

Darwin did not even coin the term 'survival of the fittest'; this honour belongs to his contemporary Herbert Spencer. Nor could Darwin claim an exclusive right to the discovery of natural selection: already in the first century BC Lucretius observed that it was by their superior cunning and strength that all existing species were different from those that had become extinct. Plutarch made a similar observation when he wrote about wolves devouring the slower horses and thus contributing to the survival of the faster ones. In the generations immediately preceding Darwin's, neither evolution nor natural selection was unknown to Lamarck, Cuvier or Darwin's own grandfather Erasmus. And Alfred Wallace, Darwin's contemporary, described natural selection independently from him and in fact passed his ideas on to Darwin in 1858, thus triggering the publication of *On the Origin of Species*.

Wallace, however, did not develop his ideas further as he was unable to explain, by natural selection alone, the human brain. No such compunctions for Darwin, the prototype of the modern totalitarian scientist. He was out to push the boat of biology towards the virtual world, and he would not be held back by a few missing links here or there.

Darwin actually admitted that there was not a single point made in his books that could not have been refuted by facts leading to the opposite conclusions. 'Not one change of species into another is on record... we cannot prove that a single species has been changed,' he wrote in *My Life And Letters*.[38]

And, considering in *On the Origin of Species* the complexity of the human eye, he went even further: 'To suppose that the eye with all its inimitable contrivances for adjusting the focus to different distances, for admitting different amounts of light and for the correction of spherical and chromatic aberration, could have been formed by natural selection, seems, I freely confess, absurd in the highest degree.' Yet history suggests Darwin was too reticent even in

38. Darwin was certain that such proof would eventually emerge. He was wrong.

his most self-lacerating assessments. In the 150 years since the publication of *The Origin*, science has never proved a single one of his conclusions of a more sweeping nature.

Unlike Darwin himself, today's politicised Darwinists do not even try to see how his assertions tally with the most elementary scientific data, such as the dearth of any intermediate forms of living creatures in the fossil records, or the fact that empirical evidence supports not the appearance and development of new species but the degradation and disappearance of the old ones. (Scientists now agree that about 99 percent of the species that have ever inhabited the earth are no longer with us. Really, the book ought to have been called *The Disappearance of Species*.) In fact, Darwinism, along with any other materialist explanations of the world, has been refuted not only by logic but also by every natural science we may wish to consider:

- *Cosmology* has reached the conclusion that our material world has not existed for ever: conclusive evidence shows it appeared more or less instantaneously at the beginning of time. The word 'God' burning the lips of modern scientists, they came up with 'The Big Bang', but that is a matter of semantics only. And today's public, with its knee-jerk rejection of anything religious, does not realise it is being tricked by semantic sleight of hand. Weaned on veneration of science, it salutes at the flagpole flying terms like 'The Big Bang', 'Intelligent Design' or, better still for being less comprehensible, 'quantum fluctuations'. What people do not realise is that they are looking at *Genesis*, encoded in scientific cant.
- *The physics of elementary particles* has reached the level where some forms of matter (particles and field) cannot always be differentiated. Their material characteristics are now often seen as secondary to their metaphysical properties describable in terms of information only.

- *Palaeontologists* have found and studied millions of fossilised remains of ancient organisms, and yet discovered practically no transitional forms in the development of species. This applies to all living beings, not just man. Deep down, scientists know that, if millions of fossils collected over 150 years have shown no evidence of macroevolution, no such evidence exists. In fact, experiments with bacteria (whose lightning-fast propagation rates make it possible to replicate within a few decades the millions of generations normally associated with the length of biological life on earth) show no macroevolutionary developments whatsoever.
- *Genetics* has demonstrated that mutations can only be degenerative in nature. Also, the amount of information in a single DNA molecule is so vast that it could not have been accidentally created even in the time exceeding by trillions of years the most optimistic assessments of the age of our universe.
- *Biochemistry* accepts irreducible complexity as fact: each molecule of living matter contains a multitude of intricate systems that in a simpler form would not have existed at all. That means they did not evolve but were created as they are at present.
- *Geology* is another example. We were all taught at school that the sequence of geological layers testifies to the gradual, smooth development of life from the more primitive to the more complex forms. That idea was so firmly entrenched in the virtual world that it became impossible to ask questions that beg to be asked. Such as: If evolutionary development was smooth and gradual, then how is it that we observe sharply defined layers at all, rather than the evidence of some species

disappearing, others appearing, and still others evolving gradually? How is it that specimens of new species always appear in fossil records instantly and in huge numbers, fully formed and lacking any obvious predecessors? How is it that many species appearing in the earlier layers are in no way more primitive than the later ones?

- In general, how can we decide which species of the organic world are more primitive than others? Studies in *microbiology* have shown that even single-celled organisms believed to be the simplest living beings are in fact incredibly complex systems of interacting functional elements. Even greater complexity is revealed at the genetic level, accompanied by much confusion in deciding what is primitive and what is advanced. Indeed, if we look at the number of their chromosomes, man, with 46, is more complex than the mouse (40), mink (30), fly (12) and gnat (6). Yet using this criterion, man is much more primitive than the sheep (54), silkworm (56), donkey (62), chicken (78) and duck (80). And the prawn, with its 254 chromosomes, leads the field by a wide margin. So is man perhaps the missing link between the gnat and the prawn? Actually, even some plants are more complex than we are. Black pepper, plum and potato each boast 48 chromosomes, and the lime tree a whopping 82.

But never mind the hard physical facts. It is the sheer beauty of the world that Darwinism or any other science has been unable to explain. Left out of their cold-blooded and ill-founded ratiocinations is something that has to be obvious to any unbiased observer: the world is organised according not only to rational principles, but also to aesthetic ones. And in many instances aesthetics comes before practicality, or even cancels it out. Not only, as Dostoyevsky suggested, can beauty save the world – beauty *is* the world.

Look at the peacock's tail for example. At first sight, this is a hindrance: after all, the oversized protuberance reduces the bird's mobility, thus making it less able to flee from predators. Darwinists explain this and many other examples of seemingly useless aesthetic characteristics, especially in males, as a factor of sexual selection.

The more striking the male's appearance, the more likely it would be to appeal to the aesthetic sense of a female and thereby pass its own genes on to the next generation. However, this raises a question that is rather awkward for Darwinism: whence do animals acquire their aesthetic sense in the first place? In the case of the peacock this comes packaged with characteristics that actively hamper the survival of the species. Clearly, metaphysical aesthetics overrides physical functionality – yet again metaphysics takes the lead.

There are many examples of that: the bright colouring of many species of both animals and plants, the beautiful singing of birds (which not only attracts females but also betrays the male's location to predators, again jeopardising physical survival for the sake of beauty), and the geometric perfection of physical bodies. The golden section is particularly telling here, for all the negative publicity it has received in Dan Brown's semiliterate fiction.

Let us have a closer look at it. The golden section is obtained by dividing a length into two unequal portions, of which the shorter one relates to the longer one as the latter relates to the overall length. Any length can be divided into an infinite number of portions, but only one division will produce this geometrically perfect ratio. Why? If no improved functionality can be held up as a possible explanation, would it not be possible to say that in this case we observe a metaphysical idea conveyed by physical means?

Modern scientists discover the proportion of golden section in the morphological makeup of birds and man, plants and animals, in the structure of the eye (which so baffled Darwin that he admitted evolution could not explain it – yet), in the location of heavenly bodies, in brain biorhythms and cardiograms.

Scientists are united in their conclusion: because this phenomenon goes across all levels of material organisation, it conveys a deep ontological meaning. But science is unable to explain it, and the best that honest researchers have done so far is admit their inability to account for the aesthetic aspect of the world.

After all, aesthetically perfect shapes add nothing to the organism's survivability and, as we have seen, often endanger it. Why, for example, do cereal plants need stalks with joints arranged according to the golden section? Such an arrangement does nothing to make the stalk stronger. Why do the bodies of dragonflies relate to the length of their separate parts according to the principles of the golden section? This does not enable them to fly any faster. Why do our fingers relate to the length of their joints the same way? This does not make gripping objects any easier. Indeed, if Darwin was right, and organisms evolve in the direction of greater survivability, then why do they have so many seemingly useless, and often potentially dangerous, features that nonetheless adhere to rigid aesthetic principles?

In other words, the aesthetical arrangement of nature points at a metaphysical, rather than physical, purpose that is not of this world. And this is revealed in so much more than just the golden section. Just listen to birdsong, to name another beautiful example.

The human ear can perceive no more than 10 modulations per second. Birdsong, however, often delivers 100-400 such modulations, making much of it imperceptible to us. The only way to hear all of it is by recording the song on a specially designed tape recorder that can slow it down when playing it back. The listeners can then be exposed to an aural canvas compared to which the nightingale, our established vocal star, does not appear all that virtuosic. In fact, many scientists regard the nightingale's songs as rather primitive compared to, say, the musicality of the hermit thrush (*Hylocichla guttata*). Played at a slower speed, his singing shows characteristics amazing in the animal world.

He repeats the passages of his music often, each time in a slightly altered version. In fact, his singing has been compared to the 'theme with variations' of classical composers. The bird follows two- or even four-beat bars, and even composes harmonic accompaniment to the main subjects, singing two voices at the same time. Actually, some of the world's leading experts in musical folklore were fooled by a clever researcher who played the slowed-down bird's music to them, having first identified it as the chant of an African shaman. The musicologists were perplexed. Understandably, none of them could identify the ethnic provenance of the music. But they all refused to believe that it came from an African shaman, insisting that it could only have originated in a higher musical culture.

Examples of this kind, and every branch of science can provide thousands, would have been sufficient to put paid to any other scientific theory a long time ago (and even the most ardent followers never claim that Darwinism is anything more than that). Generally, if a theory does not become fact within one generation, or at most two, it is relegated to the status of a museum exhibit. Yet the virtual world was prepared to throw its whole weight behind Darwinism because it needed it even more than Marxism.

The two theories dovetailed neatly and, if anything, Darwinism went even further. Not only did it attack the first metaphysical premise more effectively than Marxism did, but it also rivalled Marxism for wide-reaching social and economic implications. One no longer had to leave the realm of seemingly objective biological science to explain both socialism, with its class struggle, and capitalism, with its dog-eat-dog competition for survival. Even more fundamental is Darwinism's demotic insistence on the purely animal nature of man.

In Christendom, man was regarded as unique among all living beings because his life was believed to have a higher transcendent purpose. As long as that view was more or less universally shared, no consumer society in our modern sense could arise. There were in-built limits to man's consumption because it was recognised that there were no in-built limits to man's being. Obviously man has always consumed, but that activity could not have been the most important characteristic for someone who believed he was created in the image and likeness of God and would therefore live eternally. For consumption to be elevated to the defining feature of society, the very concept of man had to change. For consumption to reign supreme, the whole society had to become consumptive.

That is precisely the service Darwin provided, though not single-handedly. If we are nothing but highly developed apes, then we are not qualitatively different from animals. We differ only in the range of our activities that all reach their apotheosis in consumption. Thanks to our evolved minds, we do not have to stick to bananas. We can consume cars, private jets, yachts – and we can feel good about ourselves while devoting our lives to the pursuit of animal-like happiness.

(In Appendix 2 I illustrate how the West is moving step by step towards legal equality between people and apes, a development that would provide a true climax to Darwinism.)

Modern people are ever prepared to shrug their shoulders with indifference whenever yet another length of virtual yarn is spun at them. They open their arms to such manifest fallacies as Marxism and Darwinism not because they are persuaded by their rational arguments but because at heart they do not really care one way or the other. They hear vague materialist noises in those doctrines, and those are all they want to hear. The second metaphysical premise, having created the virtual world, needs nothing but virtual science to vindicate itself.

As long as money remains tangible and plentiful, people feel no need for any other reality. The assumption is that Chimaera's fire may singe everything else, including supposedly objective science, while sparing the only reality that matters. Alas, this reality is no less inflammable than any other, and more so than some.

THE TWO WORLDS CLASH

A clash between the two worlds, virtual and actual, was always on the cards. I have already mentioned that the modern state, regardless of its political denomination, strives for infinite power and centralisation. The states traditionally described as totalitarian try to achieve this end by brute force, but sooner or later bayonets prove uncomfortable to sit on. Until such time, however, totalitarians usually succeed in bringing their citizens to heel.

Their task is simplified by all the preparatory work I have described in earlier chapters. As people are convinced that their three-score and ten is all that matters, they are prepared to accept a certain, often rather large, amount of tyranny. After all, actively resisting it just might subtract a few years from the prescribed lifespan. And if a tyranny manages, or even promises, to slake modern people's material thirst, then they will accept it not only with resignation but also with alacrity (which is why the autobahn-building Nazis enjoyed a greater public support in their country than the peasant-starving Bolsheviks did in theirs).

The task facing the so-called liberal democratic states is much harder: They cannot rely on violence to the same extent as their totalitarian brethren do. If they did, then even the virtual reality of their world would soon lie in tatters. So if they wish to advance their cause, more subtle methods are required. Unfortunately for them, their cause is in direct conflict with the people's real aspirations, as defined by Weber: money and the comfort it buys.

It is impossible for a state to centralise everything in life without also centralising the economy. But doing so would make the state renege on its promise of 'happiness', for centralised economies simply do not work at the micro level of people's everyday lives. By exercising total control over the economy a state can perhaps make itself powerful for a while, but it can never make its citizens prosperous. Stalin, for example, successfully used terroristic methods to turn the Soviet Union into a global empire. However, most Russians starved, and even those who did not still lived in the kind of squalid conditions that had been unknown in the West since the early days of the Industrial Revolution.

Yet the virtual world could not abandon its innate aspiration. It had to put its foot down too, while watching its step not to smash the fragile fiscal reality underfoot. The state had to make people dependent upon it in order to cram the virtual world down their throats, and 'liberal democrats' sensed that need as acutely as did totalitarians. However, an economy based on private initiative pulled in exactly the opposite direction: by becoming good at making a living people could make themselves independent not only of the state but indeed of the economy. Once they had made a certain amount of money, they acquired the freedom to decide whether they wished to make still more or be satisfied with what they had already. And that freedom was indisputably real, a far cry from the nebulous liberties, equalities and fraternities touted by the virtual world.

Thus the situation at the beginning of the twentieth century, when the makings of the modern world were firmly in place, was fraught with implosive potential. Individually, those who manned public institutions were mostly (as they are now predominantly) out to feather their own nests. Collectively, they felt the need to increase the state's, and therefore their own, power *ad infinitum*, surmising correctly that this would make it easier for them to satisfy their urges.

On the other hand, those in the private domain, while pursuing the same individual desiderata, rightly sensed that, if the state were to be allowed to pursue its ends unimpeded, they would find it hard to pursue theirs. H.L. Mencken, the influential American writer of the first half of the twentieth century, described this dichotomy in his usual epigrammatic fashion: 'government is the enemy of all well-disposed, decent and industrious men'.

At first glance, Western governments found themselves with a losing proposition on their hands. As 'all well-disposed, decent and industrious men' were jealously guarding their real freedom against the encroachments of the virtual world, and could not yet be forced to toe the line by violent coercion, it would seem inevitable that sooner or later the state would either have to cede its position or risk a revolutionary outburst. So much more one has to admire the ingenuity and cunning displayed by the perpetrators of the virtual world in guarding, and greatly expanding, their turf. Their multifarious task consisted of many parts that at first glance look hard to reconcile with one another.

First, the state's progress towards infinite power had to proceed steadily and unimpeded, if not always at the desired breakneck speed. In economic terms, the state had to assert and expand its ability to confiscate an increasing proportion of peoples' income. This contributed directly to its own financial muscle, and indirectly to making people sink deeper into the 'pursuit of happiness'. After all, if the state could nationalise a large proportion of their 'happiness', people had to expend an ever-greater effort to make sure there was still some left for themselves.

This has to be the area where the virtual world has scored its most remarkable successes. To take America as an example, in less than 100 years since the introduction of the federal income tax the previously great number of individuals objecting on principle to the government's right to levy such a duty has dwindled to a small pool of dyed-in-the-wool conservatives. People find such objections to be blasphemous and un-American (which for most amounts to the same thing). Charles Lindbergh, for example, used to add 10 percent to his tax bill because he was 'proud to be an American'.[39] And many Englishmen claim they see nothing wrong in the state confiscating, one way or the other, the lion's share of their incomes.

39. His fire-eating patriotism did not prevent Lindbergh from admiring Hitler's pre-war achievements and in general holding pro-Nazi views.

Then again, the British tend to contort their facial features in horror whenever someone suggests that, say, the NHS is flawed not only because it is run in a flawed way but because it is based on a flawed idea (see the comments on equality earlier in this book). People in the West have been trained to treat the state with the steadfast piety formerly reserved for God.

Yet in the small pocket of the real world that still survives, denizens of both (and all other Western) countries industriously look for every legal, or at a pinch illegal, way to cheat the state out of its pound of flesh. Like Soviet citizens who mouthed cannibalistic slogans by day while reading mimeographed copies of *The Gulag Archipelago* by night, Westerners lead a schizophrenic life, with one part of their brain heeding the voices of the virtual world, and another ignoring them.

Second, the state had to make sure that in its confiscatory zeal it would not overstep a certain line beyond which people would either stop devoting themselves wholeheartedly to the economy, or else do a Don Quixote by attacking the windmills of the virtual world. The American economist Arthur Laffer explained this situation using the visual aid of his curve, which was such a blockbusting hit back in the 1980s.

Laffer began by stating the obvious: high tax rates do not necessarily deliver high tax revenues. For instance, by discouraging any economic activity, a 100-percent tax rate will produce the same amount of revenue as a zero-percent rate: none. The optimum rate was to be found somewhere in between the two extremes, and much closer to the lower one. At a tax rate within two or three points of 20 percent (I forget which side), the people would be sufficiently stimulated to work hard, while rewarding the state with more tax money than it could otherwise extort by keeping the marginal tax rates at their usual confiscatory level.

Moreover, such an arrangement would make superfluous a small army of tax lawyers and accountants who could then redirect their bubbling energy away from helping their clients avoid (or, given half the chance, evade) taxes and towards more productive activities. Prof. Laffer did not stipulate what those might be, but contextually one could infer that digging ditches would come up high on his list of employment opportunities.

The rumour has it that when Laffer drew his curve on a restaurant napkin while having lunch with Dick Cheney and Donald Rumsfeld, the key figures in Ronald Reagan's presidential campaign, their eyes lit up. They knew an election-winning trick when they saw one. The curve was immediately adopted as the intellectual basis for Reagan's ascent to power, which he effected chiefly by promising to reduce taxes without necessarily reducing government spending. By riding the Laffer curve, Reagan believed, America would be able to gallop to that unlikely destination.

Alas, neither the president nor his close economic associates, such as David Stockton, understood in sufficient depth the virtual world in which they lived. They did not realise at first that the implicit purpose of taxation is not merely fiscal. Another omnipresent aim is to extend the power of the state by limiting the people's ability to become independent of it. In that sense, taxation in the modern Western world – whatever else it might be – always has to be punitive and preventive. The whole system is designed around this desideratum, and it will fight any interloper with the kind of resolution that would put to shame the Spartans at Thermopylae.

Realising that the Laffer curve did not work by itself, without parallel reductions in government spending, the Reagan people went department-hopping door to door. Like children at Halloween they would beg to be treated to some cuts, only to be turned away. Having butted their heads against the impossibility of curbing the government's appetites, the Laffer enthusiasts were faced with an unsavoury choice. They either had to go back on their tax-cutting promise or else keep it and then plug the inevitable holes in the budget by borrowing or printing money (which these days is effectively the same thing). In theory, the choice was hard. In practice, this was no choice at all.

The myopic logic of modern politics, springing as it does from the second metaphysical premise, left them no alternative. Breaking the key pledge on which Reagan won his first term could have meant no second term, and no modern politician would ever consider hurting his own career for the *bono publico* pie in the sky. On the other hand, massive government borrowing usually does visible damage not immediately but by delayed action. And it has been known from the time of Socrates that the common man cannot perceive any damage whose consequences are extended over a long period.

In our own time this congenital defect has been canonised and protected by a variety of laws, all being a logical extension of the second metaphysical premise. After all, both the lawgivers and the law recipients believe that life ends at death.[40] Our natural egocentricity, informed by Descartes, has to make only a short jump from there to the certainty that all life ends at *our own* death. And before that happens our own good, meaning pleasure, is the highest virtue, for within this philosophy there can be no logical restrictions on instant self-gratification. And ours being a pluralistic, open-minded society, what sounds logical to most people must be made legal for all.

Thus, for instance, propaganda of homosexuality was illegal in the actual reality of Christendom, and not only because St Paul had spoken out against it. There existed a clear understanding that a spread of that practice would be detrimental to both the moral health of society and the prospects of its physical survival (if we all became homosexuals, mankind would not survive beyond one generation).

---

40. Some obviously do not, but they are completely marginalised as a social force. A demagogue screaming hatred at a stadium filled with 100,000 people can count his support as unanimous if the feeble protests of a few pariahs are muffled by the mighty roar of the rest.

And long-term thinking was a natural consequence of the first metaphysical premise, as natural as short-term thinking is to the denizens of the virtual world.

They have only a limited, and in most cases insincere, concern for any deluge that may flood society after their death. On the other hand, the phoney freedom of self-indulgence is the cornerstone of their pursuit of 'happiness'. Anyway, who are we to tell people how to pursue happiness, and what kind, as long as they do not cause the sort of immediate damage that would restrict our own pursuits? Thus propaganda of homosexuality had to be first tolerated, then legalised, then recommended. And one can confidently predict that before long it will be made obligatory, by way of expiating our ancestors' sin of finding anything wrong with the practice all those aeons ago.

Myopic thinking comes as naturally to modern men as carnivorism does to tigers. Thus Western governments routinely sell vast quantities of arms to assorted dictators for an immediate profit – only to spend, some time later, exponentially greater sums to counter the same arms now turned against them. But the profit is today, while the expenditure will be tomorrow, when these government officials might no longer be in power. No one will remember who was responsible for the original sales, and how they made the balance sheet look tastier in time for the upcoming election.

What is important to emphasise is that this mode of thinking does not necessarily make such men wicked by the standards of the society they live in. One hears from those who knew him that, as far as modern men go, Ronald Reagan was far from the worst and right up there with the best. But a modern man he was, and as such he could only think one way. So it fell upon a supposedly conservative administration to flood the market with the fraudulent IOUs of increasingly worthless bonds. Under Reagan, widely regarded as the most conservative modern president, the US public debt tripled to about $2 trillion.

Third, the state had to use its nationalised gains to create a whole class of citizens totally dependent on its largesse. Such individuals would have to be removed from economic life altogether, for if they were to remain in work there would always exist the danger that they would one day be able to loosen the state's grip on their collars. This was an essential element: creating a large group of citizens with a vested interest in the government's power to provide for them. was a guarantee of the government's self-perpetuation. Moreover, this gave a material embodiment to some of the cherished shibboleths of the virtual world, such as social justice (i.e. levelling down), equality (unachievable in any real world in any meaningful sense), and sharing twinned with caring (purloined from Christianity and perverted).

Hence the unsustainable social spending throughout the West, with pinstriped Robin Hoods in government offices robbing the similarly clad 'rich' to help (which is to say, perpetuate) the Adidas-sporting 'poor'. This situation tends to arise in moribund civilisations. According to R.G. Collingwood, it is in fact a telltale sign of a civilisation's malaise, and has been from time immemorial:

'From Plato onwards, Greco-Roman society was living its life as a rearguard action against emotional bankruptcy. The critical moment was reached when Rome created an urban proletariat whose only function was to eat free bread and watch free shows. This meant the segregation of an entire class which had no work to do whatever; no positive function in society, whether economic or military or administrative or intellectual or religious; only the business of being supported and amused. When that had been done, it was only a question of time until Plato's nightmare of a consumer society came true: the drones set up their own king, and the story of the hive came to an end.'

Fourth, those citizens who could not be made dependent on the state totally and directly had to be made dependent upon it in more subtle ways. Confiscatory taxation, supported by the law-enforcement powers of the state, is an effective method of crowd control, but only up to a point. 'Well-disposed, decent and industrious men' generally resent seeing the virtual world barge into the reality of their physical comfort. Such men tend to abhor taxation even *with* representation.

Since modernity has replaced justice with legalism, most of us anyway tend to regard laws as variously irritating regulations, or else as mere statements of intent. The dissolution, in effect, of the Judaeo-Christian basis of justice has led to the rule of law being replaced with the rule of regulation, with a concomitant loss of respect for legality. Americans used to ask, 'Is this a rule or a law?' The amount of leeway to which they would feel entitled depended on the answer: while failure to comply with either could have been punishable, rules inspired only fear, while laws also demanded respect.

For all I know, Americans may still ask the same question, but probably without realising that, while many rules have been *de jure* elevated to the status of laws, many laws have *de facto* been demoted to the status of rules. People will obey such laws under duress for as long as punishment for disobedience is assured or the laws are accepted as halfway reasonable. However, few of us will agree that a law that makes us part with most of our hard-earned income falls into the latter category. Enter the aforementioned army of tax-avoiding experts who will guide us around such 'laws' to some semblance of safe haven, thereby keeping us from destitution and themselves from the bright ditch-digging future.

So how else could the state encourage hard-working people to immerse themselves in the economy with total (not to say totalitarian) abandon but, for most, without much hope of gaining eventual independence? Or in other words, with the benefit of our terminology, how could the state move even the economy from the real to the virtual world?

It certainly was not easy, but eventually the methods were found, used and refined. This involved activating some of the same mechanisms that eventually went on to trigger the present crisis. Since they are still in working order, and their capacity for causing many future crises (until the terminal one) is unimpaired, these mechanisms deserve a separate chapter.

HOW MODERNITY TAKES REALITY OUT OF THE ECONOMY

1

Believers in the conspiracy theory of history, a group to which I proudly do not belong, can have a field day with the present situation. It is as if governments, financial institutions and the public had got together in a smoke-filled cellar to plot the destruction of the world economy – and, while they were at it, of the social order.

One can just imagine this. 'We'll create conditions in which both the banks and people will have to take crazy risks,' say the governments. 'You do that,' echo the banks, 'and we'll make it easy for people to act recklessly, and difficult for them to act responsibly.' 'And we,' contribute the people, 'will be so out of control that we'll beggar ourselves and, if we are lucky, also you two.'

Attractive though such simple theories may be to some, no such conspiracy has been hatched. A collusion does in fact exist, but it is subliminal rather than conspiratorial. Whether they realise this or not, all three parties involved are answering the clarion call of the second metaphysical premise on a rampage. Indeed, we have seen how the soil of modernity has been cultivated over centuries to accept the saplings of fiscal dementia. The question that is likely to be asked and has to be answered is this: How is it that things have come to a head now, at this particular time? After all, Western economies have suffered downturns, recessions and depressions before, without stopping the one-step-backwards-two-steps-forward march of capitalism. Why now?

The fact of the matter is that, historically, economic and social trends have a natural accelerator built into them: things that used to take 500 years to breed now take 10 or less. Before long they will take a few months. If in the past it took centuries for pressure in the boiler to build up, now this can happen so fast that the safety valves can no longer cope.

Technology has always had a big role to play in this – every development, from the horseshoe to the plough to the steam engine and onwards, would hasten the arrival of the next stage, each improving productivity exponentially. The ever-increasing speed of economic progress has also been facilitated by advances in communications and transportation. These days we can travel around the earth considerably faster than our ancestors could get from Paris to London a couple of centuries ago. And information can get from one end of the world to the other in seconds, not the weeks it used to take. However, major developments, good or bad, still seldom happen all at once: the penny has to be minted before it drops.

But when it does drop, the process is not dissimilar to Mendeleyev allegedly seeing his periodic table in a dream, Newton understanding gravity in an apple-falling instant, or Archimedes crying 'eureka!' in his bathtub. Those things may indeed have happened, but what seemed like an epiphany to outsiders came in the wake of decades of painstaking work, with crumbs of data accumulated until they were ready to add up to the loaf of knowledge.

Thus, though the mechanisms of the virtual world were integrated into Western economies gradually, they were always geared up to be activated instantly. At first, few players were aware that something odd was happening in the game; then gradually this became common knowledge. But by that time no one could do much about it: like anthropoid robots in a sci-fi novel, the mechanisms had acquired a life all their own. It was now they that activated people, not vice versa.

Faced with that situation, state officials and economists would heave a sigh and, taking a leaf out of Adam Smith's book, make some vague noises about natural market forces, the inexorable march of progress and the invisible hand. However, in this instance the metaphorical hand is very much visible: all they have to do is hold their own up to the mirror.

For example, it is not an invisible hand that has been steadily debauching Western currencies with inflation; it is state officials and economists. Their motivation is clear: inflation is a tax that requires no legislative approval. By inflating the currency, the government effectively transfers money from the people's accounts into its own, with a parallel transfer of even more power the same way. This fulfils many of the objectives modern politicians feel in their bone marrow, even if they do not always articulate them with their mouths.

A brief look at the numbers will confirm the distinctly modern flavour of high inflation. Before Western governments were allowed to meddle in economies as they saw fit, inflation was practically nonexistent, varying from 0.1 to 0.2 percent a year. If we look at Britain in the last 50 years of the nineteenth century, £100 in 1850 equalled £110 in 1900, a negligible inflation of 10 percent over half a century. That meant British subjects could confidently plan for their future, anticipating that hard work accompanied by a lifetime of thrift could make them independent not only of want but also of the government. And a baby born in 1850 with a silver spoon in his mouth, the worth of that utensil being, say, a solid middle-class income of £500 a year, could live his whole life in reasonable comfort even if he never made a penny of his own.

Conversely, if we look at the next century, £100 in 1950 equalled £2,000 in 2000 – a wealth-busting, soul-destroying inflation of 2,000 percent. This meant that the silver spoon would quickly drop out of the mouth of a similarly hypothetical baby born in 1950: unless he grew up to be successful at his job or shrewd with his investments, he would be poor. To take another Anglo-Saxon currency as an example, in the last 100 years the US dollar has lost 95 percent of its value, a marginally better, though still abysmal, performance.

Any economic primer will tell you that inflation is too much money chasing too few goods. This implies that the amount of money in circulation should be equal or at least close to the amount of goods available. Now assuming that the state stays out of the production of goods, which is more or less the case throughout the West, it has little effect on that variable: the state can neither increase nor reduce the amount of goods available. But the other variable, the supply of available money, is controlled by the state either wholly or at least largely. Crank up the printing presses, and inflation descends on the wings of banknotes gently spiralling down to the ground for the multitudes to tread on.

If we look at the same period, the last 50 years of the twentieth century, we shall notice that productivity was increasing steadily in both countries, as were the production volumes and GDP per capita. These indicators would sometimes dip for a while, but overall the curve would relentlessly zigzag upwards. This means that the only thing the state, in this case personified by our two governments, had to do to keep inflation in check was make sure that both its spending and the money supply marched in step with production, without either lagging behind it with untypical timidity or overtaking it in a burst of hubris.

Inflation figures, however, prove that everywhere in the West the state has done quite the opposite. It has been spending like a beached sailor and, whenever the money ran out, the printing press would go into high gear.

Now why would government officials do a silly thing like that? It certainly is not ignorance: as I mentioned before, we are leafing through an economic primer here, not a devilishly difficult tome full of equations and curves. And the ABC of economics has been figured out long ago. Witness, for example, Hjalmar Schacht, Hitler's finance tsar, to use a fashionable job description. When in 1943 the irate Führer complained bitterly that the reichsmark was becoming worthless, the venerable economist (subsequently acquitted at the Nuremberg trials against much evidence) retorted that it was impossible to keep a currency stable in the face of runaway government spending.

And closer to our own time, in his self-serving book *The Time of Turbulence*,[41] Alan Greenspan, former Chairman of the US Federal Reserve (1987-2006), a private organisation to which the US government delegated the money-printing function in 1913, put it even more succinctly: 'Burns [Prof. Arthur Burns of Columbia University] ... went around the room asking, "What causes inflation?" None of us could give him an answer. Prof. Burns... declared, "Excess government spending causes inflation!"'

So why do governments spend more than they take in if they know that such profligacy will predictably turn money into wrapping paper (or, in our days of electronic transfers, not even that)? The only logical answer is that they *want* money to lose value. They must feel that by acting in this manner they advance their objectives. And of course advancing their own objectives is the in-built imperative of all children of the second metaphysical premise.

One objective I have already mentioned: gradual increase of their own power, which these days comes out of the money purse more often than out of the barrel of a gun. The other is more subtle, though ultimately it amounts to the same thing: by reducing the purchasing power of a monetary unit, the state makes people seek a greater and greater number of such units to make ends meet. This works on every rung of the economic ladder: for some, the ends meet at a chateau in the South of France; for others, at a walk-up flat in the South of London.

But on any level both the overachievers and the ne'er-do-wells have to be wholly committed to economic activity to stay afloat, and to fulfil the dictates the second metaphysical premise. This commitment has to be expressed not only in working halfway

41. Actually, his book is not just self-serving – it has also served me well in providing much of the statistical data I use hereinafter in this chapter. It is noteworthy, however, that Greenspan, a key architect of the present crisis, never admits any mistakes on his own part. Surely he could have found a little space in a thickish book to own up to a teeny-weeny error of judgment?

around the clock but, whether or not they are so able or inclined, also in taking a gambler's risks with investments.

Those who fail will have to fall back on the government's largesse in order to survive – this is self-explanatory. But even those who succeed will also depend on the government, if less directly and more negatively. After all, a quick pull on the printing press lever can usher in, say, a 15-percent inflation rate. A few years of that, and a nest egg lovingly hatched over a lifetime is broken, with no omelette anywhere in sight.

The tugging on this lever is a tax in disguise, the lever itself the sword of Damocles hanging over our heads. Just like more common taxes, it is the state's way of communicating to us that our money is not really ours. We may earn it, but the state has the power to decide how much we shall be allowed to keep for our families.

This is actually the language used by politicians all over the West, which testifies both to their cynicism and our gullibility. When he was Chancellor of the Exchequer, Gordon Brown would make frequent references to 'letting' people keep more of their incomes, citing such munificence as proof of his government's generous nature and good intentions. The poor chap never realised that he was making a proclamation of tyranny as unequivocal as those made by Plato, Fichte[42] or Marx. We can only *let* people keep what in fact belongs to us.

Those with ears to hear understood what was really being said: 'be good boys, or else.' The first part of this dictum means 'vote for us and stop asking awkward questions'; the second, 'if you don't, we'll take away what's left of your money.'

2

Monetary inflation is not the only weapon in the state's armoury; it is not just money, but also assets, especially property, that become inflated. This too is easy to understand: as money is constantly

42. The statist, nationalist philosopher Johann Gottlieb Fichte (d.1814) wrote that promoting universal equality was the only real function of the state. A clever man, he probably knew that universal equality spelled universal tyranny, but that did not faze him at all.

reduced in value, people rush to convert it into something that, though it may go up and down, is unlikely to disappear altogether.

Someone who has, say, a million dollars drawing a modest interest in a savings account will in effect lose most of his money after a few years of high inflation. The same amount invested in a tangible house will be more secure come what may: even when property markets collapse, houses will always be worth something. And unlike currency that once dead, stays dead, there is a chance that property values might bounce back with a vengeance. Hence the rush to buy assets. And since the law of supply-demand has not yet been repealed, such a rush can only mean an inordinate inflation of prices.

This activates what in the real world was believed to be impossible: a *perpetuum mobile*. No such limitations in the virtual world; its motion never stops. In this case, if people are lucky with their investments, they obtain a wad of cash that has to be either spent or reinvested while it is still worth something. Investment is a gift that has to keep on giving.

When the money is spent, it needs to be replenished, and if this takes the yoke of a large loan around the spendthrift's neck, then so be it. If it is reinvested, there is always the risk that the second time round the investment will produce a loss. But the risk, however daring, has to be taken, for otherwise the money will melt away like snow on the first warm day of spring. Thus a steadily inflating currency turns everyone into either a reckless spendthrift or a freewheeling speculator, including those who are by nature neither wastrels nor gamblers.

Alan Greenspan, well-trained in the economic cant designed to lay a smokescreen over reality, makes this sound almost reasonable: 'The decline of real (inflation-adjusted) long-term interest rates that has occurred in the past two decades has been associated with rising price-to-earnings ratios for all income-earning assets. The market value of assets worldwide between 1985 and 2006 as a consequence rose at a pace faster than that of nominal world GDP.' Allow me to translate into our simple language: thanks largely to Greenspan's own policies the price of assets became even more firmly lodged in the virtual world than it ever had been before.

If I may, I would like to offer some anecdotal evidence illustrating the misleading nature of monetary inflation figures taken separately. Things can never be better than inflation figures suggest, but they can almost always be worse, as shown by the example of one of my in-laws. This gentleman retired from his job as curator at a provincial English museum in the 1960s. For reasons his family are unaware of, but which could perhaps be guessed, throughout his career he had been declining offers of more lucrative employment, preferring instead the life of a gentleman scholar, however impoverished. People used to make such choices more readily in the past, when it was still possible to opt for a modest yet dignified existence without suffering the head-splitting stresses of an economic free-for-all.

The curator's salary at the time of his retirement was about £2,000 a year, which was then roughly the value of the semi-detached four-bedroom house he shared with his wife, who did not have a job, and three children. They lived modestly by the standards of the British middle class, but nonetheless all three children were educated privately, the venerable curator wore bespoke if old suits and, and though they drank wine infrequently, when they did it was first-growth clarets. Now, adjusted for inflation, £2,000 then would be about £38,000 today, and indeed this is the salary the curator of the same museum draws these days.

Yet the very same house, now more than 50 years older, was recently sold for £250,000, thus outstripping the monetary inflation by a considerable margin of 6.5 to one. This makes (or ought to make) the house a bit too rich for the present curator's blood. And anyone familiar with the fees private schools command these days will know that his gross salary would not even cover the cost of three tuitions, never mind such trivia as taxes, food and utility bills.

Thus a gentleman scholar with no independent means who is blessed with wife and children would today be unlikely to seek such a job. If he did he would have to be prepared to accept a life of social embarrassment, not to say penury, even if his wife had a job. He would also have to drink New World wines, which must qualify as cruel, though regrettably no longer unusual, punishment.

Inflation, be that of money or assets, thus sends a loud and clear message to the people: a half-hearted commitment to the pursuit of money will not get you even a half-decent life. You cannot accept a modicum of discomfort in exchange for more freedom to pursue what really matters to you. No gentlemanly sinecures await; it is all or nothing. You must barter your soul in order to survive (in the sense in which survival is now understood). Ostensibly you may be working for your own well-being, but in fact the state, using the double-barrel weapon of taxes and inflation to claim much of what you earn, will make sure you toil mostly for its benefit. Nothing short of a Faustian transaction will do if you do not wish to tumble into the clutches of the social services.

And even if you were prepared to take such a fall, that would be fine too – your dependence on the state would become even more total and direct. One way or the other you are on a merry-go-round spinning so fast that you cannot jump off.

3

Now, if inflation is caused by 'excess government spending', then, to put it in everyday language, to keep inflation going governments have to spend more than they collect in tax revenues.[43] In other

43. If western governments stand to benefit from inflation, then why do they always make a show of trying to combat it? This would be an unanswerable question if inflation were the only weapon at the state's disposal. But it is not, and during the rare times of low inflation governments often reduce interest rates precipitously to encourage a frantic borrowing activity. Then a sudden hike in interest rates comes, and with it negative equity, defaults, bankruptcies – and a sharp increase in the number of people dependent on the government. Low interest rates act for governments the way snares act for hunters.

words, they must ignore Adam Smith with his pleas of running the state on the same fiscal principles as those we apply to our own households. This means that, if they wish to use inflation for crowd control, governments must have the ability to operate the printing press as they see fit, with no external constraints to curtail this ability.

And if Western governments or, to be more precise, privately owned central banks, such as the US Federal Reserve system, can arbitrarily issue any amount of paper currency they fancy, then such currency can have nothing but virtual value. Real money has to be replaced by the fake variety. In any meaningful terms, if we ignore the legalistic casuistry for a moment, governments have to get into the counterfeiting business, for the virtual world has no use for genuine money.

The only way of keeping money genuine would be to limit the state's ability to counterfeit it. Traditionally this used to be achieved by pegging paper money (first issued in China as far back as the ninth century) to some objective equivalent, usually precious metals. And gold eventually ousted silver as the precious metal of choice.

Step by step, Western governments adopted a system whereby the paper money they issued was backed up by their gold reserves. Every banknote was instantly redeemable in gold, and both the paper and the metal were equally real and tangible. This introduced stability into economies and greatly simplified international trade.

All major Western economies eventually went on the gold standard, if at different times. Britain did so in 1717, the USA in 1834 (*de facto*), Germany in 1871 (immediately after her formal unification). It was however understood that a rigid monetary system based on the gold standard would be hard to maintain during major wars, when deficit spending would be unavoidable ('Unlimited money is the sinews of war,' wrote Caesar to Cicero, thus striking yet another blow for the *plus ça change* view of history).[44]

44. An economist I know said recently that, 'if the gold standard can be suspended, it is meaningless'. Well, then it is about as meaningless as civil rights, which are also suspended in wartime – just ask American Japanese or British Germans (even Jewish refugees from Germany were detained on the Isle of Man for the duration of the Second World War). However, history shows that both the standard and the rights can come back once the emergency is out of the way.

Thus Britain suspended the gold standard during the Napoleonic Wars, the USA during its Civil War, and most countries during the First World War. But in that distant past they inevitably relied on the post-war return of the gold standard to bring some deflationary sanity to the crazy inflation caused by wartime spending. Where this was not done, as for example in Weimar Germany, the ensuing hyperinflation would obliterate the nation's currency altogether.

But in this example, the German government, while appearing insane, acted most rationally and deliberately: wiping out their currency would come close to wiping out their post-Versailles reparation debts. However, governments that did not have such a millstone hanging around their necks would do their best to bring their currencies back in line with the gold standard.

This was the case before modern governments realised that inflation could be a useful power tool – before they became fully aware of their inner imperative. Once that realisation, or rather post-rationalisation, sank in, the gold standard had to go. Wishing to bind its citizens hand and foot, the state itself had to slip the tethers of fiscal responsibility.

It has to be said for the sake of fairness that, in a real world, the gold standard has its downside. For one thing, it limits the government's ability to increase the money supply as a means of combating recessions (these inevitably occur whenever supply and demand get out of synch, which in a free economy they are bound to do occasionally). This time-honoured salvage operation has often been successful in the short term, though some eminent economists, such as Joseph Schumpeter (d. 1950), have argued against it on principle.

They would maintain persuasively that, unless an economy climbs out of a recession organically, it will show a remission, not recovery. This argument rings true, but I do not need it for my purposes because there is even a stronger one. For the gold standard limits not only the state's flexibility but also its capacity of increasing its own power by using inflation the way Robin Hood used his bow for redistributive highway robbery.[45]

In a real world, the two sides would have to be weighed against each other, and a serious debate could be possible. But since, as we have seen, the modern state's inner imperative calls for replacing any real world with the virtual kind, the flip side of the gold coin can be safely ignored.

We do not want the modern state to have the short-term flexibility to steer the economy into safe havens, for we can be certain that in the long term the state can only steer it into dire straits. As a matter of fact we must do all we can to deprive modern governments of their flexibility to meddle in the economy.

Hence the attraction of the gold standard, at least to those who value their freedom above an ability to ride the economic rollercoaster through hair-raising rises and dips. It puts people, as opposed to the state's whim, in control of their own pecuniary destiny. The gold standard may make an economy less upwardly mobile, but in return it will definitely make it more stable and free. For that reason, it is anathema to any modern government.

That is why governments have seen fit to devote much energy, which could have been more profitably applied elsewhere, to wage a sustained war of extermination against the gold standard. The will to conduct such a war had been brewing for a long time, only the weapons had been missing. Finally the right tool for the job was found.

It was perhaps partly for the purpose of phasing the gold standard out that the quasi-independent[46] Federal Reserve system was created in 1907: the US government wanted to abrogate some

45. The gold standard may also limit the state's ability to increase its power by waging wars. It is conceivable, though far from certain, that some governments might think twice before embarking on an adventure they are unsure they will be able to finance. The gold standard would not be an insurmountable obstacle, for it could be temporarily suspended. But it just might be an obstacle nonetheless.
46. The Fed is only *quasi*-independent because it is the US government that appoints, and the Congress that approves, its board. So the 'Federal' part has somewhat more meaning than it does, say, in Federal Express. After all, we would not regard a country as totally independent if its government were appointed by a foreign power. To what

responsibility for what was bound to follow. And in 1913, the year the Federal Reserve Act came into effect, the Sixteenth Amendment to the US Constitution was passed, empowering the Congress to levy federal income tax as it saw fit.

(In debating the bill, the honourable gentlemen laughingly mentioned 10 percent as a nightmarishly high rate never to be achieved. A generation or two later their colleagues were joyously taxing high incomes at 90 percent, thus vindicating the thin-end-of-the-wedge theory of state aspirations.)

These two power tools were plugged into the mains at the same time, a two-prong strategy that was to be used by modern states over and over: the shock of one blow can affect the people so deeply that they may hardly notice the second one.

It took 20 years and a major depression for the state to get its way, but eventually it did: in April, 1933, shortly after his inauguration, Franklin D. Roosevelt abandoned the gold standard. In this he displayed the same speed of action as did Lenin, who 'monopolised' (which is to say confiscated) all gold and silver plate in Russia in December 1917, a mere couple of months after the revolution.

The methods the two men chose to enforce their decrees were different, but rather less so than one would expect on the basis of the clear difference in their political environments. Roosevelt operated in a country that perceived itself to be free. Consequently such Leninist expedients as summary executions were beyond his reach, as was Lenin's favourite trick of having men (or, better still, their wives and children in front of them) tortured until they surrendered every gram of gold in their possession. Robbing the churches of their valuables, and murdering the priests for good measure, *à la* Lenin, could also have been frowned upon in a country that still retained some

extent the US government indeed appoints the board, rather than rubber-stamps the banks' appointments, is open to debate. Interestingly, though each president replaces upon his inauguration most of the senior government officials appointed by his predecessor, Chairmen of the Federal Reserve tend to keep their jobs. Greenspan, for example, served continuously under four presidents, both Republican and Democrat. And Ben Bernanke, appointed by the *soi-disant* conservative George W. Bush, has been re-appointed by the socialist Barack Obama. Conspiracy theorists, wipe those smug smiles off your faces.

vestigial attachment to religion. Given such annoying limitations, one has to admire Roosevelt for doing his level best.

In the same April of 1933 Roosevelt issued Executive Order 6102, 'forbidding the hoarding of gold coin, gold bullion, and gold certificates' by U.S. citizens and demanding that they sell all their gold to the government at the price set by the buyer. Failure to comply was punishable by a fine of up to $10,000 or imprisonment of up to 10 years, or both.

The amount of the fine is staggering, especially in relation to the one dollar a day being paid to the millions employed in public works. As to the threat of a tenner in prison for failure to hand in all privately owned gold within a month, Roosevelt, as we have seen, was treading a well-beaten path: the Bolsheviks had shown the way in Russia directly they had grabbed power.

But FDR added an elegant touch that was beyond the crude Bolsheviks: having forced Americans to sell their gold to the treasury for $20.66 an ounce, the next year he used the Federal Reserve machine to ratchet up the price to $35 an ounce, a level at which it stayed fixed for the next 38 years. However, at that point it was allowed to float, and in the 35 years thereafter the price of gold has increased almost thirty-fold, in parallel with the practical pulping of paper money.

The difference between private citizens keeping their assets in gold or in currency is critical to my thesis. Gold coins or ingots sitting in a bank vault are a factor of their owner's independence: the money is beyond the state's reach, more or less. Not so banknotes: we are welcome to stuff suitcases full of paper, but the government has an almost absolute control over its value.

The gold standard is thus a factor of freedom, while its absence is a potential factor of tyranny. Since all modern governments are tyrannical in their aspirations, and as tyrannical in their actions as they can reasonably expect to be able to get away with, we ought not to be unduly surprised that a totalitarian Russia and a liberal-democratic USA followed the same course of action, if by different means.

If you can stand a few more numerals, we can see how far the world economy has veered away from the real-world discipline imposed by the gold standard. The total amount of gold that has ever been mined in the world is estimated at around 142,000 tonnes. At $1,000 an ounce, roughly the price at the time of writing, give or take a couple of percent, all the gold that Egyptian, Soviet and South African slaves, American forty-niners, Inca and Aztec Indians or our contemporary miners have ever extracted out of the ground would today be worth about $4.5 trillion. This is approximately half the value of the paper money currently circulating in the USA alone, never mind the rest of the world.

Thus, barring a catastrophe of a magnitude we dare not imagine, a return to the gold standard would be impossible (or at least would take many years) even in the unlikely event that the state would show willing. Like death and taxes, the virtual world never relinquishes what it claims.

Gordon Brown drove this point home when he was still Chancellor of the Exchequer. In a series of auctions between 1999 and 2002 he sold off more than half of Britain's gold reserves at a rock-bottom price that represented a 20-year low. That fire sale cost the taxpaying public about £2 billion (not including any inevitable future costs), as the Bank of England had predicted it would. But Brown had no time for the old bankers' advice. Those fossils were terribly behind their time, as far as he was concerned. They just could not grasp that, as long as the gold stayed in the country's coffers, it represented a potential loss of power for himself and his ilk. That pernicious yellow stuff has no place in a virtual world.[47]

However, until 1971 some tenuous link between paper money and gold still existed, as America was still prepared to settle her foreign debts in gold. In fact, once the Western countries had

47. It is the most baffling triumph of virtual-world propaganda that Brown, easily the most disastrous Chancellor of the Exchequer in history (and the field of aspiring candidates is crowded), is hailed as the most successful one. Then again, his tenure does appear to be a success by contrast to the self-evident ineptness of his subsequent performance as Prime Minister.

abandoned the gold standard, the Bretton Woods Agreement of 1944 established a virtual-world version of the same system. The signatories to the Agreement agreed to peg their post-war exchange rates to the dollar, while the US government undertook to keep the price of gold fixed at $35 an ounce, thus linking all the participating currencies to gold at one remove. Not a bad idea, considering; but, as such a link ran against the grain of the virtual world, it could not last.

In 1964 this point was made abundantly clear by the French president Charles de Gaulle who sent to the United States a cargo ship loaded to the gunwales with paper dollars. He then demanded that his right to exchange the banknotes for gold be honoured. That first jab at Bretton Woods involved a manageable sum of $150 million, but de Gaulle made no secret of his intention to follow up with the right cross of another $150 million soon, and more later. This was consistent with the French president's understanding of economics and, truth be told, also with his well-documented dislike of Anglo-Saxons. The present-day world, he explained, needs 'an indisputable monetary base, and one that does not bear the mark of any particular country. In truth, one does not see how one could really have any standard criterion other than gold.'

What was worse, other countries began to follow suit, with, for example, Spain exchanging at least $60 million for gold. A run on Fort Knox looked like a distinct possibility. Added to the staggering cost of President Johnson's egalitarian 'Great Society' reforms, to say nothing of the Vietnam War, this attack on the dollar left Bretton Woods dead in the water in any real sense. What was immediately worrying was the growing US budget deficit, which was threatening to undermine the country's economic clout abroad.

In 1971 President Nixon (another 'conservative') severed the vestigial link between gold and the dollar by declaring that thenceforth the US government would only settle its foreign debts in paper, be that in the shape of dollar banknotes or treasury bonds and bills. Using the same double-whammy trick we have already seen in action, Nixon simultaneously introduced wage and price controls, a temporary measure he claimed would only be in force for three months. In fact, it lasted three years – with predictably appalling results.[48]

In the previous 25 years the US economy had been growing at an average annual rate of four percent; since then the rate has dipped to only about one tenth of that. But interestingly, the country's political power in the world did not decrease in consequence; quite the opposite. For the all-virtual paper dollar had to replace the semi-real pre-1971 unit as the world's reserve currency, with the lever of the printing press firmly in the hands of the Federal Reserve. Thus the state's thirst for global power was slaked at the expense of the long-term health of the world economy. That, as far as the state was concerned, was a fair price to pay. We care about ourselves only, do we not? Hail to the second metaphysical premise.

Since then the USA has run up a debt equal, when various social guarantees are taken into account, to more than $100,000 for every American. (In Britain the public debt at the time of writing stands at close to £1 trillion. This spells bad news for our projected fiscal health, even though we are not the world's biggest offenders in terms of debt as proportion of GDP. In fact, Britain, at 77 percent, is at Number 12 on the list headed by Japan that owes a staggering 225 percent of her annual GDP.) This means that the US has progressed, if this is the right word, from being the world's biggest creditor in the 1950s to her present position as the world's biggest debtor of all time. In a real world such a debt could never be repaid, especially since it is growing by the day.

(But in our virtual world this does not matter any longer, and nor do domestic budget deficits. One year, President Eisenhower actually apologised to the American people for running a $3 billion deficit. In 2009 President Obama ran up a $1.6 *trillion* deficit, with no

48. It is refreshing to observe the ease with which 'conservative' politicians adopt socialist, which is to say statist, measures when in power. The whole taxonomy of modern politics ought to be scrapped – and, in a real world, would be scrapped. In the virtual world, however, what politicians say matters infinitely more than what they do.

apology uttered within anyone's earshot. But then he was busy preparing his Nobel speech.)

After all, the debt is denominated in dollars, and the US government can manipulate this currency as it sees fit at a stroke of a computer key, even if this means that Big Macs and hotel rooms will cost Americans more in foreign lands. Nor does it matter to the state that foreigners now own about 80 percent of American assets, which to an outsider may look perilous. If foreign governments were to fancy some serious asset stripping, one would think the USA would lose its strategic supremacy in short order.

But for the creditors that would mean cutting off their fiscal noses to spite their foreign faces: they would lose the world's biggest market and, as an important corollary for some of them, America's military protection. As they seem to be unwilling to take such consequences yet, for the time being they go along with the pretence that all those trillions they are owed will one day be repaid. How long the pretence will last is anybody's guess.

Meanwhile, Americans, along with many other users of their reserve currency, palm off worthless paper to 'outsource' most production to countries like China, whose population is consigned to what only Protagorian sophistry would prevent one from calling slave labour. In the good, if relatively recent, tradition of materialistic amorality, we choose not to ponder the ethical implications. When paying $1 or, for that matter, £1 for a pair of cotton underpants made in China,[49] where the average labour cost is one-thirtieth that in America, we refrain from doing simple mental arithmetic. Most of us would be incapable of such mental exertions anyway, after a couple of generations of equal education for all.

Yet if we were to add up the cost of the cotton, utility prices, depreciation of the factory plant, manufacturer's mark-up, cuts taken off the top by various middlemen and retailers, cost of transportation and storage, customs duties, and many other things I have undoubtedly left out, we would realise that the poor devils who

---

49. The forensic evidence was recently gathered by the author at a local department store.

stitch those underpants together probably still subsist on a small bowl of rice a day.

We congratulate ourselves on thus greasing the palm of capitalism. More power to the elbow of the invisible hand. After all, without us those people may not even have that bowl of rice. They are better off, we are better off, what is there to worry about? Our souls, ladies and gentlemen, would be one answer to that. But this is not the kind of answer many would understand these days. We have become desensitised to the suffering of those who oil the works of our own consumption.

Staying on the more accessible material plane, let us ask another question, utterly hypothetical of course: What would happen if the Chinese ever became reluctant to toil for sub-coolie wages? What if they began to crave the modest prosperity similar, say, to that of Rumania, the poorest country in the European Union?

To fulfil such an aspiration they would have to, among other things, match Rumania's per capita consumption of electrical energy. Given China's population, the country would then be using up almost half of the world's electricity, which is a patently impossible proposition. This alone means that China can never be free while continuing to act as the West's factory: only a totalitarian regime can prevent the people from harbouring even such humble hopes as keeping up with the semi-impoverished Rumanians.

It is instructive to observe how 'conservative' economists defend the seemingly indefensible growth of America's negative trade balance. In his bestselling book *Free to Choose* the Nobel-prize winner Milton Friedman explained: 'Another fallacy seldom contradicted is that exports are good, imports are bad. The truth is very different. We cannot eat wear, or enjoy the goods we send abroad Our gain from foreign trade is what we import. Exports are the price we pay to get imports.'

This would be true if the exports exchanged for the imports were goods and services. The statement, however, is false when the exports consist chiefly of worthless paper, of which the Chinese now own the better part of two trillion dollars' worth. It is true that 'we cannot eat... the goods we send abroad.' Unfortunately for them, neither can the hungry Chinese slaves.

What would happen to the US economy if China (followed by Japan and Russia) were to transfer her assets into another currency is something too scary to think about. A step like that would not be in China's short-term economic interests, but – and I know we find this hard to fathom – some countries may at some point put a long-term political objective before immediate gain. This is to say that a foreign debt of astronomic proportions may just put America, and with her the rest of the West, at a strategic risk.

4

If we proceed down the descending order of culpability, financial institutions will have to be mentioned next. Such delineation can only serve the purpose of convenience, for in essence the state and the financial system are one. They are fused together by the second metaphysical premise, and propelled by the engine of naked self-interest. Yet structural integrity demands that some fragments of the whole be chipped off and analysed separately. And if we regard financiers and corporate executives as marginally less blameworthy than politicians, it is only because the former do not have to mask their cynicism behind the shroud of mendacious verbiage invariably worn by the latter.

In every other sense, people who run either financial or manufacturing concerns are these days no different from those who run governments. For old times' sake we still talk about free enterprise as the cornerstone of our economies, and we do not stop to think if the term still applies. In fact, the modern tendency to dissipate ownership by financing *ad infinitum* expansion through stock market flotation, leads to a situation where 'free enterprise' becomes neither. The 'capitalist', Marx's bogeyman, is eliminated in modern liberal democracies as efficiently as he used to be shot in totalitarian regimes.

Supporters of free enterprise *über alles* would be well advised to take a broader look at society. This would enable them to see that although competitive free enterprise may be a necessary condition for civilised society, it is certainly not a sufficient one. For one thing, men who these days find themselves at the cutting edge of free enterprise do not believe in competition. Quite the opposite, they would like to nip it in the bud by bankrupting every business but their own.

A free entrepreneur *par excellence* can exist today only in a start-up mode, or else at the level of a corner sandwich shop. Once his business has grown, his thoughts gravitate towards putting an end to competitive activity. He wants to put competition out of business. At that end of economic thought he is greeted with a fraternal embrace by his brother the democratic bureaucrat who, for his part, used to believe in pluralism while he was clawing his way up the party ladder. Now he has reached the top, pluralism means only one thing to him: a threat to his position. The modern brothers instantly recognise their kinship and have no difficulty in striking a corporatist partnership.

True free enterprise in the West today occupies about the same slot as it did in Lenin's Russia during the New Economic Policy (NEP). Faced with an economic collapse, mounting famines and peasant revolts, Lenin allowed most of the service industries as well as some small-scale manufacturing to go private. But what he described as the 'commanding heights of the economy', which is to say banks, heavy industry, foreign trade, large-scale manufacturing, exploration and control of the natural resources, remained firmly in the hands of the Bolsheviks.

Replace 'Bolsheviks' with 'the bureaucratic corporatist elite', and today's situation in the West is not dramatically different. For all the Sherman Acts and Monopolies Commissions in the world, big business has to gravitate towards monopoly, which is the only thing Marx got right. A modern businessman has a psychological need to achieve total control of his market in the same way, and for the same reasons, that a modern politician wishes to achieve total control of his flock. Class has no role to play here, which is one of the many things Marx got wrong: The virtual world prays at the altar of uniformity, and it melts down any class differences until they are reduced to quaint idiosyncrasies.

What propels the modern 'free' businessman towards mono-poly is the same utilitarian impulse that paradoxically drives many aristocrats towards socialism: they know that putting the clamps on the socially dynamic strata of the population will prevent any serious competition appearing. Here the entrepreneur's longings converge with those of his employees who tend to act as a collectivist bloc. Their motivation is old-fashioned envy coupled with the deep-seated belief that it is possible for some to rise only at the expense of others falling.

At the same time, the ruling bureaucracy has a vested interest in keeping businesses as large, and consequently as few, as possible for this will make control easier and more total. In short, the only people who sincerely believe in free competition are big businessmen waiting to happen, those who are still climbing towards the summit and do not want their rope cut. Once they have got to the top, they will realise the error of their ways and start acting accordingly.

Another dynamic at work here is a tendency towards the globalisation of business, closely mirroring a similar trend in modern politics (witness the EU). Like modern life in general, business tends to lose its national roots. In the absence of protectionist tariffs, known to be counterproductive at least since the time of Adam Smith and David Ricardo, an aspiration to monopoly drives a big business towards foreign expansion *ad infinitum*, which is another form of protectionism but one that does not provoke retaliation in kind.

Most international corporations are neither run nor controlled by capitalists, if we define the breed as the owners of capital. Modern captains of industry do not necessarily own the capital of which they dispose, and they do not live or die by their success or failure. The risks they venture are usually taken with other people's money, and they stand to gain untold fortunes by achieving success, while personally risking next to nothing in case of failure.

If they fail, they take the king's ransom of redundancy and either move on to the next bonanza or, should they so choose, retire to some tropical paradise of philistine comfort. Those suicide shots reverberating through empty boardrooms are hard to imagine these days: shame and dishonour are alien concepts to today's lot. And even in the slightly older days they were mostly figments of Ayn Rand's fecund imagination.

Rand, incidentally, is the Archangel of crude materialism, the nexus at which all strands of modernity converge. Naturally, she exerted a formative influence on Alan Greenspan, the Virgin to her Gabriel. Even today, almost three decades after her death, this objectionable woman still claims apostles, most no doubt attracted by her fanatical championing of free enterprise.

Few are repelled by the way Rand fuses the values of cutthroat capitalism with fascist philosophy and aesthetics. At the centre of all her musings stands the fiscally virile superman, towering over a godless world. This is couched in the literary equivalent of Nazi and Soviet paintings depicting, respectively, a muscle-bound chap sporting swastika insignia or a muscle-bound chap raising high the hammer and sickle. Replace those attributes with a wrench and a balance sheet, keeping every other detail intact, and Rand's clumsily painted picture will be complete.

To reinforce the parallel, whenever Rand delivers herself of views on religion, she matches the hateful rhetoric of her fascist contemporaries, such as Lenin and Stalin or Mussolini and Hitler. Nor does she defer to them in the hysterical pitch of her effluvia, except that she chooses as the object of such outpourings the *übermensch* defined in economic terms, rather than those of race or class. Just like Marx, Rand creates an imaginary economic world that has as little to do with any observable reality. Just like him she belongs in the virtual world.

Indeed, the qualities essential for a rise through modern corporations are different from those needed in the early stages of the Industrial Revolution. They are, however, close to those required for careers in government bureaucracies. Today's multinational corporations bear much more resemblance to government departments than to entrepreneurial concerns. Thus, even as modern governments grow more corporatist, so, tautologically, do actual corporations.[50]

A new elite is thereby formed, and it is a homogeneous group whose members, such as the sainted Alan Greenspan himself, are indistinguishable from one another regardless of whether their original background was business or politics. Witness the ease with which they switch from the corporate to the government arena and back again, especially if they come from the international side of either. (Both Republican and Democratic administrations in the USA provide ample proof.)

As their budgets begin to rival Belgium's GDP, international corporations forge even closer links with financial institutions. The latter form part of the corporatist-government world not just by

50. Some scholars argue that the US economy is not really corporatist because small businesses contribute more to the GDP than do great corporations. That may be, but small businesses do not act as a bloc, and big corporations do. The owner of a restaurant may make more money than a corporate (or government) bureaucrat, but he has no power outside his own walls. The bureaucrats, by contrast, run the country and, should they so wish, can curb even the independence of the restaurateur by, for instance, taxing most of his money away. He, on the other hand, is helpless to do anything about it.

inclination but by statute, having to forge a unity with the quasi-independent set-ups that control the money supply. Organisations like the Federal Reserve, the Bank of England, Bundesbank and Banque de France are more independent of their national governments than they are of one another.

Like today's businessmen and politicians, they do not feel they owe loyalty to their people, much less to any moral principles. Their loyalty, what is left of it once the Number One has been taken care of, is pledged to the international elite that increasingly supersedes national governments.

5

The situation bears every hallmark of the virtual world, and that is precisely the address at which our financial system can be reached. Those wishing to contest this observation could do worse than look at stocks and shares, which these days are owned by most people either directly or indirectly, typically through pension funds.

In the real world, the proposition was aboveboard. A company wishing to raise some cash divided its assets, both current and realistically projected, into units of stock. These were then bought as shares by those who understood the business and found the projections to be indeed realistic. The buyers thus acquired a part of the company, and this was commensurate with the size of their holdings. As effectively partners in the firm they were entitled to their share of the profits, payable in the form of dividends. If the company performed well, their dividends were high; if it performed badly, they were low. In that case any shareholder, even a small one, would have been entitled to voice his concerns at a general meeting.

If he had valid suggestions on how the business could be improved, the management would consider, and usually act upon, his ideas. If the management and other shareholders disagreed with him, his proposals would be rejected. In either case there would be a serious and informed discussion. There existed an understanding all round that the dividends reflected the actual, rather than virtual, reality. They were linked to how well the company was doing, and if that could be improved the dividends would go up.

Frenzied urgency, so typical of today's markets, was nowhere in evidence. There was seldom any rush. The company was in it for the long haul, and so was the investor. He could have put his money in a bank, but he had chosen to invest it more aggressively for a chance of higher return. But in principle the investment in shares was the same as a deposit into a savings account. In a bank the invested capital produced an interest, in the stock market it produced a dividend. The former was guaranteed; the latter involved a risk. A conservative investor could reduce the risk to an imperceptible minimum by investing only in strong, well-established companies. A more daring chap could take a bit more of a chance. A wise investor would mix up the two options in his portfolio.

However, these days we hardly ever buy shares for the sake of the dividends. Let me illustrate this by asking a personal question (I promise this is strictly between us). If you own any shares, do you remember offhand the amount you have earned from the dividends so far this year? If you are like most people, you probably do not. However, most people will have a fairly accurate idea of whether the cost of their share portfolio is going up or, more likely in today's climate, down.

This is because we no longer treat the stock market in generally the same way as we treat a bank, or rather used to treat it. For most of us today the stock market is a giant casino, a chance of getting something for nothing. (Actually banks too are beginning to look more like a chancy proposition than a rock-solid depository of our money. In fact 'casino banking' is much talked about these days.)

Let us be kind and describe investment in shares, as it stands now, as a highly speculative venture, rather than a gamble. Even so, as with any other highly speculative investment, what we are after is not to secure a stable income (this is nowhere near so secure as it used to be anyway) but to score a quick killing.

So it is no wonder that the average length of share ownership has plunged tremendously, from decades a century ago to years in mid-twentieth century to months or even days now. In fact, some Japanese businessmen have abandoned even the vestigial pretence that investing in securities is any different from spinning the roulette wheel. They reduce the turnaround time to seconds: by way of post-dinner entertainment the jaded tycoons go to cafés equipped with terminals and gamble on next-instant's changes in the spot market for currencies and securities. This may be an extreme example, but the general tendency to treat shares as roulette chips results in huge volumes of trading and, consequently, immense fluctuations in share prices day to day.

Computer technology promotes this tendency. For example the practice of High-Frequency Trading (HFT) would be impossible without the lightning-quick computing power of modern machines. They enable traders to track the market trends in real time, instantly taking advantage of equity positions open for seconds only. The second is thus rapidly becoming the standard unit for measuring the time it takes for shares to change hands, and most high-frequency traders tend to liquidate their entire portfolio in one day. As this sort of thing is consonant with modernity, in 2010 HFT accounted for over 70 percent of all US equity transactions.

Under such circumstances the old certitudes sail right out of the window, and the gulf between actual and virtual reality widens beyond the horizon. If the shares of Disunity United have gone up 15 percent today and then dipped 25 percent tomorrow, this no longer reflects anything the company may be doing. The traditional logic of the market with its hands, visible or otherwise, has nothing to do with it.

The stock exchange operates according to its own logic, or rather absence thereof. So every day we can observe a situation where the stock price of a company may dip below the total value of its hard assets. And it is far from unknown for it to drop even below the amount of cash the company holds in its current account. Just consider it: a company can be bought for less money than it has in the bank. In other words, you can pay £10 to buy £20. Most people would regard this as an attractive proposition.

This makes asset stripping such a widespread activity these days. An eagle eye is all it takes to be an effective asset stripper: spot a disparity between a company's stock price and its assets, and in you move. The company is doing well, its profits are healthy, and its hundreds of employees all look forward to a secure future. Suddenly a blip in the stock market sends out a pulse triggering frantic activity. Predators converge and make an acquisition offer way in excess of the virtual, depressed market price of the company's stock, but still much lower than the value of the company's assets. Members of the board, who own a large block of the shares, vote to sell: the second metaphysical premise they proceed from makes it impossible for them to ignore their own immediate good. The liquidators move in, close the company down and sell off everything of value. As a result, they turn a huge profit, the managers a smaller one, and the employees who have made the firm a success in the first place are out in the street.

But many of them were also shareholders, if minor ones. Why did they not join forces with thousands of other small shareholders outside the company to stop the deal in their tracks? Or at least to argue against it? Alas, as companies began to grow to today's megalomaniac proportions, the voice of a small shareholder could be heard no more loudly than the voice of a single voter can be heard in a modern democracy.

The management is as far removed from the shareholders as our governments are from the voters. And the greater the distance between the two, the easier it becomes for the increasingly bureaucratic management to act upon the imperative imposed by the second metaphysical premise. Their company's success only matters if it coincides with theirs. In case of a contradiction, for all they care the company can disintegrate and its employees join the queue at the unemployment office.

One would think that a manager can only be successful if his company is, and vice versa. That type of thinking is so firmly entrenched in the real world as to be irrelevant. For in the virtual world the face that a business presents to the public has nothing to do with reality. If the firm puts up a good front, and consequently attracts investors, the manager is successful. If it does not, he is not. No other considerations even come into it. The aphorism 'perception is reality' may be vulgar, but these days it is true. This was once illustrated, with quite some wit, by a genius in an unrelated field.

The sublime Canadian pianist Glenn Gould had a good business head on his shoulders, and a keen understanding of virtual reality. This he once proved by buying a large block of shares in a small oil-tool company. He then casually mentioned to a few gossipy people, including his barber and the head waiter at his favourite restaurant, that Sheik Yamani, then the Saudi Oil Minister, had told him over dinner that he was seriously considering the oil-tool company as a potential partner in a major venture. The news spread instantly, the company's stock shot up against the background of a general slump, and the wily musician cleaned up, prompting his broker to suggest that perhaps he had missed his true calling.

Leaving aside the dubious ethics involved in that little caper, a myriad developments had to come together to make that trick playable. Collectively they all mean the same thing: the perceived, which is to say virtual, value of a business had nothing to do with its real value. Perception is no longer merely divorced from reality; it has indeed become reality.

In other words, the old philosophical problem of appearance and reality has finally been solved by the removal of the second concept. Plato and Aristotle have been replaced by Marshall McLuhan. Otherwise it would be impossible to explain today's world in general and specifically the wild fluctuations in the share prices of so many companies.

Let us say Company X makes some kind of widgets. The company is publicly owned, and its stock was worth Y at the close of business yesterday. Suddenly, when the Exchange opened in the morning, the stock of Company X shot up 10 percent. Does this mean that overnight X had increased its productivity? Modernised its plant? Begun to be managed better? Cut its overhead? Found new markets? It does not.

The increase had no more to do with the company's good performance than tomorrow's possible 15 percent dip in its share value will result from its poor performance. It is just that the virtual world has passed its verdict.

6

Mostly it speaks in the language of advertising and its related disciplines, such as public relations and political propaganda. Like everything else in the virtual world, including politics, this language has its own logic. A modern advertising copywriter reverses the traditional logical process by always starting with the conclusion (*'Brand X offers what the much-touted Brands Y and Z can't possibly offer'*), and only then sometimes touching upon the intermediate steps. Once the conclusion has been understood, the copywriter (PR executive, politician) fills in the blanks by putting together a list of desemanticised verbal stimuli best suited to achieving the goal. This is the nature of commercial brand building.

The word 'brand', with its 'personality' matched to the 'market profile', is a virtual-world invention. Brand characteristics have little, often nothing, to do with real product characteristics. If they in any way overlap, it is by serendipity. Any similarity between the two is no longer needed: the public, resident in the virtual world, has been conditioned to think brands, not products. A pub crawler selects a brand of lager not because he really believes that by doing so he appears more intelligent to his friends, but because he is satisfied that the marketers of the brand have activated the correct mechanisms of virtual-world response. What those mechanisms are differs from brand to brand, but only superficially. By and large, they can all be grouped according to which of the seven deadly sins they not only expiate but indeed glamorise. The appeal of the virtual world is not only not modern in any true sense, but is downright atavistic.

Lust, for example, has been shown to be particularly effective for the marketers of personal-hygiene products, underwear, cosmetics and some cars. This appeal has become a self-fulfilling prophecy, which is a sine qua non for closing the virtual-world loop. Thus a belief that some brands of motorcar have a strong 'pulling' power has been communicated to the male of the philistine sub-species directly, and to the female vicariously. Men residing in the virtual world expect, and their women accept, that the thrust generated by a powerful engine will reflect or perhaps even enhance the sexual potency of the man who drives a car thus equipped.

That a real-world holdout may wince at this kind of transference is neither here nor there. What matters is not semantics but semiotics; not substance but form; not reality but make-believe. Similarly, the modern political process has practically nothing to do with actual reality, which is reflected in the imprecision of the words that convey the meaning, or rather the symbolic meaning, of political concepts. If even the names of the parties mean nothing in any of the leading parliamentary democracies, then it is little wonder that the modern political process almost entirely by-passes reason, in whose name it was devised in the first place. Modern politics is neither democratic nor autocratic; it is virtual-world.

Modern politicians follow the same logic as modern marketers, which is why they share the same techniques. Marketers have benefited from the polling tricks first conjured up by politicians, while the latter are relying ever more on focus-group research that has stood marketers in such good stead. Focus groups are put together for the purpose of identifying the semiotic actuators of the basic, not to say base, response mechanisms.

Let us say research reveals that the public responds better to an appeal to lust than greed in the marketing of a car. The resulting TV commercials will then show, say, a leggy creature, all billowing hair and rock-steady bust, running towards the car in which a muscular chap awaits. That is, if the intended target audience is male. If it is female, then a tall, dark and handsome chap will be shown first in close-up, contorting his unshaven features into a semiotic message of an impending erection, and then in a medium-wide shot, rolling his pectorals as he john-waynes towards the car and its pouting female driver.

Had the focus groups suggested that avarice would be a more promising deadly sin to target, exactly the same product would acquire different brand characteristics. It could for example come across in a commercial depicting the driver as an astute youngster who has saved a fistful of cash by buying this car. The payoff for his thrift could again be sexual (a girl realising he would be a better father of her unborn children than the square-jawed apparition who had wandered in from the adjacent lot) or it could be professional (his boss realising that a young man who looks after his own money so well can be trusted to look after someone else's). In any case, the car's real characteristics will not come into it.

A marketer who wants to include some latent appeal to reason will be helped in his effort by an elaborate code of practice frowning upon outright falsehood but making up for it by countenancing more subtle deception. To that end, our modern 'brand builder' will be encouraged to use any number of tricks, of which the most illustrious are the Unique Selling Proposition (USP for short) and its derivative Pre-Emptive Benefit.[51]

The concept of the USP springs from the correct evaluation of the audience brought up in the virtual world as an aggregate of persons who are incapable of responding to more than one message at a time. Thus, the marketer of a brand uses his own judgement, fortified by every manner of market research, to 'position' the brand in a unique way. If this bears some semblance to reality, so much the better. If not, that is just fine too.

Let us suppose two brands of soda are identical in every respect, except that one has a twist-off cap and the other has not. The twist-off cap becomes the brand's USP, and every piece of communication for this soda will feature comparisons between a silly lad who has to look in vain for a bottle opener and his clever rival who neatly opens his bottle in one graceful motion. The pay-off will most probably be sexual, with the latter chap claiming the affections of a girl who looks down with contempt as the other suitor tries to open a bottle with his teeth.

Such communications will not tell a lie by stating that one brand of soda has a twist-off cap when it has not. But they will deceive by blowing this minute detail out of all proportion and by omitting the fact that in every other respect the two sodas are identical.

If even such a minuscule USP cannot be found, which is increasingly becoming the case in the conditions of uniformity so beloved in our virtual world, then the Pre-Emptive Benefit makes an

51. A closely related derivative of the USP is the so-called 'top parity' claim ('nobody does it better'). When the maker of a car, or rather his ad agency, claims 'you can't buy a faster car for the same money', he omits the fact that there exist a dozen cars that are just as fast. Legally he is in the clear because he did not lie. Morally he is dubious because he deceived by implying his car is the fastest. Lewis Carroll anticipated this marketing trick in his *Alice*: 'There's nothing like eating hay when you're faint,' he remarked... 'I should think throwing cold water over you would be better,' Alice suggested... 'I didn't say there was nothing BETTER,' the King replied. 'I said there was nothing LIKE it.'

appearance, which is a characteristic shared by all or most brands but claimed by only one. The marketers of this brand thus pre-empt the benefit of the whole product category by claiming it to be the unique property of their own brand.

Many years ago, for example, the marketers of a mass-produced American beer proclaimed that all their bottles were 'washed in live steam', implying pristine sterility. The campaign was swallowed hook, line and sinker by the public, unaware that all beer bottles were sterilised the same way. But they would not have cared even had they known. Any sane individual would assume anyway that a commercially distributed liquid comes in a clean bottle, however this is achieved. What matters to a modern consumer is the mating ritual of the virtual world, not facts.

The modern consumer of political messages responds in exactly the same way. If we look at the slogans of any political campaign, we shall discern 'USPs' and 'pre-emptive benefits' galore: meaningless shibboleths, not real ideas. But the situation in politics is even more pernicious than in commerce because there are few legal restrictions on what a politician can promise.

Unlike a marketer, a politician is not prevented by law from telling a lie, such as issuing a promise he knows he is not going to keep. He may suffer for a broken promise in the next election, but in all likelihood will not. The electorate is, after all, like a market: short on memory, long on the desire to see the game played by the rules of the virtual world. And veracity is not one of those rules. Thus, when a politician promises to look after the least fortunate, only the most backward voters expect him actually to do so.

A majority of both politicians and voters are middle-class people proceeding from the second metaphysical premise. They could not care less about the poor. But voters who gravitate towards the left pole will not plug themselves into the virtual-world loop until they hear the right words, the eenie-meenie-miny-mo of politics but without the politically incorrect brutality towards a person of Afro-Caribbean descent.

Whether the politician actually intends to help the poor is immaterial. It would matter, however, if he announced that such mythical help would be financed by tax increases. The voter must be re-assured that this is a game played by the rules, but a game nonetheless. Politics is played in the virtual world. But money, especially his own, is real life. So a good politician will mollify the philistine voter by promising to increase government spending without increasing either the taxes or the money supply (which was Reagan's promise we discussed earlier).

The voter could, of course, ask where the money is going to come from in that case, especially if the economy is sluggish, but he is unlikely to do so. He is, after all, satisfied that the right virtual-world noises have been made. He is ready to consent to be governed. In other words, he is ready to accept the pre-emptive benefit as real.

If a voter regards himself as more right than left, then he will want a guarantee that his taxes will not go up. A politician seeking his vote will grab the USP opening by issuing such a guarantee in as emphatic a fashion as it takes. The elder George Bush's 'read my lips, no new taxes' was a good example of such a USP positioning. Of course, both the politician and his 'conservative' supporter know that taxes will go up – they usually do.

You can emulate George Bush Sr by inviting friends to read your lips: taxes will go up, whichever party is in power. If the rate of income tax remains the same or even drops (the favourite trick of 'conservative' politicians), then some other, less visible taxes will make up for this generosity in a stealthy way. Under Tony Blair, for example, the amount of money we paid in tax increased considerably, though the income tax rate remained the same. Thus the difference between 'right-wing' and 'left-wing' politicians lies not in their actions, much less in their principles, but in the response they wish to elicit from the electorate in the virtual world.

7

Just as a modern state cannot exist without the consent of the governed, however fraudulently such consent was obtained, a modern financial system relies on the consent of the multitudes firmly rooted in the virtual world. The consent can be either passive or active. Some may meekly acquiesce to pump their money into the system's veins, some will do so enthusiastically. But none has either the strength or desire to revert to the real world. In that sense, while governments and financial institutions are the main culprits in the catastrophe, the public cannot be exonerated either.

The whole process looks insane, if we define insanity as losing touch with reality. Allow me to illustrate this by a hypothetical version of a real situation. Let us just assume for the sake of argument that you are on a reasonable but unspectacular middle-class income. Now imagine this kind of telephone dialogue between you and a stranger whose name sounds vaguely familiar. The phone rings:

You: Hello.

Stranger: Hello. This is John Doe speaking. You may've heard of me.

You: Yes, Mr Doe, your name does sound familiar. What can I do for you?

JD: I'd like you to give me twenty thousand.

You: Why on earth would I want to do that?

JD: Because I may pay you a high rate of interest.

You: How high, exactly?

JD: Well, that's the rub. I don't really know how high. It may be ten percent. It may be five percent. And, truth to tell, it may be nothing at all. We'll find out later.

You: But surely, if I want my money back, say a year from now, you'll return it with a little extra? At least a sum equal to the kind of interest the bank would have given me?

JD: Well, I may. Then again, I may not. You may get your twenty thousand back, possibly with interest. But then you may also get only fifteen thousand back. Or, if things don't work out for me, nothing at all. It's impossible to predict. Are you willing to give it a go?

You: But of course! Sounds like a splendid investment idea! Wouldn't pass it up for anything in the world. Oh by the way, what exactly are you going to do with my money, er... John?

Here there are two possible replies.

Version 1:

JD: Don't know yet. I'll probably find a few other investors like you, and then try to sell the whole amount on at a profit, in which you may or may not participate. Naturally, I'll take my cut off the top first, regardless of what happens. Anyway, it won't matter to you. You'll have no say in how the money is used one way or the other.

You: So much the better. I wouldn't trust myself with my own money anyway.

Version 2:

JD: I'll spread it around. Give forty chaps in different markets five hundred each, see what they can do with the money. If they do well, you may (or may not) do well too. If they don't do so well, you'll lose it all, or much of it at any rate. Once again, my cut comes off the top in any event. Now doesn't this sound good?

You: Wonderful! I'll go along with this.

This imaginary dialogue is based on exactly the same logic we follow when investing in the shares of a modern, which is to say virtual-world, company (Version 1) or buying into a hedge fund (Version 2). When presented this way, any reasonable individual will probably hang up, expletive deleted, halfway through such a phone call. And yet financial advisers lead us along exactly that very garden path every time we discuss investment options.

Nor does it look odd to us that people who manipulate our money to give us, at best, a modest return are themselves drawing millions every year. It does not strike us as out of order that a young hedge-fund manager can pull down 100 times more than a history teacher with 30-years' experience. The financial chap neither trains longer nor works harder. What makes him worth his king's ransom? He does not produce anything; unlike the teacher's work, what he does has no social or cultural value. In fact all he does is shuffle someone else's money around to make a huge profit for his employer, a large bonus for himself and a modest return for his investors. His motto is not 'Defeat ignorance!' It is 'Beat the index!'

Sometimes he makes less profit for his employer, sometimes none at all, and sometimes he destroys his employer altogether, which is a service the barely post-pubescent lout Nick Leeson provided in 1995 for Barings, Britain's oldest investment bank. But, such a calamity apart, all the youngster risks is the sack. Even so, at an income of millions for a few good years, he would not be unduly inconvenienced. After all, how many years of £2,000,000 bonuses does it take not to fear the bread line too much?

Not so long ago every London paper carried the story of a young female executive working at a hedge fund whose louche manager had treated her inappropriately. Sympathetic as we all are to the young lady's actionable plight (she was made to attend a couple of strip shows and listen to endless dumb-blonde jokes interspersed with stories of her boss's amorous conquests), it is hard not to notice that her starting salary immediately out of university was £60 thousand a year. In the next five years, while she was still in her mid-twenties, her annual salary rose to £577 thousand, and that is not even taking into account bonuses (£1.4 million in one year) and other perks.

Now even assuming that the young executive in question is an intuitive financial genius of J.P. Morgan proportions, this sort of compensation can under no circumstances be explained by market forces. Markets work by buying things at the lowest possible price and selling them at the highest possible price. Would the girl still wet behind the ears not have consented to do the same job for £300,000? Or, pinching at every possible turn, even for a paltry £150,000? Plus bonuses of course? You bet she would. Her naughty boss thus violated elementary market practices by paying well over the odds. And we would probably have to study the theory of exponential numbers to calculate *his* income.

Naturally while the papers were all righteously indignant at the young lady's ordeal, none found anything wrong with this outrageous skimming of other people's money. This is regarded as par for the course: do these financiers not provide a valuable service? The answer to that is no, they do not. And even if they did, their remuneration would not be based on that. They pay themselves obscene amounts for the same reason dogs in a popular joke do something too crude to mention here: because they can. The market has not spoken; the second metaphysical premise has.

Usually these people have not even started the companies they work for. Had they done so, one would be hard-pressed to come up with valid arguments against any rewards they would draw for themselves. It would be their money after all, at least at the beginning, and they would have run considerable risks to be in the position they are now.

Conversely, all the woman in question ever did was persuade people to make chancy investments into the hedge fund that employed her. Judging by others working there at the same time, the hiring policy was geared to attract nubile girls, on the correct assumption that they would have greater persuasive powers than a bald middle-aged man with a bottle of Rioja on his breath. Given the period in which the harassment victim operated, most of her investors probably lost a bundle. No matter. 'I'm worth every penny,' she proudly declared against the most elementary common sense, to the accompaniment of loud hosannas screamed by her colleagues.

Yet people only ever think there is something wrong with this kind of virtual-reality show when the bottom falls out of the market (or, on this evidence, sometimes not even then). Suddenly seven-figure bonuses commanded by the new breed of City barrow boys, or barrow girls as the case may be, begin to look irritating. At other times we may, for example, cite footballers' salaries by way of a comparison designed to defend the youngsters who gamble investors' money away. Yet the defence does not quite work.

Yes, for purely aesthetic reasons one winces whenever a tattooed ignoramus with a useful left foot signs a five-year contract worth £150 thousand a week (replace the left foot with the jump shot, and corresponding numbers may be even higher in America). But for purely practical reasons one has to agree that the virtual world is not the sole provenance of his remuneration. The real-world law of supply and demand is at play too, however obliquely.

It is bread and (or, in this case, for) circuses: The walking canvas for body art is the circus for which people, in their millions, are happy to part with their bread. And, unlike the 'service' provided by our fund-managing youngster, there are no strings attached, no risks involved. People always get what they pay for. Sixty thousand of them may each shell out £50 of their hard-earned to watch the winger dribble his way to fortune every Saturday, but in return they get the kind of fulfilment they cannot really find anywhere else – not these days, not with the puny values burnt into their brains by the second metaphysical premise.

Moreover, in the absence of any community spirit, people seek the surrogate of shared tribal loyalty, which they find among the fellow fans of their team. This is worth a lot to them, and they are prepared to pay through the nose to the leaders of the tribe, which is to say footballers.[52] The exchange between the player and the paying public is therefore fair, which is more than one can say for a little financial wizard who displays considerably less ingenuity than a half-decent midfielder, while producing the kind of results that usually disappoint people or, at worst, leave them destitute.

This goes to show that not only is the financial system lodged in the virtual world, but the public is as well. Anaesthetised by virtual reality, people no longer realise that what they thought still resided in the real world, their money, does not live there anymore. They are being duped because they are begging to be duped.

Not that, to be fair, they have much choice anyhow. After all, our virtual governments and financial institutions have succeeded in destroying actual reality. That is why, even if our hypothetical investor were actively looking for a real-world opportunity to put his money to work, he would be unlikely to find one, for practically none exists any longer. This is not his fault. But what is his fault is that he is eager to play by the rules of the virtual world. He is a Prometheus who loves eagles, a chicken that loves battery farms, a slave who loves slavery.

The same logic that compels a modern financier to maximise his own returns at the expense of his investors' drives potential investors into his clutches. I refer to this logic here as the second metaphysical premise. Our modern investor lives by it and he dies by it. But fear of fiscal death does not slow him down. His nerve endings have been

52. In ancient Rome, race chariot drivers were quite wealthy too, although, if you trust historiography, their supporters did not use mobile phones to prearrange punch-ups after a few amphorae of Falerno.

deadened by hysteria: I must make it! Now! I'll be old before long, and unable to enjoy money! And then I'll be dead! If I don't make it soon, I'm worthless!

It is no accident that in America the question 'How much is he worth?' has ousted 'How much money does he have?' from everyday parlance. Colloquialisms ought not to be taken literally, but then neither must they be dismissed as linguistic mishaps. They always reflect a real state of affairs in some way.

Indeed, in a materialistic world, how else can the human worth of a person be judged objectively? In the old days describing someone as a good man was an unequivocal statement: the standards of goodness were laid down in Matthew 5: 3-12, and there was no quibbling about them. Thus, though an argument on whether or not a person was indeed good could have been possible, no disagreement on what constituted goodness could have arisen.

In our anthropocentric days the standards are different, and everything is open to doubt. You say someone is a good man, but that is only your opinion. In my opinion he is a bounder. No, I do not know anything you do not. We both know the same facts about the man; we just assess them differently. Who is to say which of us is right? Show me your criteria of goodness and I shall show you mine.

Money, on the other hand, is objective. Someone who has a million in the bank is indisputably twice as rich as someone who makes do with merely half a million. Let us just cut to the chase by saying he is worth twice as much. Our interlocutor, craving objectivity and finding it only in money, will know exactly what we mean. Repeat the process a few billion times over a century or so, and in most people's minds money will equate human worth. What started out as a metaphor has become a descriptive term.

Another folksy phrase every American knows is, 'If you're so smart, how come you ain't rich?' As many other half-jocular phrases, this one communicates a half-truth by half-implying that getting rich is the only valid test of intelligence. Conversely, a poor man, such as for instance Socrates, can be safely presumed to be stupid. After all, he wasted every opportunity to make money by wandering around the city, accosting strangers and asking them impertinent questions, for which he eventually was killed in a perfectly democratic way. The simpleton could have been starting hedge funds instead.

Thus the happiness everyone has an inalienable right to pursue acquires a dimension that goes beyond mere physical comfort. It now equates self-respect, and people have been known to commit reckless acts in search of that elusive commodity. If soldiers charge into machine-gun fire not to lose face in front of their comrades, then it is easy to understand why people are ready to risk their fiscal future for public approval.

It is in our nature to seek peer endorsement of our own self-assessment. Informed by the second metaphysical premise, we measure our human worth in money and communicate it to the outside world through spending. That is why in the last 20 years the average household spending in the US outpaced income by three to one. Just think about it: *on average* people have spent three times what they have earned over 20 years. And the pattern is heavily skewed towards the last decade, putting us all under an increasingly greater strain. It is hard to keep up with the Joneses when they are running away at an Olympic-calibre speed.

Obviously, it took an inordinate amount of credit to encourage such profligacy, and easy availability of money has traditionally been a telltale sign of an economy doing well. However, in the first years of the new millennium America's real GDP was sliding down, which means the country was, and has been since, in recession.[53] Yet, against both tradition and considerations of plain prudence, consumer credit and consequently reckless spending continued to climb. Encouraged by politicians, bankers and economists, people simply could not control their urge to declare their human worth to

---

53. Official GDP figures ought to be taken with a bag, as opposed to merely a pinch, of salt. For example, if one bank lends another £100, and the second bank then issues a derivative bond on that loan and sells it on to a third party for £120, the country's GDP has increased by £220 without adding any actual value to anything other than the virtual world.

the world by the only means at their disposal. The sociologist Thorstein Veblen (d. 1929) coined the term 'conspicuous consumption', and it is very precise, with the adjective just as important as the noun. 'Happiness' is not just in consuming; it is in being seen to consume.

A couple of decades of such freewheeling profligacy can bankrupt any country and certainly any financial system. Indeed, America is now technically bankrupt: her present liabilities greatly exceed her assets, and 80 percent of those are in foreign hands. The only thing missing is a formal declaration of bankruptcy, but politicians do not make such frank pronouncements in the virtual world. More in their nature are statements like 'we owe it to ourselves,' FDR's economically illiterate response to concerns about the growing national debt.

These days any American who reads the papers knows that the country's staggering debt is primarily owed to outsiders, most of whom do not share America's warm feelings about herself. Like vultures, they circle overhead waiting to pounce. After all, if asset stripping can work at the micro level of a company, who can guarantee it would not work at the macro level of a country?

The only thing that keeps America from total collapse is the dollar, the tottering, moribund reminder of past grandeur that by default still remains the world's reserve currency. For as long as America can manipulate the currency in which her debt is denominated, she can stay afloat and even make triumphant noises about the end of recession and the recovery of her sick economy. Only hopeless ignoramuses can think this situation is healthy. Only inveterate optimists can think it will last for ever.

THE PLOT SICKENS

1

The current crisis is a direct result of our three culprits, the state, financial institutions and the public, acting in unison. Then again, why would they not? They do share common goals, aspirations and morality, all deriving from the second metaphysical premise. Naturally they all pull in the same direction.

The unwitting collusion has worked in any number of ways, and these have been described in great detail by people more knowledgeable in the mechanics of finance than I am. Yet as the theme of this essay cannot be properly developed without some attention paid to finance, I shall do so anyway, while begging your forgiveness in advance if what I say sounds too basic.

It is widely known that the crisis of the world's financial system was caused by the collapse of the mortgage market in America. In broad strokes, towards the end of his presidency (1993-2001) Bill Clinton decided to encourage a wider spread of home ownership, just as Margaret Thatcher did in Britain a decade earlier. In both instances the politicians were hailed as the present-day answer to Moses, Aaron and Joshua, leading their people out of the wilderness towards the promised land.

Yet the journey left a legacy fraught not only with opportunities for short-term gain but also with potential for long-term disasters. In Britain, for example, over the last decade the property business has outstripped manufacturing as the largest contributor to the nation's GDP, which is hardly a healthy situation. The underlying assumption seems to be that we can all get rich not by making things others would want to buy but by selling houses to one another. We probably can at that, but only in the virtual world.

Owning one's residence, provided one could afford it, was an attractive proposition then, and had been for centuries before the world was blessed with the arrival of Mrs Thatcher (as she then was) and Mr Clinton. Largely the attraction was emotional: in the real world, house and hearth used to represent a warm, safe place to raise a family and to take refuge from the raging elements outside, those both natural and man-made. It was an anchor, securing people to the land of their ancestors and to their community. Moreover, a freehold entitled the owner to vote, as it was presumed that only such civic attachment would enable him to cast his vote responsibly.

But in the conditions of a fully mature virtual world, owning a house became an opportunity for a quick gain, and often nothing but that. There certainly was no longer any civic reason to own a house: with virtual form counting for more than real substance, casting a responsible vote was no longer an objective for either politicians or voters. Even living in a cardboard box under a bridge was no longer seen as a disqualifying circumstance. In parallel, the requirement of being able to afford what one buys began to apply no more rigidly than it did in casinos. People were not buying an abode; they were taking a punt. 'Have a hunch, bet a bunch,' was the Las Vegas motto they heeded.

Answering the battle cry of Clinton's legacy, the Federal Reserve, led by the self-admittedly infallible Alan Greenspan, gradually lowered the prime interest rate from six percent in 2001 to one percent by 2006, an all-time low at the time. Clinton's firm belief in the redemptive value of home ownership was therefore shared by his Republican successor – another example of two minds (great or otherwise) thinking alike, provided they start from the same premise.

Heeding the clarion call, millions took on mortgages to the absolute maximum they could possibly carry even at rock-bottom lending rates. Then, out of the blue, the Fed increased the prime interest rate to five percent. The ensuing rise in mortgage repayments pushed many into default, thus precipitating the present crisis.

This gave proof, if any was needed, that in today's economy, home ownership is an imprecise term that reeks of virtual world. Someone who takes out a 25-year $450,000 loan to buy a house worth $500,000 does not really own the house. He owns $50,000; the bank owns the rest. (This means that 'mortgage loan' is another misnomer coined by the virtual world: when spread over 25 years a loan is not really a loan; it is equity.)

So what does our homeowner actually own, in addition to the $50,000? The answer is, he does not own anything else; he controls. The bank has transferred to him the temporary control of the capital, not the ownership of it. In that sense the homeowner is not unlike a modern corporate executive or a trader: he disposes of the capital that does not belong to him, treating it accordingly.

Typically, how does he dispose of it? By now we know enough to realise that a modern 'homeowner' can only treat the capital under his control in the same way a stock-market investor treats his share portfolio: as an opportunity for highly speculative ventures. In colloquial parlance this is called taking equity out of the property, which is another way to describe gambling with someone else's money. As in any other game of chance, the gambler has to have highly optimistic expectations for the future. If such expectations are confirmed, he gains. If they are frustrated, he loses, triggering off a chain reaction of losses.

This is how it works. Let us say the market value of the same house has increased by 20 percent in the first year, not an unrealistic scenario considering the inflation of assets that inevitably accompanies the debauchment of currency. The house is now worth $600,000, of which the 'owner' still owes only $450,000. The remaining $150,000 is his original down payment plus paper profit, which for the time being is only that: he has to live somewhere, and if he were to sell the house, the 'profit' would be eaten up by the cost of buying a comparable residence whose value has similarly increased.

Apart from moving to a smaller place or a less prestigious neighbourhood, the only way of profiting from the bullish market would be for the owner to take out another mortgage worth $150,000 that he could collateralise against the paper value of the house. He could then reinvest the new wad of cash into another house, if he so wishes, or else into some other speculative deal.

Let us say he does it for two consecutive years, with the house price growing another 20 percent in the second year as well. Now he has taken out cash, or rather taken on two additional mortgages on the first house, in the overall amount of $390,000. On top of that, he has probably added at least three times that amount in mortgages on the two new houses, but for the moment we can disregard that in our calculations.

His investment begins to resemble an inverted pyramid, with the tip of the original house supporting the growing structure at the top. True enough, the pyramid scheme provides the model for all such investments. And not only investments in property: one can say that this is the principle at the foundation of all modern finance, both public and private.

Witness the fact that the government has no pot of money out of which it pays state pensions. Instead it hopes that the money paid in by some people today will be sufficient to pay for other people's pensions tomorrow. What if it is not? The state spends next year's increase in revenue expecting that the economy will grow enough to justify such generosity. What if it does not? Banks pass on loans to one another in the expectation that the underlying value of the collateral will increase. What if it does not? The investors act in the expectation that their stake, as a minimum, will never go down. What if it does? It is better not to think about it.

When this pyramid-shaped logic is applied in an honest, if ill-advised, hope for the future, it is called aggressive entrepreneurship. When used with criminal intent, it is called Ponzi scheme. The perpetrators of the former are patted on the back if they succeed and commiserated with if they fail (usually with equal insincerity in both instances). The perpetrators of the latter, such as Bernie Madoff, are sent to prison in either event, often for peculiar terms exceeding the miscreants' life expectancy by hundreds of years. The difference in the explicit motivation of the investor and the criminal is indeed real, but the difference in their underlying animus is nonexistent. Both are driven by the second metaphysical premise.

Getting back to property, when the market climbs steadily, as our intrepid investor hoped it would, his risk pays off. He can make a fortune, and many have. But Newton postulated that everything that goes up must come down, and gravity works in investments too. At some point estate prices will fall with the certainty of a ripe apple falling off the tree.

Some lucky individuals will catch the moment when this is about to happen and get out while the getting is good. Most will not. The pyramid has grown too heavy at the top, the needle point at the bottom can no longer balance it. The structure comes down with a big thud, and the 'owner' now sits on negative equity. His house, from whose 'value' he has already 'taken out', on top of his original $450,000, another $390,000 in two separate gambles, is now only worth $350,000 (again, not an unrealistic drop). That leaves the chap almost $600,000 in the red, and this does not even include the losses he might have suffered by investing the extra $390,000 in the same fashion, and taking on additional loans. The combined mortgage repayments become an intolerable burden.

Most people who find themselves in that situation default on the loan, hand over the house keys and walk out. This does not place an undue emotional burden on them: in all likelihood they have not lived in the house long enough to develop any attachment to it. Even though illiterate, or else devious, estate agents routinely replace the word 'house' with 'home' (as in 'attractive, beautifully proportioned three-bedroom home'), in reality for most 'owners' a house is no longer a home. The word has lost any warm, emotional connotations, having acquired instead those of a commodity or stock certificate.

The last few decades have marked the first time in history when people treat their dwellings as short-term investment. In boom times, they are prepared to move every year if that is what it takes to turn a profit.[54] After some cosmetic improvements to their 'homes', they sell and move on to the next project. If things do not work out, they shrug their shoulders and default. In some countries, such abject surrender may involve declaring personal bankruptcy; in some others it may not. One would expect that in all countries this would be the end of it, one way or the other. Alas, it is not: things are only beginning to get interesting.

2

For the mortgage lender was more prescient than the wannabe borrower cum speculator. Bankers know how to protect themselves, or so we were taught to believe. In our scenario the bank did not just proffer the original $450,000 loan hoping that the borrower would dutifully repay it, with interest, over 25 years. The prescient bank issued a derivative bond on the loan that it then sold to another bank. To make it worthwhile, the value of the bond was stated as $600,000, which the buyer accepted. After all, the price of property has nowhere to go but up, has it not? So what is a $150,000 surcharge among friends? Just in case, however, the buyer then issued his own bond, this time for $900,000, and sold it on. And so forth, until in some instances the combined value of the derivative bonds would reach 15 times the original value of the house.

In our hypothetical case, the needle point of the $350,000 (formerly $500,000) house must now support a much heavier institutional pyramid of up to $7.5 million in combined derivatives.

---

54. Some intrepid Londoners would strike a package deal with a removal firm to get a volume discount on, say, three moves over the next four years.

The expectation that the market value of the property will reach this figure in any foreseeable future is no longer merely optimistic. It is insane. Any tenuous link with the real world that may have existed has been severed. The virtual world has triumphed again.

If the banks play their derivative hand more conservatively, and if house prices go up as optimistically predicted, then obviously everyone benefits. Just as obviously, when house prices fall, the pyramid heavily loaded at the top by the weight of virtual-world derivatives comes tumbling down; there is nothing left to support it. Now imagine this type of collapse repeated thousands of times, and you will realise that few banks would be able to take such calamitous falls in stride. Repeat it millions of times, and few are the countries that would be able to remain upright. But did the banks not protect themselves against such a development? They thought they had, and not only in their mortgage loans.

Without going into much tedious detail, as derivative markets in mortgages tottered, exactly the same disaster was brewing with other bank securities. There too the banks thought they had protected themselves by using a most ingenious safety valve. Called Credit Default Swap, CDS for short, the valve has existed in its modern form since 1997.[55] The details were worked out by a team at JP Morgan Chase, a bank that had intimate links with Alan Greenspan, an unabashed fan of the idea.

(It is worth mentioning parenthetically that various Morgan outfits usually tend to contribute more than their fair share of weapons to the armoury of the virtual world. For example, Morgan bankers were the principal architects of the Federal Reserve system, masterminding its strategic offensive against the gold standard.)

Essentially, a CDS means that the seller of a security assumes a certain amount of risk in case of some specified future events, usually defaults. Just like mortgage bonds, CDSs can act as secondary derivatives; they too can be sold on at a profit. Before long the idea

55. For the sake of brevity I am focusing on the CDS, though many other similar tools have also been concocted by the hyperactive minds of our financiers. In effect, using such tools, they have acquired the power to increase the money supply in circumvention of governments and central banks.

turned into a standard practice all over the world: you buy my CDS, I buy yours. A few spins of that particular wheel, and everybody was insured, including the insurers. Unfortunately for the virtual world, reality has its own logic, and this has not yet been universally repealed. And simple logic, unsullied by any intricate expertise in finance, suggests that, when everyone is insured, no one is. To mix the metaphors ever so slightly, when the penny drops, the piper has to be paid. Western financial institutions have learned this to their detriment.

In this instance the piper was demanding rather exorbitant amounts. The Bank for International Settlements currently estimates the total paper value of outstanding derivatives, including CDSs, at $592 trillion, which is roughly 10 times the annual GDP of the whole world, with its five continents and variously industrious populaces. The face value is only about one tenth of that amount, but even such a paltry sum is clearly repayable in the virtual world only. In other words, what could have been a straightforward, real-world transaction between a chap who wants to borrow a couple of hundred thousand to buy a suburban semi and a bank willing to lend it to him, provided he proved his ability to pay off the loan, turned into a worldwide virtual game played with funny money.

Even as this was happening, towards the end of 2007, early 2008, the Financial Accounting Standards Board's (FASB) directive loftily called Fair Accounting Practice went into effect in the US. In broad outlines, FAS 157, as the directive was designated, ruled that a bank's assets must now be calculated on the basis of their current market value, not the original purchase price.

Since by that time the negative disparity between the two had on average grown up to 90 percent, banks had no option but to start dumping their devalued securities in order to plug some of the more gaping holes in their balance sheets. The supply of such securities instantly exceeded demand, with predictable results. The market tumbled from its stratospheric height, shattering on the flinty ground down below.

3

But while the going was good, the second metaphysical premise was working overtime. Driven by it, our three culprits (government, banks and the public) went to war to make the virtual world safe for profligacy. With prime interest rates at an all-time low, courtesy of the 'liberal' Bill Clinton, 'conservative' George W. Bush and 'non-partisan' Federal Reserve System, the orgy of irresponsible lending and reckless borrowing proceeded unabated.

With interest rates unrealistically low, the bankers now had to expect a smaller return from every mortgage loan, so predictably they needed more customers to make sure their own bonuses would not suffer. Thousands of mortgage brokers went on the prowl looking for willing takers. There was no shortage of those: even economically and mentally disadvantaged people could sense that they were being offered something for nothing. But in a real world nothing comes out of nothing, and eventually even the virtual world had to realise that. *Ex nihilo nihil fit* used to act as proof of God's existence. Now the same principle went on to strike a blow for common sense.

The vetting system that used to be unrelentingly rigid was gradually relaxed until it disappeared altogether for all practical purposes. Those of us who in the distant past applied for a mortgage in America still cringe at the recollection of the strict requirements: 20 percent down, plus an annual income equal to at least 25 percent of the property value. No longer: such requirements were first lowered, then dropped. A penniless, unemployed and possibly unemployable gentleman in his advanced middle age could now realistically expect to obtain a mortgage as high as that only available in the past to a wealthy executive with a high life expectancy.[56]

56. The situation in England was no different. A freelance copywriter I know got a mortgage for a Pimlico flat by claiming his income was £100,000 year. In fact it was a fraction of that, but no one bothered to check.

Not only did the banks stop demanding any down payment, but in many cases they were now willing to add a $15,000 closing cost to the 100 percent mortgage loan. Since in reality closing costs rarely exceeded $10,000, people soon figured out that they could get a quick $5,000 cash simply by buying a house (or, to be precise, by taking out a mortgage) – a painless way of paying for a holiday on some tropical island.

Traditional morality no longer applied, as it never does in an environment where punters are attracted by the possibility of getting something for nothing. It is not by accident that Las Vegas was built by the mob: it takes a criminal mentality to cater to essentially immoral cravings. Whatever the laws say, and whoever owns or patronises casinos and race courses, they are corrupt establishments because their underlying assumptions are corrupt. It therefore stands to reason that the modern state would get into the gambling business too: state lotteries do not just levy a tax on people who are poor at maths; they promote the same immoral something-for-nothing mentality that fuelled the borrowing frenzy.[57]

The message both the state and the banks were sending out screamed, 'Borrow! Don't save! Spend!' More and more frequently the message came scribbled on credit cards. In America these never were particularly difficult to obtain, but some loose vetting criteria used to be applied. These now went out of the window. Moreover, Americans, including those who in the past would not have qualified even for a department-store charge card, were now receiving in the post credit cards with $10,000 spending limits or higher. All they had to do was open the envelope and start spending with the card thus received, which was tantamount to signing the contract. The temptation proved irresistible to hordes of people worshipping at the altar of the second metaphysical premise: by the end of 2008 credit card debts in the US approached a trillion dollars.

57. An accountant of my acquaintance has suggested an ingenious, if not quite serious, scheme. Income tax could be replaced by a lottery held every day instead of once a week, with both the ticket price and the prize fund tripled. As a result, he claims, the state would derive the same net revenue as from taxation, but without having to run a collection service: people would be delighted to give their money away in the hope of getting something for nothing.

Divide all those zeroes by the number of heavy card users, and you will realise that a spate of defaults were inevitable. Sure enough, they arrived. In fact, defaulting on credit card loans became a growth industry in America, and not only for conspicuous but honest consumers. Many unscrupulous individuals would simply assemble a pack of all available credit cards, then spend to the limit of each, sometimes using one card to pay off the debt incurred on another, sometimes not even bothering. When the combined debts reached the maximum amount the pack of cards could allow (often measured in hundreds of thousands of dollars), the enterprising chap would simply file for personal bankruptcy and wipe the slate clean.

The punishment for that would be slight: he would not be able to get any more credit for a few years, usually five, at which point he could start afresh. Chapter 7 of the US Bankruptcy Law thus makes it easy to act in an immoral manner without overstepping the boundaries of legality. Even though he acted in a premeditated fashion, the bankrupt crook has done nothing illegal. He has merely played the game by the rules. A new chapter has thus been written in the history of the second metaphysical premise: Chapter 7.

The banks would be left to count the cost of their generosity in having offered unrepayable credit, either as mortgages or credit cards. Since the cost is staggering, one would expect many of them to go bankrupt.

Such an expectation would be frustrated: thanks to the centralising tendency of modern business, paralleling the same trend in government, most banks have grown too big to be allowed to fail. Should they do so, the state would have to pay off the insurance costs to the depositors who have prudently stayed within the limits covered by such policies. Those who have unwisely strayed beyond such limits would lose money, which could make them unlikely to vote for this government again.

By now we know enough to realise that modern government bureaucrats are prepared to endanger anyone but themselves. Hence their liberal use of the printing press in aid of the failing banks. Inventive PR hacks have come up with an imaginative term for printing money: quantitative easing, presumably *queasing* for short. In the virtual world such a euphemism is considered to be a neat verbal trick. It masks the underlying reality, which is simple enough: modern politicians pay for their votes with our money. Quantitative easing spells qualitative disaster.

4

Observing gleefully the current crisis, many on the left of the political spectrum talk about the collapse of capitalism. Considering that the command economies for which such misguided individuals pine collapsed a long time ago, we seem to be at a dead end. There appears to be nowhere to go.

So has capitalism really collapsed? To answer this question, we must first note that neither capitalism nor any other economic system has ever existed in its crystallised form. The most socialist Western economy ever, that of Soviet Russia, always left room for individual economic self-expression, some of it even legal. The most capitalist Western economy ever, that of the USA until the First World War, always left room for government regulation, some of it even just.

Words like 'capitalism' and 'socialism' thus describe not an exclusive, simon-pure formation but rather the dominant ingredient in a mix. The best proportion of the ingredients is easy enough to determine by trial and error, especially if we keep it simple by concentrating on matters economic only.

On these terms, there can be no doubt that a mix in which the main ingredient is capital-fuelled economic self-expression, other-wise known as capitalism, works better than any known alternative.

Observation shows that Jeremy Bentham's utilitarian desideratum of the greatest good for the greatest number of people is fulfilled far more effectively in societies where people fend for themselves with relatively little state interference.

We know why: when it is allowed into the economic game in any other than a refereeing capacity, the state will always prove to be singularly inept. Even worse, it will be likely – nay, certain – to manipulate the economy for its own benefit, rather than that of the people. This, irrespective of whether or not the government has been voted in by an electorate.

As a general rule, therefore, we can accept the practical proposition that the wealth of a society is inversely proportionate to the size and activism of its government. And one would find it difficult to argue on any moral grounds that an economy that delivers widespread prosperity is inferior to one that delivers widespread penury. To put it crudely, freedom pays.

However, any freedom, be that of economic, political, artistic or religious self-expression, presupposes a discipline of some sort. Without discipline economic freedom becomes gangsterism, political freedom becomes anarchy, artistic freedom becomes incoherent self-indulgence, and religious freedom becomes sectarianism at best, and paganism more usually.

In all these types of freedom, discipline can be imposed from either without or within. However, to achieve its desired aim it has to be both external and internal. The first without the second is tyranny; the second without the first is egotism. Either will ultimately prove to be unsuccessful.

If we delve a bit deeper, we shall find that even externally imposed discipline has to originate from within, from the character of those in a position to impose it. Thus proper discipline, wherever it comes from, can only emanate from trustworthy individuals, for otherwise we could always find any number of easy ways around it.

And here we go back to the central proposition of this essay: when government officials are driven by the second metaphysical premise, people cannot trust them; when it is the people who are thus animated, they should not trust themselves; bankers proceeding from the same philosophy ought to be trusted by neither.

Discipline is needed to direct freedom towards a desired end. Yet the nature of our modern, which is to say virtual, world is such that human lives lack a purpose worthy of the name. Thus it is the process of life that remains the sole focus of popular aspirations. This finite concept is naturally transferred on to every aspect of life: more and more we busy ourselves with procedures and details, while losing sight of any ultimate objective. The question we tend to ask ourselves is 'How?', not 'What for?'

For example, a staunch supporter of Western modernity would identify achieving and maintaining democracy as the universal goal of politics. But democracy cannot be the aim of government; it is merely its method. And no method of government should be assessed in separation from the type of society it fosters.

Judged by that criterion, and it is the only valid one this side of ideology, both Britain and the United States were better countries when democracy was balanced and limited, as in Britain, or at least just limited, as in America. But that was before the triumph of the virtual world. In the real world there was much argument on whether or not the end justified the means. In our virtual world the means *is* the end.

The same applies to freedom, be that in the proper, inner sense of the word or as it is these days misused to denote liberty. Freedom is the road, not the destination. It has to be a necessary condition of human life, but it cannot be its goal.

In the past freedom was seen as a tool of salvation (or damnation, as the case might have been). In the virtual world, people talk about it as salvation itself. Freedom is thus first misused linguistically, then abused substantively. It is turned against itself, and before long the word begins to mean whatever we want it to mean. That is to say it becomes meaningless in any Western context. For the founding tenet of the West was that life is not just about *being*, it is about *becoming*. Remove that understanding, and we begin to move in a circle that will become vicious sooner or later. Freedom will stop being real; it will become virtual.

True freedom can exist only in a society with a clear sense of direction. Otherwise it is licence, these days issued *en masse* to porn and pop, euthanasia and abortion, perversion and corruption. And, relevant to our theme, to economic irresponsibility.

Free enterprise, a term that is somewhat loosely used as a synonym of capitalism, is another example of such circuitous viciousness. When capitalism is but a process of economic life, enabling people to live without much deprivation while still on earth, then it is impossible to fault on either moral or empirical grounds. But when it turns into the be-all and end-all, pursuit of happiness begins to come with an awful price tag.

Define happiness in strictly materialistic terms, and misery beckons. Remove morality that comes down from an authority infinitely higher than human regulators, and a country like Britain morphs from a nation of shopkeepers into a nation of shoplifters. In the old days, when shoplifting was technically easy, it was much less widespread than it is in our technologically advanced days of computer barcodes and screaming door stiles. When happiness was synonymous with righteousness, it was to be found in poor areas just as easily as in stately mansions. When it became synonymous with money, it proved illusory in every part of town.

Before the twentieth century reached its halfway mark the publisher Henry Luce described it as the 'American century'. We can accept that definition within our own framework not because the United States was solely responsible for ushering in the virtual world, but because she derived the greatest benefit from it. But actual reality can sometimes peek through the virtual kind, and then we realise that the country that has gained the most can also lose the most, taking the rest of us down with her in the name of globalisation.

When the reality of the first metaphysical premise is extinct, every small gain comes with the flipside of a big loss. Take for example the progress in science and technology, held up by advocates of virtual reality as its vindication. Every critic of modernity is bombarded with variously inane sound bytes. Do you not prefer driving a car to riding a horse? Yes I do, though more people are killed in car accidents than ever were killed in carriage accidents. Isn't it better for surgery to be painless? Yes it is, though as a result we probably have more surgery than is strictly necessary. Wouldn't you hate to write with a quill? Yes I would, though more great books were written with that implement than ever will be written with a word processor.

But all those drugs, nuclear power stations and motorcars only constitute progress if they are used to good ends by good people. When this condition is not met, progress begins to look rather less progressive. Suddenly we notice that the same company that gave us the Beetle car also gave us the V1 rocket; the same conglomerate that first synthesised aspirin also mass-produced the Zyklon B gas; the same American automaker who pioneered mass production of cheap cars also delivered 20 percent of all vehicles used by the Wehrmacht, not to mention thousands of lorries that carried millions to Soviet concentration camps. And, as some unfortunate Japanese could have testified, the same technology we use to illuminate our houses can also be used to incinerate them.

Of course the moment we mention human goodness as a necessary precondition, we leave the domain of material progress and enter the realm of metaphysics. It is there that modernity has failed. And it is this failure that is putting dents, soon to become holes, into material progress as well.

That is why the balance sheet of the 'American century' is not all credits. It is not just the left-hand column of computers, cars, cheap food, antibiotics and scented lavatory paper. The debits on the right side of the ledger include the number of violent deaths in the twentieth century. Variously estimated between 300 and 500 million, this exceeds by an order of magnitude the score achieved by all previous centuries combined.[58] To keep the accounts straight, when we boast of modern life expectancy, which is so much higher than in less progressive times, do let us remind ourselves of all those hundreds of millions whose virtual life expectancy might have been long, but whose actual lives were cut short.

The same double-entry approach would help us assess economic progress. There is no question that the overall standard of living (not to be confused with quality of life) is higher now than it ever was in the distant past. But blanket statistics are not much help to today's pensioners whose life savings have been wiped out by the crisis or to the millions of jobless, approaching 20 percent of the labour force in the US and probably exceeding that proportion in the UK,[59] who subsist on handouts.

Nor are they much consolation to the majority of Westerners who spend their lives scrambling to put 'two cars into every garage and two chickens into every pot', to borrow another pithy phrase from John F. Kennedy. They dream not of salvation but of prosperity, but their small dreams are turning into great nightmares. They wake up covered in sweat, hoarse from their own screams.

When Joseph Schumpeter introduced the concept of 'creative destruction', he gave us a terse explanation of dynamic economic development. But not all modern destruction is creative. Some of it is very destructive indeed. When candles are replaced with electric

58. This cannot be attributed solely to advances in killing technology. At least sixty million Soviet citizens, for example, were killed by low-tech executions, slave labour and artificial famines – expedients long in the public domain.
59. The official unemployment figures in the UK are artificially low because they do not include those on disability benefits. Their number suggests we have more cripples now than in the wake of either world war. This leads the cynics to believe that most of those benefit recipients are disabled only virtually, not really.

bulbs, ploughs with tractors or gramophones with CD players, the creative aspect of destruction outweighs all else. New entries appear in the credit column of modernity. But when stable families are replaced with 'partnerships', cohesive communities with social atomisation or responsible investment with frenzied gambling, the debit column becomes so full that awkward questions are begging to be asked.

Recent history shows that modernity in general and capitalism specifically can neither wipe out the debits nor even invariably keep the balance positive. Socialism, which in any real terms equates rampant statism, can have even less of a claim to being a panacea. It is part of the disease, not a cure.

If the twentieth century and the first decade of the twenty-first have taught us anything, it is that modernity is fraught with disaster. Capitalism deprived of its moral underpinnings has ended up in the virtual world, where old certitudes no longer apply. To become a paragon of creative destruction, rather than of the tautologically destructive kind, capitalism must move back into the real world. To be able to do that, it needs help from an authority that can let it run free, while mitigating its soul-destroying potential.

We know exactly what such an authority must be. The history of the West shows that only Judaeo-Christian morality, or rather the Judaeo-Christian way of life as a whole, can counterbalance the destructive, and self-destructive, power of capitalism. The error of the Enlightenment economists was in believing that capitalism was self-correcting. They thought that, by disavowing what I here call the first metaphysical premise, man could create a society that would be a towering monument to reason.

However, upon closer examination the monument begins to look more like a tombstone. Simply adding millions of private self-interests together does not produce public virtue. It produces instead a frantic traffic in buying and selling with no red lights, except those found in the district known for such fixtures, and with morality as the burnt-out cars by the roadside.

To answer the question at the beginning of this section, no, capitalism is not dead. But something else is, or rather will be soon: society defined in economic terms only or even primarily, one that worships at the altar of the second metaphysical premise. If we understand this, then perhaps we can take a stab at answering the perennial question that inevitably crowns any ratiocination by the pragmatic Anglo-Saxon mind:

So what are we going to do about it?

WHAT NOW?

1

This big question has millions of small ones spinning out the moment it is asked. In broad strokes the answers to them all can be divided into two large groups: what ought to be done ideally, if we still lived in a real world, and what can reasonably be expected to be done in our virtual world.

The answers belonging to the second group are easier to figure out. After all, some steps on the virtual road to recovery are already being taken, some others have reached the stage of a firm statement of intent, some others still can be confidently inferred from all of those. Even in these early stages one can predict what will happen: The more visible symptoms will be relieved, which for a while will mask the original disease. In short order it will return, deadlier than ever.

Western governments are throwing virtual money at the real problem, hoping to drown our sorrows under a waterfall of counterfeit currency pouring into the leaky coffers of the banks. Our governments could not have allowed the big banks to fall, because such a calamity would have buried under the rubble the livelihood of hundreds of millions – at least that is the accepted line. The governments are thus administering the iatrogenic medicine that largely created the problem in the first place. In the process they hope to build up the banks (and other financial institutions) to a point where they can return to their old ways – the same ways, in other words, that contributed to the disaster.[60]

Banks will get up from their knees, start walking tall, and resume the financing of the American dream (this has become generic, shared as it is by most countries in our globalised world tending to uniformity), the same dream that has produced the

---

60. This, to the predictable accompaniment of empty promises that there is no return to the old ways.

current nightmare. In fact, early evidence shows that the newly nationalised British banks have begun to use public money to finance bonuses that are scarcely lower than the pre-tempest windfalls. The managers of those banks are even threatening to quit if they are prevented from signing seven-digit bonus cheques. They want to feed their addictive habit that has been proved to be detrimental to our financial health. Oh well, one expects nothing else from these people. The discipline they lack is not being imposed from without, and they certainly cannot find it within. The second metaphysical premise will not let them.

At the same time, the governments will announce higher taxes, sold to the public as a way of soaking the rich. In Britain, Gordon Brown's government already raised the top marginal tax rate from 40 to 50 percent. And Vince Cable, Business Secretary in the new coalition government, recently supported the 'symbolic value' of this measure, even though he acknowledged that no additional revenue had resulted from it. The new (Conservative!) Chancellor obviously feels the same way, for the confiscatory bracket is to remain. Yet again virtual trumps real.

Our politicians provide material for this book faster than I can write it. One wonders if they have ever heard of Arthur Laffer and his curve. But then again, we already know that taxation is there for PR and punitive purposes, not just as a way of keeping the state solvent. Under the coalition government, other similar taxes will follow, whose sole effect will be reducing the state revenue by driving the wealthiest and most productive people, not to mention businesses, out of the country (180,000 British high earners have left the country in the last two years, and that is only a warm-up). But then people's envy and desire for revenge will be assuaged for a while. They will get the impression that the government is doing something, and creating false impressions is the essence of the virtual world.

The assumption, peddled by government mouthpieces, and bought by the duped masses begging to be duped some more, is that the whole process of recovery will be bothersome but relatively painless, like today's dental surgery. Yes, there is a need for some cuts – even the most statist parties can see the necessity. And yes, the unions are striking in protest, the papers are writing about the poor being hurt and the rich being favoured. Yet if one looks at the cuts proposed in the new government's first spending review, one finds it hard to believe that Britain's trillion-pound debt will be reduced soon, if ever.

The 'cuts' are in fact as virtual as everything else emanating from any modern Western government. In nominal terms, the coalition will be spending 10 percent more per capita than the last Labour government. Depending on inflation, it is conceivable, though far from certain, that government spending will be reduced by about a negligible five percent over he next five years. In effect, the 'cuts' are tantamount to pushing money around, not spending less of it.

The defence budget, already pitifully inadequate, has indeed been slashed to a point where Britain can barely launch police, never mind military, operations. At the same time foreign aid (once accurately defined as the transfer of capital from the poor people in rich countries to the rich people in poor countries) has been increased by 37.5 percent – God forbid we shall seem insensitive to the suffering of African millionaires. The shamanistic dances involving mythical man-made climate change will also receive more funds – God forbid we shall ignore the needs of politicised scientists shuffling data with the skill of a riverboat gambler. Just as our Harriers become scrap metal, our contribution to the EU will go up – God forbid we shall let a few hundred million stand between us and our bureaucrats' job security. And of course the sainted NHS will not suffer even virtual cuts.

In fact, the 'cuts' only mean that government spending will, one hopes, be growing at a slower rate. But one would not know this from the hysteria in the press, especially of the leftish variety, with hacks serving up the literary equivalent of rolling on the floor and frothing at the mouth.

To help the medicine go down, PR flaks who these days pass for statesmen smile bravely and admit with self-deprecating honesty that the treatment may take some time, perhaps as long as a year or, 'in a worst-case scenario', even two. To extend the medical parallel, a doctor who deliberately lies to terminally ill patients that there is nothing wrong with them would be censured or at least reprimanded. A politician who makes promises along similar lines may look forward to winning the next election, and this is all that matters. Who cares if a subsequent deluge washes the whole society out into the sea?

However, let us pretend for a second that we still live in a real world. Let us admit to ourselves that no general anaesthetic for this kind of operation exists, nor any arsenic to stuff into a dental cavity. One way or the other, we shall not just suffer some mild discomfort. There will be agonising pain, lots of it. All we can realistically hope for is that it will not be endured in vain. To make this more likely, we must choose the right type of surgery.

2

Let us look at the examples of three different approaches to similar situations, all supplied by the same country. For it was Germany in the twentieth century that provided the three possible models of handling catastrophic economic meltdowns, only one of which worked.

The first model was introduced by the Weimar republic in the aftermath of the First World War. Faced with ruinous reparation payments, the government welcomed hyperinflation as a means of wiping out its currency, thereby claiming that its Versailles obligations could not be met. Widespread misery ensued, with the country going hungry and growing despondent. Being modern, the socialist Weimar government also used Versailles as a convenient scapegoat for its own incompetence in managing the economy. The other scapegoats, identified either explicitly or implicitly, were speculators and Jews, which created the troubled waters in which the Nazis could then fish so profitably.

Hyperinflation, or at least very high inflation, is a distinct possibility today, considering the suicidal abandon with which our governments have been printing money. In Britain, for example, more currency has been churned out in the last two years than in the previous century, and government spending shows an inordinate potential for growth. To cite one example, in November, 2009, the British state increased its borrowing to 88 times (sic!) the corresponding figure of the previous year, when the crisis was already in full swing and 'queasing' in full flow.

Such cavalier practices never go unpunished. Without going into much detail as to what unpalatable forms the punishment could take (high inflation being the most likely), let us just agree that a Weimar-style debacle is not the pain we wish to suffer. Most of us would love to drive a million-pound car, but not if it is a Vauxhall or a Kia.

The second model was put into effect by the Nazi government that succeeded Weimar: militarisation followed by a world war. A global military conflict is indeed an effective method of boosting the economy, vacuuming loose cash out of people's pockets in the process. However, while we can debate whether or not the world has ever recovered from the wounds of the first two world wars, there is no arguing about the likely consequences of a third one. These can only be so cataclysmic that we cannot even imagine the ensuing devastation. The technological advances of which modernity is so justly proud make the second model even more undesirable than the first.

That is, the first two models may be undesirable to us, but not necessarily to our governments, if their past performance is anything to go by. What is indisputably undesirable to them is the third model. This would be based on the miracle (*Wirtschaftswunder* for short) worked by the German economy starting in 1948 and throughout the 1950s. The country's rapid recovery after the Second World War was indeed nothing short of miraculous, and contrary to the common misapprehension it was not all due to the aid offered by America under the Marshall Plan.

In fact, the reparations Germany had to pay after the war exceeded the total amount of that aid, and systematic dismantling of German industry by the victorious allies did not improve matters either. This included the annexation of Germany's coal producing regions, confiscation of the plant of 700-odd factories still standing after the wartime bombing raids, and wholesale prising of German intellectual properties off patents. And, as if to prove that American aid had little to do with economic performance, Britain, which had received much greater infusions under the Marshall Plan, took 40 years to recover after the war. Germany (West Germany, that is) did so by the mid-fifties.

Whether critical junctures of history produce misery or joy largely depends on the key personages who find themselves in charge at the time. Granted, it was not just barbarian attacks that brought Rome down, but her own metaphysical crisis. But without Alaric on the scene, she may have been able to hang on for a while longer until she found a second spiritual wind. Similarly, there were conditions in place for Napoleon to appear. But without Napoleon, France would not have conquered most of Europe. The Bolsheviks destroyed a consumptive Russian democracy, but without Lenin they would not have destroyed it. Nor would Nazism have become a powerful evil force without Hitler: the evil was in the air but the powerful force came from him.

That was the nature of the German miracle: the right men at the right time were Konrad Adenauer and his economics advisor (later the Federal Republic's Economics Minister, still later Chancellor) Ludwig Erhard. It is to them that Germany owes her Phoenix-from-ashes rise. Adenauer and Erhard exceeded their authority under the law imposed by the occupying powers to shift the economy from the virtual to the real world. Rejecting the Keynesian practices mandated by the Anglo-Saxons, Erhard freed up the economy in one fell swoop by removing price controls and introducing a stable currency.

He took that plunge on a Sunday, when American and British Keynesians had a day off and were thus in no position to stop him, as they surely would have done on any other day of the week. At the same time, Adenauer and Erhard told the Germans in no uncertain terms that there would be no huge deficit spending on a Bismarck-type welfare state, not in the immediate future at any rate. This would come when the economy got up on its feet. Until then the Germans were told to tighten their belts, work hard and count their pfennigs. The ploy worked to perfection, and within a few years of low inflation and rapid industrial growth the country climbed to the economic summit where it has more or less stayed to this day, despite the combined ballasts of the reunification and the EU pulling it down.[61]

The Germans suffered much deprivation for a few years, and enjoyed much prosperity thereafter. The pain they suffered was acute, but it was in a good cause. It was a necessary precondition for their future gain, which, under the guidance of two sage men, they understood and accepted – and acted accordingly.

Looking around, one has to acknowledge that regrettably no Western government is being blessed with the leadership of such

61. Germany of course is the primary force behind the EU, but her aims have got to be political because they clearly cannot be economic. For example, as the world's second biggest exporter of value-added products, she is being hurt by the artificially high rate of the euro, which she is powerless to lower – as she would certainly do with the Deutschmark if it were still in circulation. By contrast, China boosts her exports by keeping the yuan artificially low.

273

men at this critical juncture. This is proved by the measures the governments are taking. For example, the first tentative steps of the British powers that be towards combating the present crisis suggest they have rejected the third, and the only successful, model. In all likelihood they never even considered it for being politically unfeasible.

After all, austerity imposed by a drastic cut in public spending can never work as an election-winning slogan. In an atomised society driven by the second metaphysical premise, the people have been corrupted too much for too long ever to accept the idea of immediate sacrifices producing long-term benefits. Long term, they seem to be saying, we shall be dead. We want our handouts here and now. Civic pride that used to be such an engaging feature of Western societies has been replaced by myopic greed. And the government goes along with almost indecent readiness.

According to HMG, this is a wrong time to cut public spending dramatically, beyond a cosmetic nick here and there, for doing so would exacerbate the unemployment problem and create a double-dip recession (the government plays both ends against the middle, by reassuring the right of the political spectrum that the current cuts are significant, while at the same time trying to convince the left that they are not as significant as all that). Alas, that is true, but this kind of truth makes one cringe.

First the British government hugely increases the publicly financed workforce. Then it claims that a sorely needed deep cut in public expenditure is impossible because it would make many of those jobs redundant. As if they were not redundant already in any reasonable sense: do we really need all those directors of diversity, ministers for equality, culture, sports or women,[62] facilitators of optimisation and optimisers of facilitation?

Nor can the government reduce the money supply straight away, it is claimed: to do so would slow down our virtual recovery.

62. Another proof that equality is an empty word in our virtual world. After all, though we have a ministry for women, we have none for either men or herma-phrodites. Most unfair, that, especially considering the important contribution made by the former to science and the latter to women's athletics. Something must be done to correct this injustice, and in our virtual world it probably will be.

274

That is true too: first we create a monstrous mass of funny paper that has any value only in a virtual world, then we become so dependent upon it that it becomes indispensable. Yesterday's emergency measure turns into today's permanent fixture.

Yet even a virtual recovery will be impossible if some of those banknotes are not removed from circulation. In the absence of an immediate 50 percent cut in public spending that is really needed, the government has only two options: either to encourage a high inflation rate, Weimar-style, while hoping that hyperinflation can be avoided, or to increase taxes beyond their already confiscatory level (not that one necessarily precludes the other). In fact, the leaders of all three major British parties are already dropping broad hints that they will support a further increase in the tax burden. And if there is one promise made by this lot that we can take on faith, it is the promise to raise taxes.

America's present-day answer to FDR would not be outdone. His bailout of a failed General Motors sent the first and biggest chunk of money not the way of the shareholders who rightly felt entitled to it, but into the coffers of the unions, the principal political force behind Obama's election. (The popular saying used to be 'what's good for GM is good for America.' GM went bust – so where does it leave America?)

Also, President Obama recently pushed through Congress a healthcare bill whose cost, even conservatively estimated, will run into trillions, a numeral that by attrition has become part of everyday parlance. Nothing like good timing, one might say. This measure, which even in brighter times could only charitably be described as ill-advised, is simply barmy at a time when the economy is reeling from one blow after another. Add to this similar or even greater amounts that are being foolishly pledged to reverse the mythical man-induced climate change, the scientific evidence for which is at best dubious (and at worst, falsified,) and one is stuck for a rational explanation.

That is, one would be short of explanations in a real world. In our virtual world, the motivation of both the British and American governments is painfully clear. To reiterate what I have explored in the earlier chapters, politicians are out to increase their own power, a purpose they know from experience will be well served by inflation, tax increases and madcap spending schemes. One expects nothing else from those who have devoted their lives to worshiping the golden calf of the second metaphysical premise. If it takes 'queasing' on a Zimbabwean scale to advance their personal agenda, then so be it.

The outlook is therefore bleak. It is very likely that within a year, two at most, the West will be hit with a double-digit inflation rate, and I have already outlined the modes of human behaviour such further debauchment of currency will promote. We do not have to leave the domain of common sense to know what they will be.

To start with, a high inflation rate will greatly reduce both savings and debts. People will therefore be discouraged to save and encouraged to borrow. We need no crystal ball to know that, after the smokescreen of PR effluvia has been lifted, our current problems will thus be not so much solved as perpetuated. Another crisis, more devastating than the present one, will be just round the corner, with a massive war looming as the last resort. God save us.

So much for what is likely to happen. Now let us consider in brief some of the things that I think ought to happen. In doing so, I shall not for the time being touch upon the political, social or cultural feasibility of the measures that fall into that category. This we shall discuss later. It is their desirability that is the subject of the next section.

3

By now we must have realised that our governments and financial institutions will not come up with right measures because they are manned by wrong people who are driven by the wrong metaphysical premise. If such individuals cannot be removed from their positions of power, then the power vested in those positions must be curtailed. Only this would enable us to lift the fog of the virtual world.

Therefore the people must claim the powers vouchsafed, but so far denied, to them in the virtual world. Or rather we ought to reclaim what we used to have in the real world: the political power of citizens (or, in Britain, subjects) and the economic power of consumers. Our mandate must expand *pari passu* with the central government's mandate shrinking, which is a precondition not only for economic but also for moral recovery. As the writer R. Austin Freeman reminded us a century ago, 'The corporate conscience is an altogether inferior product to that of an individual.'

There is nothing new in the thought that people can do a better job looking after themselves than any government can. The statement 'that government governs best which governs least' was true even when it was first uttered in the eighteenth century. Variously attributed either to Thomas Paine or to Thomas Jefferson, this aphorism is even truer today, when the democracy of one man, one vote, boosted by the second metaphysical premise, has plunged the West to its current abysmal level. If two centuries ago people only suspected that, democracy or no democracy, great power was likely to be abused by any government, then these days we are certain of it.

Earlier in the book I suggested that, when we travel in the wrong direction, we can do only by undoing. In the case of state authority, we must therefore revert to a constitutional arrangement that concentrated the greatest power at the level of the individual and his local community. By way of divesting the state of some of its power, it must first be forced into a statutory obligation to run a surplus, or at least balanced, budget, while reducing public debt to a level not exceeding a small proportion of the country's GDP.

Just a few years ago public debt in Britain stood at 40 percent. It is now 77 percent, and the measures either on line already or about to be introduced will soon push it to 100 percent of the GDP. One does not have to be an expert to realise that a catastrophe beckons.

At the same time, the government's ability to tax must be rolled back. A maximum take of 20 percent of the GDP, give or take a couple, would be ample for the state to fulfil its legitimate functions, of the kind that brought it into existence in the first place. Above all, these include providing for internal and external security – an objective that has to be financed out of public funds, for every member of the public stands to gain equally.

We must have armed forces strong enough to protect us from any foreign menace, and we must have a law enforcement system strong enough to keep any homespun menace at bay. To achieve these objectives we would need a substantial hike in defence and law-enforcement budgets, but, with the government curtailing its self-serving generosity in other areas, we shall be able to afford it. (Naturally, huge cuts in those budgets were among the first proposed by the new coalition government. Britain can afford foreign aid, we have been told, but she cannot afford a strong enough navy or enough prisons. This when the country is fighting a war, and crime is at its highest level for centuries.)

This means that the government must be banned from extorting huge proportions of the people's income to bankroll a giant welfare state (in the jargon of the virtual world, this comes under the rubric of 'public services'). For reasons we have already discussed, this practice is unworkable financially and corrupting morally. Its chief purpose, gloriously realised in every Western country, is to create a permanently dependent class that can be counted upon to perpetuate itself and therefore the modern state.

The fiscal deficit resulting from such an arrangement pales into insignificance when compared to the moral cost equally borne by the givers, the takers and the society at large. The welfare state must go not just because it is unaffordable, but because it is immoral.

Granted, certain provisions ought to be in place to take care of those citizens who for one reason or another are incapable of looking after themselves, and who cannot be taken care of in any other way. In civilised countries, helpless people do not go without food, shelter and medical treatment. However, providing for its able-bodied citizens indiscriminately is not a legitimate function of the state. Those who can look after themselves must do so, and a vibrant economy including a strong manufacturing sector would offer ample opportunities for that.[63] Only those truly infirm or destitute due to incapacity must be helped.

To that end, private charities must be financed at a level sufficient for them to reclaim some of the functions that have been usurped by the state. This means that, in the morally questionable atmosphere of our virtual, post-Christian world, people must be motivated to donate large proportions of their incomes to those charities that would be responsible for running hospitals, schools, nurseries, alms houses and so forth.

Such motivation could come from either human goodness or, more reliably, from large tax breaks, way in excess of those that are in place already. Given the choice of donating money to a worthy charity or handing it over to the state as tax, most people would probably choose the former, provided they do not suffer financially for it.

---

63. The Conservative governments of Margaret Thatcher and John Major contributed to a decline in Britain's manufacturing sector. To them the paragon of economic virtue was a hedge fund or an estate agency, not a car factory. Amazingly, since the misnamed (virtually named?) Labour Party took over in 1997, British manufacturing has shrunk a further 60 percent. That is understandable: Tony-Gordon had to find panting takers for the myriad public jobs they dangled in the air.

4

With that as a general principle, we can look at any number of details, starting, and for the sake of brevity ending, with nationalised medicine. First, one has to demythologise the National Health Service in Britain, which evidently serves as a model for some of President Obama's more imprudent ideas.

This gigantic organisation has used every trick known to the virtual world to create a saintly aura around itself. Many brainwashed Englishmen honestly believe that using private medicine, even if it means salvation from misery or death, is tantamount to moral turpitude and treason. And in Canada private medical care is banned altogether, which greatly increases the workload of private hospitals in the adjacent areas of the USA. If medical care is not free, claim the sorely misguided champions of this arrangement, poor people will be dying in the street like stray dogs.

But outside the virtual world the term 'free medical care' is mendacious. 'Free', to a semantic rigorist, used to mean something one did not have to pay for. To an adherent of the virtual world it means something different. If pressed, he would admit reluctantly that of course somebody has to pay for all those MRI and PET scans. Such things are expensive; and the more inefficiently provided, the dearer they get. If patients do not pay for them direct, the payment comes from the government, which can only make money the old-fashioned way: from taxes or 'queasing'. (In Britain, 'national insurance contributions', a tax by any other name, amount to 11 percent of personal income, and are about to go up another penny.)

In the virtual world, 'free medicine' thus means that the transfer of money from patient to hospital is mediated by the state acting as a general contractor with megalomania. But governments are always less efficient, more cumbersome and usually more corrupt than private enterprise. So we must assume that mastectomies are more expensive when one pays for them through the government, whether one needs them or not, than they would be if one paid for them direct, and only when one needed them.

But when today's Englishmen pay for state medicine, they do not just pay for mastectomies and scans. An ever-growing proportion of their money pays for the ever-growing state bureaucracy required to administer 'free' medical care, something for which we would pay less if medical care were not 'free'.

Yet the British do not mind paying taxes or at least claim they do not – just as Soviet people claimed they did not mind donating, on pain of imprisonment, huge amounts to government bonds that never paid up. In both cases, it is the tyranny of the virtual world, sometimes reinforced by the Stockholm syndrome and sometimes by coercion, that is responsible for such acquiescence. True enough, in any real sense it is a patriotic duty to pay taxes, but only to a government that pursues patriotic ends. Otherwise it is our moral duty to avoid tax to a point of civil disobedience.

Since steady growth of nationalised medicine is tantamount to the state extorting increasingly larger sums from the people, 'free' medical care places an increasing proportion of the nation's finances and labour force under state control, thus increasing the power of the state over the individual. The NHS is already by far the biggest single employer in Britain (and Europe) and it will soon be the only one, if the current crisis proceeds apace.

In other words, 'free', translated from the virtual-world cant, means 'serving the state, not the citizen, and therefore being more expensive than it otherwise would be, not to mention less efficient'. Doctors complicate matters even further. In a UK survey of a few years ago, 90 percent of 'medical professionals' stated that people suffering from smoking-related diseases ought to pay for treatment direct, on top of getting it 'free' by paying taxes. Why? Because these diseases are behavioural, self-inflicted by obtuse bloody-mindedness. How about AIDS? asks a holdout from the real world. Just goes to show how little he understands the virtual meaning of 'free'. Off with his head.

Incidentally, that medical care can be used as an instrument of tyranny has been demonstrated by every unsavoury state of modernity, not least by Nazi Germany. Reading about Hitler's healthcare, one cannot help noticing parallels with today's West. Firm believers in state medicine, the Nazis showed how it could be used for crowd control. Like our bureaucrats today, they emphasised prevention, with proper nutrition featuring prominently in their health propaganda. Every German had a duty, according to the Nazis, to look after himself in order to prolong the state-serving part of his life.

Likewise, in today's state medicine the need to relieve financial pressures on the state's purse can be neatly converted into a blanket control of citizens' lives. Conditioned to accept the dictates of the state, Europeans do not cringe upon hearing from yet another health official yet another admonishment on their dietary habits. We do not even notice that from one year to the next the government's dictates may be mutually exclusive. 'And exactly what makes this your business, Minister?' is a question seldom asked. But if it were asked, the truthful answer would not be far removed from the Nazi rationale: the good of nationalised medicine and therefore the state.

The Nazis waged an anti-smoking campaign that would be the envy of today's EU or USA. It was the Nazis who first established the link between smoking and lung cancer, and as a result lung-cancer statistics in Germany continued to be better than in other Western countries for a couple of decades after the war. Like many other forms of research, this proceeded from the starting point of an axiomatic assumption, in this case that smoking had to be bad because the Führer was good, and he did not approve of lighting up.

Chemical additives and preservatives were roundly castigated by the Nazis, wholemeal bread was depicted as morally, not to mention nutritively, superior to breads made from blanched white flour. Like today's bureaucrats, the Nazis promoted vegetarianism (practised by Hitler, Hess and many others) and attacked medical experiments on animals (unlike us, they had no shortage of enthusiastic human volunteers). As the Nazis were godless, animals were to them not principally different from humans, and were in fact superior to some. Hitler loved his Alsatian Blondie more than any woman in his life; in today's Britain veterinary medicine is organised considerably better than the care of humans.

Of course, doctors in Nazi Germany were involved not just in preventive medicine but, most of them eagerly, in such less benign pastimes as eugenics and enforced euthanasia. It is comforting to observe how medicine in today's West is inching in the same direction. Euthanasia, in particular, is custom-made for the virtual world, what with its adulation of the state. One cannot open the papers these days without reading a thinly veiled lament about the burden placed on the fragile shoulders of state medicine by an aging population. And euthanasia is steadily moving towards the forefront of potential remedies.

At the moment Swiss clinics offer 'mercy killing' as an expensive optional service, but the time cannot be far away when our governments will make it compulsory. This is a paradox, for the governments' tireless propaganda of healthier 'life styles', coupled with advances in pharmaceuticals and hygiene, is designed to help people live longer. In reality, it is designed to increase the power of the state but, when medicine is used for that purpose, one cannot be had without the other: life expectancy will increase. This creates yet another vicious circle of modernity: the state uses medicine to advance its own good by tightening its control on citizens' lives; but as a corollary to this, the state hurts itself by creating a multitude of wrinkly freeloaders who do nothing but sap the state's resources.

The British are unhappy about waiting lists at hospitals, caused by a chronic shortage of hospital beds, but they miss the point. In a virtual world, state medical care does not need hospital beds to perform its principal function: control over people's lives.

To make this point, one British hospital recently created a new post of Director of Diversity at a cost of £100,000 a year,[64] while at the same time cutting their number of already scarce beds for lack of funds. All such travesties proceed to the accompaniment of PR noises to the effect that before the NHS descended upon us ill people had been treated inadequately, if at all. In fact, fewer hospitals were built in Britain during the first half-century of her nationalised medicine than in the 1930s, hardly the most prosperous decade in British history.

Driven by the second metaphysical premise, servants of the state have to look out for Number One, which means promoting state power. And in order to be truly successful, state control has to extend to people's private lives, not just public activities. The virtual world can achieve this end by itself – for example, by brainwashing people into believing that there exists a valid moral distinction between driving after two glasses of wine or three.

To speed this process up, why not help it along by issuing a direct threat: if you smoke and get emphysema, you can croak without any medical help, see if we care? No reason at all; every little bit helps. At least, medical care remains free.

Exactly the same arguments can be made against state education and every other department of the welfare state. Dismantling this Leviathan would go a long way towards moving the economy into the real world and therefore towards solvency.

Thinking small, or at least smaller, can also be expected to produce moral benefits, especially if the charities filling the void formed by the demise of the welfare state could be numerous enough to prevent them from falling into the same trap of institutional megalomania.

---

64. His first act was to issue a memorandum on the importance of appreciating religious differences. It included, among other stunningly ignorant assertions, the statement that Islam is the principal religion in the People's Republic of Congo. In reality, it is a distant and almost negligible third.

But the principal financing of medicine has to come from personal insurance policies. Before excessive litigation compromised this system in the USA, it had functioned well enough. Even then the usual objection, which by now has reached a fervour pitch, centred around those people who could not afford private insurance.[65] The current solution, coming straight out of the virtual world, is that the US government must step in and buy it for them, at however staggering a cost. But in a real world, if private medical care could indeed be financed by the state, it would be by expedients other than robbing Peter to pay Paul.

The state could do a much better job by introducing negative taxation for positive purposes. The underlying principle is that, rather than taking money away from the people and then supposedly trying to use it for their benefit, the state would leave the money in people's wallets and let the citizens fend for themselves. In our example, rather than taxing people into submission, the state would exempt from tax the full cost of premiums paid for medical insurance. This would make private medicine not just tax-deductible but tax-free, and consequently affordable to just about everybody.

Every taxpayer would have the choice of either handing his money over to the government or using the same amount to provide for his own health. The choice is not at all difficult: most patients even now would rather keep themselves out of the government's clutches if they could afford it. The third-world standards of medical care in the NHS are hardly news any longer, and people would happily welcome the alternative system. Not only would such a system be infinitely more efficient, but it would also be more moral – if merely by eliminating all those tax collectors and optimisation-facilitating, facilitation-optimising directors of diversity cum equality.

Morality, however, must be not only the upshot of private medicine (or, by extension, any private endeavour) but also its

---

65. US municipal hospitals catering to such patients were at least equal to the best the NHS can offer.

starting point. It was not for any systemic failure that American medical care developed structural defects, but for exactly the same reason as that behind the current crisis: a moral, which means at base a metaphysical, deficit. The unholy trinity of the culprits was also the same: patients whose venality and unshakeable belief in the pursuit of happiness compelled them to seek legal restitution whenever they could smell money; similarly motivated government and private lawyers who encouraged litigiousness;[66] and like-minded doctors who charged exorbitant fees while frequently recommending surgical and other procedures for their own benefit, rather than that of their patients.

The same system of negative taxation would work just as well in education, with most schools going private, and with all school fees becoming tax-free. In both instances, most people would be considerably better off. However, those who do not pay any tax anyway, for whatever reason, would not derive an immediate benefit from negative government taxation (they would derive a vicarious benefit though, as the quality of both medical care and education would improve). If they do not pay tax for reasons of poverty or incapacity, they must be provided for in other ways. In the case of medical care, help could come from private charities, sufficiently funded due to the same negative-taxation approach. In the case of education, the slack could be taken up by parish schools, or those run by secular charities, similarly financed.

The state would only step in to help those who slip through the net altogether. As the number of such individuals would be small, this arrangement would not place an unduly heavy tax load on the public. Moreover, before long the state would begin to shrink to manageable proportions, and much of the power hitherto vested in it

---

66. An amusing anecdote to illustrate this point: when I lived in New York many years ago, I mentioned to a lawyer at a party that I might have got a raw deal from a doctor. 'Sue!' was his instant advice. 'But I'm not really sure it was his fault... ' I protested feebly. 'That's not up to you to decide,' exclaimed the lawyer with righteous indignation. 'That's what we've got judges and juries for. It's their business to decide who's at fault. Your business is to sue everyone you know whenever anything goes wrong.' It was that kind of attitude that compromised a system that, though obviously as imperfect as any human institution will always be, used to function well enough. Otherwise it would be hard to explain why these days exactly the same procedures often cost twice as much in the US as in British private hospitals.

would be transferred to the people. They themselves would be able to decide where they would be treated or their children educated. And, with personal income tax not exceeding, say, a flat 20-percent rate, significantly lowered due to personal allowances and negative taxation, they would be able to back up their decisions with cash. Reducing the state's capacity to extort tax is thus tantamount to reducing its capacity to impose tyranny.

The cost of government would come down tremendously, releasing hosts of well-educated people into productive employment. That their work is less than productive now can be proved by their sheer numbers. As a random example, one out of many, the numerical strength of the British Defence Ministry is approaching that of the armed forces. The Royal Navy, which has dwindled away practically to nothing, is being supervised by 30,000 bureaucrats; in the nineteenth century, when Britannia ruled the waves, the same job was done by 3,000. Surely most of today's bureaucrats could more profitably satisfy their craving for public service in the defence arena by enlisting into our frontline troops in Afghanistan.

5

At the same time it is essential to stabilise our currencies once and for all. For reasons we discussed earlier, reverting to the gold standard would be impossible now, what with enough funny paper floating about to fill an ocean. But this ought to be the goal towards which to strive, and it can be achieved after years of prudence, austerity and reduced ability of the government to increase money supply at will.

As a stable currency is essential for a healthy economy, and modern governments clearly demonstrate their inability and reluctance to keep the currency stable, one is hard-pressed to come up with an alternative to the gold standard, with all its flaws. If we do not choose the lesser of two evils, we shall be stuck forever with the evil of two lessers.

Checking the power of the state would also have another consequence, one less immediate but perhaps ultimately even more important. Power-hungry, money-grabbing careerists would have less motivation to enter politics, a trend that could be encouraged by cutting politicians' pay dramatically, or perhaps even reducing it to just legitimate expenses. Our institutions would then be able to attract more people committed to serving others before themselves.

Also, this would mean that the average age of our politicians would rise, as they would have had to make a success of private life before entering public service at little or no pay. In any case, the statutory age limitations on public service that exist in some Western democracies are too low, with pedocracy an unfortunate consequence. (England's goalkeeper at the last World Cup was older than our present Chancellor of the Exchequer.)

For example, Article 1 of the US Constitution stipulates a minimum age of 25 for the House of Representatives, 30 for the Senate and 35 for Presidency. This may have made sense at the time the Constitution was adopted, when the average life expectancy was around 40. Today, when it is twice as high, the minimum requirement must be raised by at least 15 years and, in those countries where it does not exist, it ought to be introduced.

We would then have more of a chance of being governed by older, sager people who do not look upon public service as a self-aggrandising possibility, something to stand them in good stead later in life. They would also have had a rich experience of life outside politics, thus gaining both knowledge and empathy. Admittedly, such a system would preclude the rise of a present-day Pitt the Younger, who became Prime Minister at 24, but then one does not see many such figures on the political horizon.

Also, in Britain, it is essential to undo the constitutional mayhem perpetrated by post-war governments, but particularly by the last one. The English constitution represents, or rather represented, the highest political achievement of the West. Based as it was on a fine balance among the estates, it guaranteed that none of them would become too powerful.

This Aristotelian balance evolved over centuries, obviating any need for a blanket code contained within a legislatively approved document. Foreigners, especially those whose understanding of political science is primitive, point out that Britain has no constitution, by which they mean no written document similar to those produced, say, by the USA, Stalin's Russia and – in all but name – the European Union.

In fact, with the possible exception of the USA, which at the time her constitution was adopted was just being born, a written constitution is akin to a prenuptial contract stipulating the frequency of sex: if you have to write it down, you might as well not bother. If the constitution is not written in the citizens' hearts, to borrow de Maistre's phrase, no document will be effective. If it is indeed written there, no document will be needed.

Yet this absence of a written document left an opening for constitutional vandals driven by venality and self-aggrandisement. Animated by such shameful motives, all springing from the second metaphysical premise, they destroyed the unelected, hereditary House of Lords whose historical function had been to counterbalance the democratic power of the Commons and the royal power of the crown.

Having first brainwashed the people about the redemptive value of unchecked democracy (see earlier chapters), the vandals raised a hue and cry about the unfairness of it all. They could not abide any counterbalance to their own power, any viable government body driven by considerations other than political expediency. They did not want democracy to be the *primary* power. They wanted it to be the only one, for they knew that this would perpetuate their own rule by bureaucracy.

6

But even a limited democracy can never work in the absence of a strong electorate. It goes without saying that only responsible voters can elect a responsible government. Edmund Burke, who, along with Aristotle, was arguably the greatest political philosopher ever, estimated the number of those fit to vote in his contemporaneous eighteenth-century England at 400,000, which then constituted about eight percent of the country's population. The same proportion today would produce an electorate of approximately five million. Since the actual number is almost 10 times as high, one may be forgiven for getting the impression that the requirement for responsible voting has been dropped somewhere along the way.

Limiting the franchise would be the only way of reverting to a democratic arrangement that would have a sporting chance of elevating to government only those fit to govern.[67] This thought would sound less blasphemous if we took the historical perspective. For franchise was severely limited throughout much of the West's history. The most notable limitation was the disfranchisement of women in all the established democracies. In the US women got the vote as late as in 1920, in the UK in 1921, in France in 1944 – and in Switzerland the fair sex had to wait until 1971 to start dropping those papers into the ballot boxes. Restricted suffrage does not therefore contradict the founding tenets of Western democracy; the relative size of the franchise is a matter of transient consensus, not transcendent principle.

What sort of restrictions would be desirable today? A detailed proposal on constitutional reform is not the purpose of this essay, but some remarks are appropriate, if only as trial balloons. Let us start with a general statement: voting should be not a right all citizens are born with but a privilege to be earned. To do so, people must

---

67. As I write this, HMG has just extended the franchise by bowing to the EU's dictate on prisoners' voting rights. If disfranchised, prisoners will now be able to seek eight-figure compensations, something HMS can ill-afford at the moment. Never mind that its abject surrender reverses a practice that has existed for 140 years.

demonstrate their ability to cast votes in the interests of the whole community, which may not always coincide with their own interests.

The idea that the sum total of a few million citizens exercising naked self-interest would somehow add up to public virtue is as ill-advised in politics as it is in economics. Without going into the theory of it too much, let us just cast a look around us to notice that this manifestly does not work in practice – unless you think that the current crop of politicians really is the best we can do. In that spirit, and in no particular order, let is consider a few, far from exhaustive, possibilities.

1) Anyone deriving more than half of his earned income from the state, be it in the form of salary, fees or handouts, should be disfranchised. Such people have a vested interest in the perpetuation of the current government, which can only fortuitously coincide with public interest. Moreover, this measure would preclude the unsavoury TV spectacles of incumbents voting for themselves with a big grin on their faces.

2) If the first shots of the American Revolution were fired to the accompaniment of demands for no taxation without representation, then surely the reverse must apply as well: only taxpayers should be able to vote. Consideration also ought to be given to attaching a quotient to each vote, in proportion to the amount of tax paid. This would restrict equally those who are good at exploiting either welfare provisions or tax havens.

3) A length-of-residence requirement must be introduced: in order to vote a citizen would have to have lived in the area for a minimum set period, let us say two years. This is to replace the freehold qualification of yesteryear: for reasons we discussed earlier, freehold ownership just does not have the same cachet as it used to have. However, the idea behind both is the same: promoting community spirit and the feeling of social attachment.

4) For immigrants whose length of residence in the country qualifies them for citizenship, an additional voting test must be administered to determine their agreement with the basic values of our society. For example, a firm belief in the stoning of adulterers, much as some wronged spouses may welcome it, just might be seen as a disqualifying circumstance. An English-language test is a must as well: fluency in the language of public life ought to be a self-evident precondition for taking part in it.

5) One household, one vote would be a better principle than one man, one vote. On the assumption that people living together as a family have the same vested interests in the community, the single vote ought to be cast by the head of the household, either man or woman.

6) As we discussed earlier, one problem with today's democracy is that people do not know those they are supposed to elect. To remove one degree of separation, candidates for national offices ought to be nominated not by their parties, but by the people elected to local offices (in communities not exceeding a population of 10,000), such as town or borough councillors, village mayors, magistrates and so forth. After all, if we know such people and trust them to run our community, we ought to rely on them to put forth those *they* know and trust.

7) Voting age, which is being lowered in most Western countries, must instead be raised to at least 25, and possibly older. Until age 25 or so people's brains are not even wired properly, but their emotions are at a lifetime high. This is a wrong combined premise from which to contemplate community interests and decide which candidate would serve them more effectively.[68]

8) Some basic IQ testing is essential. One does not have to be particularly intelligent, or God forbid educated, to cast a responsible vote, but neither must one be feebleminded. (Sorry, this word constitutes an egregious violation of virtual morality. Shall we settle

68. The common argument against this is that, if people are old enough to die for their country, they are old enough to decide how it is governed. This is as dubious as suggesting that an 18-year-old footballer is old enough to manage his team.

on 'differently [or alternatively] minded?') An IQ of no more than 20 points below the community average must be a requirement.

9) Consideration also must be given to weighing the citizen's vote on the basis of his familiarity (or lack thereof) with the key issues of the election. For example, if the rival candidates diverge on the issue of compulsory euthanasia, or, say, post-natal abortion,[69] a potential voter must demonstrate a most rudimentary awareness of the moral, legal and historical implications of such desiderata.

This is far from a full proposal on democratic retrenchment. It is but a sketch of what ought to become a carefully drawn picture depicting those fit to vote electing those fit to govern. The purpose here is to empower more of those people who can handle power with prudence, sagacity and disinterested commitment to public good. This includes both politicians and voters, for in a democracy anyone taking part in elections is thereby exercising power.

7

The same logic ought to be applied to big financial institutions and other businesses. It is clear enough that, in our virtual world animated by the second metaphysical premise, they are incapable of disciplining themselves from within. Therefore they must be disciplined from without.

Some of this discipline can legitimately come from the government, acting as the chair umpire of the economic game, though this will have to be kept down to a minimum until the human material of which our governments are made has been significantly upgraded. Meanwhile, most of the discipline can be imposed by citizens exercising their free choice and thus ascending to the lofty perch that is rightfully theirs.

For the choice to be not only free but also informed, people must have a clear idea of what sort of behaviour they wish to

---

69. I have yet to hear a persuasive argument on the moral or any other valid difference between aborting a child three months before birth or three months after.

promote on the part of the commercial world. For a couple of centuries now we have been told that businesses exist to advance consumers' benefits, succeeding inasmuch as they manage to do so. This principle must still apply, but perhaps we ought to reassess our understanding of exactly what constitutes a benefit. Let us look at an example familiar to all of us, that of food retailing.

Whereas even half a century ago most Europeans and many Americans went food shopping on foot, trundling from one local shop to the next, wicker basket in hand, today they usually drive to a supermarket with a large car park attached. They then pick up a trolley and in the next half an hour fill it with enough provisions for a few days, sometimes a week. This is undeniably a more convenient way of doing it and, assuming that supermarket chains pass on some of their economies of scale, a cheaper one.

Indeed, if in 1930 Americans spent 24.2 percent of their disposable income on food, in 2008 this proportion stood at only 9.2 percent. Even if we were to make allowances for the general rise in disposable income since the time of the Great Depression, it would be undeniable that throughout the Western world food is relatively cheaper these days. And a general shift from neighbourhood shops to supermarket chains must be a factor in this.

If we define public benefit in monetary terms only, that must be seen as a positive development. However, if we shift our vantage point, things appear to be less clear-cut. First, though a supermarket sitting on two acres of land can offer a greater variety of food than a local butcher, fishmonger and greengrocer, the small shops generally offer better quality. When old people complain that tomatoes have no fragrance these days, and chicken no taste, they are not just grumbling for the sake of it. And, contrary to the popular adage, nothing is worse than sliced bread peddled by supermarket chains.

Supermarkets have to buy centrally, which means that, say, fish would first have to be delivered to some large distributorship and only then taken all over the country (or the region). This normally takes several days, and by the time the fish reaches your frying pan it will have lost much of its taste, texture and nutritive value. By contrast, a local fishmonger goes to a wholesale market at six in the morning, opens his shop at nine and sells you fish caught within the last 24 hours. He and his colleagues, dealing in other foods next door, thus offer a valuable service, which supermarket chains would be unable to match. And even the price difference can be reduced in a variety of ways.

This brings us to another benefit of local shopping, one that goes beyond the freshness of the food you buy. The local shop provides a personal service. The fishmonger knows his customers; they are also his neighbours, occasionally friends. He is aware of what they like and what they can afford. If some of them live in strained circumstances, he could perhaps charge them a little less, and he certainly would if they came in just before closing time. In addition, he would be pleased to give them a few choice bits, such as heads and bones for stock, free of charge.

On balance, customers may still perhaps pay a little more than at a supermarket (then again, they may not – visiting a friend in Shropshire, I chanced upon a superb butcher who undercut the local supermarket by a wide margin), but such a small difference could be worth it to those who would rather be treated as individuals than as ciphers, and also to those cursed with sensitive taste buds. Old people also used to look forward to their daily shopping trips as a chance to have a friendly chat with the owner and other neighbours who happen to be there at the same time.

In short, the local shops promoted the community spirit and a sense of togetherness – something one would not normally expect from a sprawling U-Save-$$ miles away. Add to this the better quality of their food, and we see a clear incentive to curb the natural tendency to monopoly so typical of big modern businesses.

This is observable in every industry. Companies merge into giant conglomerates, and as the number of such Leviathans is reduced they become less inclined to compete in general, and on price in particular. In the pharmaceutical industry, for example, if two companies market two drugs with a similar active ingredient, the price they charge will always only vary within a few pennies, if at all. The two conglomerates have strong legal departments prepared to work overtime and so are unlikely to be convicted of forming a cartel. However, that they cannot be caught does not mean no cartel is in place. This stands to reason: the fewer competitors, the less the competition, the more will consumers ultimately have to pay. A multitude of companies that are big enough to produce things efficiently, yet not so big that they can operate as a near monopoly, would be the best answer.

Yet modern governments are unlikely to favour small over big. They welcome in businesses the same megalomania of greed that drives them themselves; kindred spirits always find it easy to see eye to eye. That is why any hope that businesses could be made smaller while governments remain big is misplaced. Therefore, for example, the current plans of the British government to break up the already nationalised banks are doomed to failure, even though this is a good idea in theory. (If these days banks are too big to be allowed to fail, then surely they would become more competitive if brought down to a size where their failure would not spell a global catastrophe.)

Alas, as a big modern government itself is *ipso facto* corrupt, it cannot expurgate corruption in business enterprises. But consumers can force the issue themselves by, in our example, shunning supermarkets and shopping locally whenever possible. If enough of them did so, before too long supermarket chains would have to start reducing their number of outlets. Eventually, some chains would go out of business altogether. At the same time, more local shops would open (or rather reopen), which would encourage competition, both from other shops and remaining supermarkets, thus keeping the prices down and the quality up. Food would still probably cost a little more, though in relative terms much less than it used to cost in the past. But people would also eat better stuff and, more important, have better communities.

Following the same path, we can extrapolate into other areas, from finance to manufacturing. In doing so we again may be sacrificing some short-term standard of living for long-term quality of life. Admittedly, there is little doubt that, if it is run by capable and incorruptible people, a huge international bank can offer a variety of financial services that an independent local bank would be hard-pressed to match. On the other hand, there is even less doubt that a small bank would not be able to bring down the world's whole financial system, a service that banking conglomerates have amply demonstrated their ability to provide. One begins to suspect that 'capable' and 'incorruptible' may not be universal attributes of the ladies and gentlemen currently engaged in looking after our financial health.

The same kind of pressure we have discussed in relation to supermarkets can be brought to bear on financial institutions and manufacturing concerns. The aim would be to mitigate not their competitiveness but their craving for monopoly. For example, we could withdraw our custom from banks that combine commercial and investment functions. Before long they would get the message and begin to specialise in one or the other. We could also spread our money over several banks, thus preventing any one of them from growing too big.

At the same time we could reassess our whole approach to investments: any meaningful change must start from within. This may involve doing ourselves much of the work we currently trust assorted advisers to do for us. If we remember that, as they are driven by the second metaphysical premise, these people are more interested in their own cuts off the top than in our benefit at the bottom, perhaps we should trust them a bit less.

Eschewing, or at least restraining, our craving for a quick killing, we must study the businesses whose shares we consider buying. The principal consideration ought to be the company's ability to pay dividends in excess of the interest one may expect from a savings account. A steady appreciation of the company's stock must be an important but secondary consideration. And ideally we should invest within the area of our expertise. Someone who works, say, for a pharmaceutical company would be better equipped to invest in a Glaxo (or rather Glaxo SmithKline, as it became after an endless series of transatlantic mergers and acquisitions) than in a Microsoft.

We should also curb our appetite for things we cannot afford and can therefore only buy on credit. At different periods, particularly those of high inflation, taking on large debts may look like an attractive proposition. We may be tempted to disregard calculations showing that, by taking out long-term loans, we shall illogically end up paying double, triple or more for what we could not afford in the first place. Granted, most people cannot avoid some personal credit, for example when buying a house. But here we must make our desires and aspirations commensurate with our incomes, current and realistically projected. Above all, we must look upon a house as a residence – not, at least not primarily, an investment.

True enough, by acting in a more prudent fashion we may miss out on some opportunities for ending up in a stately mansion. However, we would also be less likely to end up in a cardboard (or, prematurely, wooden) box. Many an otherwise honourable man has developed ulcers, cancers and coronaries worrying which of the two possibilities was more likely to be realised. Investing prudently and saving up to buy things we want could under some circumstances reduce our standard of living. But under all circumstances acting in that manner would improve our quality of life.

8

My practical proposals cannot help being radical: they illustrate how the first metaphysical premise could be applied to everyday life in the modern world. They are designed to signpost possible roads we ought to consider, not necessarily to provide the specific vehicles we can drive down those roads. The overall long-term aim is to reverse the damage done by the virtual world – even if doing so would produce much pain. My immediate aim is to emphasise yet again that much damage has been done, and if we wish to reverse it, palliatives will never be good enough.

None of the measures I have outlined is impossible to imagine: all we have to do is look at a rather recent past to see that they are all reflections of the real world in which we used to live. You may find that you agree with some of my suggestions and disagree with others, or you may dismiss all of them out of hand. You may then come up with your own suggestions, all doubtless better than mine. However, for them really to be better than mine, they too will have to be launched off the same platform, that of the first metaphysical premise and the behavioural shift it would bring about.

However, one feature will unite all such radical ideas, yours, mine or anyone else's: though easy to imagine, they are impossible to carry out. That is, they are impossible to act upon in a society animated by the second metaphysical premise. Driven by materialistic self-interest, politicians will not relinquish any of their power; financial institutions will not begin to act in a prudent fashion; and Western countries will not stop 'outsourcing' (dread word) their manufacturing to countries where people are prepared, or rather forced, to live from hand to mouth. Above all, having been utterly corrupted by the unsustainable hedonism of the last few decades, we are unlikely to accept willingly any initiatives that rely on our prudence, sensibility and the kind of austerity that comes from a healthy disdain for material possessions.

Every nation, said Joseph de Maistre, gets the kind of government it deserves. The same holds true for the economy. We have got the economy we deserve, and the only way for us to get a better one is to deserve something better. Much as we may resist it, austerity will sooner or later be imposed on us anyway by another economic catastrophe, the next instalment in the drama unfolding before our eyes. But by then it may be too late to do anything about it.

Nor can we do anything about it now, in the absence of a tectonic shift from the second to the first metaphysical premise. For, as I have argued in these pages, the systemic problem facing us is metaphysical. The problem can therefore be solved only by metaphysical means. It is perfectly true that a free society cannot exist without a free economy, or a free economy without credit. But it is as true that real freedom comes only from God – and real liberty, in the West, from institutions that derive from the Judaeo-Christian view of the world.

It is patently impossible, especially after centuries of ever-accelerating secularist propaganda, for all of us to start believing in God. Faith is a gift in the very precise sense of the word: it is bestowed by an outside donor. Not everyone can be a recipient of this gift – any more than everyone can have a gift for music or poetry. But everyone can act as if he indeed believed; everyone can organise his life along the lines laid down by the first metaphysical premise. Though I am not an unequivocal admirer of Pascal's wager, it does work at the quotidian level of our physical life. We can all bet on God's existence – if we are wrong, we have nothing to lose; if we are right, we have much to gain.

Then perhaps we shall see that some of the suggestions in the previous section may not be so unrealistic. Nor will the kind of economic activities we take for granted be wholly off-limits. However, they will have to be leavened with the prudence and self-restraint that are incompatible with the second metaphysical premise.

We shall still be capable of making as much money as we need.[70] We shall still be able to invest our surplus income in whatever manner we find reasonable. We shall still be able to function in a competitive business environment. We shall still be able to live in decent comfort, eat good food and wear stylish clothes. We shall still be able to trade freely with other nations, exchanging our exports for their imports. Yet we shall be able to do all those things without destroying either our souls or our societies. I claim this on good authority:

'... With men it is impossible, but not with God: for with God all things are possible.' (Mat. 19: 26)

---

70. Packing for their boat trip, Jerome K. Jerome's eponymous three men finally decided to take only those things they could not do without, rather than those they could do with. This approach to life in general would do wonders for our peace of mind.

AFTERTHOUGHT: IRISH STEW

Just as this book was going to print, Ireland set out to validate its most important assertions, thereby earning my gratitude and inspiring these concluding remarks. It is as if the Irish had decided to stage an accelerated small-scale experiment for my benefit, offering themselves as guinea pigs.

In the last 15-20 years Ireland went from being one of the poorest countries in Western Europe to becoming one of the richest. During exactly the same period, what used to be the most fervently pious nation in Europe channelled the same fervour into militant atheism. The priest who until recently had enjoyed the greatest veneration in Ireland now draws the bitterest hatred; many are scared to wear the clerical collar in public for fear of verbal or even physical assault.

With the benefit of our terminology, a shift from the first metaphysical premise to the second is very much in evidence, and it occurred in record time. Naturally no one was complaining; the country seemed to be going from rich to richer.

She owed her new wealth to three factors: EU subsidies, which this sinister organisation uses as a means of conquest; a highly educated and well trained labour force; and a low corporate tax rate, which attracted foreign investment thereby keeping the labour force in Guinness. The future looked bright.

Alas, even as the shift from one metaphysical premise to the other was quick to occur, so were the consequences quick to arrive. The newly materialistic Irish instantly created a bubble of debt and pumped it full of hot air. An orgy of irresponsible spending and suicidal borrowing (both public and private) followed and the bubble burst.

What was left behind was a gross foreign debt amounting to $500,000 per capita. That is hardly surprising, considering that banks all over Europe had been falling over themselves trying to force unsecured loans on the Irish who, to be fair, did not resist very hard.

The Royal Bank of Scotland alone lent a sum amounting to $12,000 per Irish capita. Predictably the country went bankrupt, and an EU bailout to the tune of 100 billion seemed like the only salvation.

The European Union, however, is more like Mephistopheles than St Francis: its largesse comes with strings attached. One such string was that Ireland was told to bring her corporate tax rate in line with that of Germany and France where it is almost three times as high. Low taxation, be it corporate or personal, explained a high EU official, is 'predatory.' A denizen of the real world would be tempted to put this astonishing statement down to the gentleman's insufficient command of English. Surely he meant 'competitive'? How, he would wonder, could the desire to take less money from people be deemed to be more predatory than the urge to grab as much as possible? But this was no linguistic solecism – all we have to remember is that we now live in a virtual world, and every erstwhile certitude is inside out.

The Irish government had to come up with some decisive action fast, and the Prime Minister acknowledged as much. *'There are occasions,'* he said, 'when the imperative of serving the national interest transcends other concerns, including party political and personal concerns.' I added the emphasis out of admiration for Mr Cowan's innocence, something hard to preserve in our cynical world. It is only this quality that can explain how he could utter something as monstrous as that, and also why he was unaware of its monstrosity. He spoke like a true child of the second metaphysical premise – and tellingly his little admission drew no comments.

For contextually such 'occasions' are rare (permit me to doubt that they come up at all). Most of the time 'party political and personal concerns' are everything for a modern politician, and the national interest is nothing. Welcome to the virtual world shaped by the second metaphysical premise.

What I find amazing is that a country that fought for her independence so valiantly is now willing to sell herself into vassalage to the European Union. The times they are a-changing, was how Bob Dylan translated *tempora mutantur*.

At the time of writing, the Irish are still fighting tooth and nail, trying to keep their low corporate tax rate. They know that without it foreign concerns will move out, and the country will become impoverished again. The government has announced a truly drastic cut of 20 percent in public expenditure, hoping that this will mollify the European Union. They miss the point. The Irish can have another potato famine, for all the EU cares. The bailout is about controlling, not helping out.

How much longer the Germans (who, let us not forget, were overwhelmingly opposed to the introduction of the euro) will be prepared to use their money the way their ancestors used *panzer* pincers, is anybody's guess. Judging by the rumbling audible at the grassroots there, not indefinitely. But for the time being the virtual world is alive and well. The Irish, along with the rest of us, are just alive.

APPENDIX 1

A FOOTNOTE ON PLATO

By way of a starting point, early in the book we agreed on three things. The first is self-evident: our thinking affects our behaviour in general and our economic behaviour specifically. The second is that the metaphysical premise from which we proceed will affect the type of our thinking, though not necessarily its acuity. The third is that, in solving both intellectual and practical tasks, the type of thinking is often more important than its acuity. A correct metaphysical premise may thus enable even a modest thinker to work out a useful philosophy of everyday life, while a wrong one can lead even a great mind astray.

Searching for illustrative examples, we may be well advised to have a look at one of the greatest and most influential minds ever, that of Plato. There has never been a serious thinker who was not, at one time or another and in one way or another, influenced by him. This observation holds true over the whole history of subsequent Western thought, from Aristotle to the first Christian philosophers and all the way down to modern times.

In fact, the twentieth-century thinker A.N. Whitehead went so far as to claim that, 'The safest general characterisation of the European philosophical tradition is that it consists of a series of footnotes to Plato'. Indeed, when Plato postulated that the visible is rooted in the invisible, and separated the idea of a thing from the thing itself, he charted the course for Western metaphysical philosophy, influencing thinkers as far apart both in time and in their thought as Origen and Bergson, Plotinus and Kant, Augustine and Schopenhauer, Clement of Alexandria and Whitehead himself.

Nonetheless, when we apply the test of practical eating to Plato's metaphysical pudding, we wince. The taste in our mouth is decidedly rancid. And the reason is that the philosopher, while skirting around the outer edges of the metaphysical truth, never did manage to reach it. Living three centuries before Christ made his appearance, he could not rise to the height of the Christian synthesis of God and man. That meant he started from a wrong metaphysical premise.

And it was wrong not because I say so but because it demonstrably led Plato, step by logical step, to the kind of ideas that were to be realised in practice only by the less savoury regimes of modernity, Bolshevism and Nazism. Nazi ideologues, such as Carl Schmitt, extolled Plato's perfect *polis* as 'the highest ideal of a totalitarian state' and Plato himself as 'the true founder of the national-socialist concept of the state'. Marx too could have offered a similar plaudit but did not, probably because he did not wish to trace his lineage back to yet another idealist philosopher. That slot was already occupied by Hegel.

While following the rational process that led Plato to the dubious honour of such recognition, let me remind you that my intention here is not to try to refute Plato's metaphysics in theory. It is only to show how it led him to many ideas that refuted themselves the moment others applied them in practice. He himself never managed to do so, though not for any lack of trying. However, political upheavals in Sicily, where, in today's parlance, Plato was employed as policy consultant, prevented the philosopher from besmirching his reputation by attempting to implement in practice the measures he advocated in theory.

Nor should we ever forget the importance of Plato's thought not only in general but specifically to Christianity. Karl Jaspers (d. 1969) was right when he identified Greek, and especially Platonic, thought as a key constituent of Christian philosophy. True enough; for lack of any other ready-made philosophical tools the earliest Christian thinkers, regardless of whether or not they reached the same conclusions as Plato, often relied on his methodology. Moreover, they acknowledged their direct debt to Plato's teaching on the highest deity, the spiritual world and, in *Phaedo*, the immortality of the soul.

If for nothing else, Plato ought to be put on a metaphysical pedestal for having led Augustine out of the intellectual cul-de-sac of his early life. Without Plato, Augustine may not have been able to exert his lasting and deep influence on all subsequent thought – including, as we have seen, economic ideas. And even though the other seminal theologian, Aquinas, was perhaps more influenced by Aristotle, he too owed a debt to Plato.

But while praising the Athenian, many early Christian thinkers also pointed out, either in so many words or obliquely, the fundamental and irreconcilable differences between Platonism (and, by inference, any philosophical idealism) and Christianity. For example, St Justin Martyr (d. 165 AD) showed that in his *Timaeus* Plato foretold the cross. However, Plato's demiurge, having first arranged matter in the shape of a cross, then bent it into a circle. As an ideal symbol of life that geometrical shape has a decidedly Eastern feel to it, and Plato was influenced by Indian philosophy in many ways, not least in his cosmology. In common with Vedic authors, Plato did not believe that God had created the world. Matter to him was eternal (the first law of thermodynamics had not been discovered yet), and the demiurge only rid it of its chaotic state, organising it into an orderly entity. Plato put this thought quite succinctly: 'God changed [all visible things] from disorder to order.'

The Eastern circle in Plato differs from the Western cross not only geometrically. While the horizontal strut of the cross traverses the universe from east to west, joining it into a whole, the vertical post links man with infinite heaven – the cross affirms the unity of the physical and the metaphysical. The circle, on the other hand, links nothing to nothing, which is why in the West it can only be vicious.

Yet Plato did not, nor could not, consider the true implications of the cross. The circle was to him a perfect symbol because Plato's metaphysics lacked an eschatology. While for a Judaic, Christian or Islamic thinker life on earth represents a teleological, dynamic progression towards the kingdom of God, for Plato it was cyclical and therefore static. From there it was but a small step to regarding the physical world as at best meaningless or even unreal, and at worst evil.

As quite a few other thinkers both before and after him, Plato was better at diagnosis than at treatment. He correctly identified many of the ills of the world in general and of Athenian democracy in particular. He even suggested 'timocracy', which he narrowly defined as rule by the honourable and valorous, as a preferable (though still flawed) alternative to democracy.

However, Plato saw the danger of timocracy degenerating into an oligarchic plutocracy, rule not by honour but by money. This was fraught with all manner of dangers, the main one being the ensuing likelihood of class struggle. Society would be divided into the haves and have-nots, with the latter putting their greater numbers to telling effect. The inevitable victory of the paupers would result in the ultimate political calamity: democracy, which to Plato was nothing but mob rule.

Yet his response to the evil he so clearly saw in the world was not dramatically different from that of Buddha or for that matter Pythagoras and other pre-Socratics. Instead of considering ways of combating evil, a thought process that comes naturally to an exponent of any Abrahamic religion, Plato escaped from it by claiming that the physical world was largely an illusion anyway. It was but a cave where the spirit was imprisoned, with reality (or what lesser minds would see as reality) merely shadows on the wall.

Our own selves were therefore the principal depository of reality, a view whose echoes were to reach Descartes and other like-minded thinkers of modern times. The main difference between Buddhism and Platonism is that, though both regarded the physical word as evil, Buddha preached escape into nothingness while Plato believed in the possibility of an ideal world.

Dualistic separation of body and spirit was a blunder later expunged by Christianity, though, alas, not without trace. But the Christian rehabilitation of the body was still some time off, and meanwhile Plato would often quote the orphic aphorism 'the body is a tomb'. Elsewhere, he described the physical world as a nasty place where the spirit is exiled.

And while the spirit was perfect, the body was the source of all evil: 'Who is to blame for wars, riots and battles,' he asked, 'if not the body and its passions?' Trying to answer that question, one could mischievously put forth as likely culprits such widespread failings of the spirit as pride and envy, but Plato did not even consider this. The body was the only transgressor.

When translated into early Christian thought, this idealistic contempt for the flesh contributed to the kind of asceticism and, mostly through Origen, institutional monasticism whose genesis is wrongly ascribed to the New Testament only. In fact, in its Western context disdain for the body was born not in Jerusalem but in Athens, and from there it spread not only to the Hellenic world but also to early Christianity and other contemporaneous religions.[71]

For example, it was largely on the basis of Plato's ratiocination that Manicheans and other Gnostics came to believe that the physical world was created by the devil and only the soul by God. Augustine himself fell under the spell of this belief as a young man, though he later abandoned it.

Since the Platonic Greeks regarded the spirit as pure in its perfection and the body revolting in its filth, it was no wonder that St Paul's proselytising efforts made little headway in Athens. Neither

---

71. Christian asceticism has indigenous roots as well, both in the Old and New Testaments. In the first couple of centuries after Christ, however, monasticism was the lot of isolated hermits inspired by the life of John the Baptist and Jesus's forty days in the desert. The movement gathered momentum only in the late Middle Ages, partly, one suspects, out of disappointment with the way the church conducted itself in the physical world.

the Incarnation nor the Resurrection could have possibly made any sense to the Athenians. What they sought was not salvation of the flesh but salvation *from* the flesh. Thus post-Platonic idealism predictably led to the denial of the Christian synthesis. And it stands to reason that some of the deadliest heresies ever to endanger Christendom, such as Catharism, were also based on the dualism of an ideal soul and wicked body. Nor is it hard to understand why the most prominent idealist philosophers of the German Enlightenment were all either atheists or, at best, deists.

Yet in practice, for all the similarity between his and eastern metaphysics, Plato was a European, not an Indian. Therefore, although he was perfectly capable of looking upon life on earth with nothing but contempt, Buddha-style, he could not wholly detach himself from it. Hermeticism was not a possible salvation for which Plato could reach in practical life. Affairs of the state in particular were never far from his mind, and it was only logical that sooner or later Plato would juxtapose the evil Greek democracy and the ideal he saw in his mind's eye. This was first laid down in *Republic* and developed *ad absurdum* in his last dialogue *Laws*.[72]

Reflecting his cyclical view of life, Plato's ideal was almost Confucian in its striving for static order. Dynamic development towards a specific goal was alien to his politics because it was alien to his metaphysics. Yet social dynamism presupposes freedom, and freedom presupposes social dynamism. The two are inseparable. Therefore Plato's political philosophy of stasis left no room for freedom, either personal or collective.

And because the very idea of freedom was alien to him, Plato did not recognise the significance of the individual. People were for him but structural elements in the edifice of the *polis*, to be put together so that the building would work functionally and aesthetically. In fact he claimed both in his *Timaeus* and *Critias*

---

72. Some analysts ascribe the more extreme ideas in *Laws* to Plato's old age, and possibly dementia, at the time of writing. This ignores the unimpeachably rational link between his metaphysics and practical thoughts. In general, suggesting that ideas we find objectionable could only be inspired by madness is seldom credible. For example, though both Stalin and Hitler were evil, neither was mad, as popular mythology would have it.

dialogues that this laudable subjugation of the individual to the collective had already been achieved in Atlantis, Plato's imaginary island organised along primeval lines. Atlantis was his ultimate, which is to say primordial, society where the tribe was everything and the individuals nothing. Rousseau later expanded upon this ideal of a Golden Age, but without invoking mythical continents. Replace 'state' with *'polis'*, and his conclusion could have come from Plato's tracts:

'The state should be capable of transforming every individual into part of the greater whole from which he, in a manner, gets his life and being; of altering man's constitution for the purpose of strengthening it. [It should be able] to take from the man his own resources and give him instead new ones alien to him and incapable of being made use of without the help of others. The more completely these inherited resources are annihilated, the greater and more lasting are those which he acquires.'

But what if people refused to act in such a subservient capacity? Well then, they had to be taught the true facts of life. And if they would not learn, they had to be coerced into toeing the line. Thus, in the absence of any metaphysical concept of freedom, the practical Platonic order could only be imposed by coercion. And, considering the kind of order it was, such imposition necessitated the amount of force that only a totalitarian state could bring to bear.

Plato divided people into three broad classes, assigning specific and more or less immutable functions to each. According to him, some people were called upon to run the state, some others to guard it against external and internal enemies, and most to toil away for the common good. And who should make up the ruling class? At the risk of being accused of partiality, Plato answered categorically: philosophers. 'Until [political power and philosophy] have not merged into one whole,' he wrote, 'the state will not expunge evil.'

A FOOTNOTE ON PLATO

This idea was rooted in the moral theory of Socrates, Plato's mentor, who regarded morality as a by-product of reason. If that is so, then of course thinkers who operate at the outer reaches of reason, philosophers, must rule the roost. People only ever do evil things because they do not realise they are evil. It takes philosophers to sort those simpletons out by appealing to their reason. Explain to the dunces what is right and what is wrong, and they will instantly turn into little angels. Or better still, they will become placid slaves who, out of gratitude for having been taught proper morality, will accept their lot and welcome the teachers as their rulers.

If at this point you were to suggest that Plato's philosopher kings looked suspiciously like our modern Bolshevik or Nazi leaders, his warriors like the KGB or the SS, and his toilers like the rest of the population of those unfortunate countries, you would find no argument in these quarters. Just look at the details of his prescriptions.

Plato's ideal *polis* was to be the freeholder of all land.[73] Hard agricultural work was to be done by slaves and outlanders. In education, an accent was to be placed on sports and military training. At the age of twenty all men were to be conscripted for long military service. Slavery was to be codified for ever. To nip any possible, and likely, resistance in the bud, the state would keep a watchful eye over everybody by encouraging universal snitching and denunciations. And, as the devil finds work for idle hands, people should be kept busy at all times, preferably with physical labour or military exercises, the more exhausting the better. If they still had time left over and wished to indulge a passion for the arts, the state would tell them which arts were allowed and which were proscribed.

'Music is the moral law,' wrote Plato, and his disciple Aristotle added that this law was to be strictly enforced. 'Any musical innovation is full of danger to the whole state, and ought to be prohibited when modes of music change, the fundamental laws of the state always change with them.'

---

73. I shall not bother to draw modern parallels each time. They are too obvious to point out.

Aristotle's wrath was caused by the addition of the Phrygian mode to the Dorian, which to him made music much too sensual. Plato too believed that one had to be alert to the possibility of music appealing to the baser passions of man, not to the higher faculty that he regarded reason to be. To become a high art, music therefore needed the ennobling effect of words, just as Eros needed the mitigating effect of philosophy. Thus, according to Plato, musicians were never to be allowed to compose merely instrumental music. They were to write songs, and only those with patriotic and educational lyrics. No songs without words for our hero (Felix Mendelssohn, call your office).

The same principle applied to the theatre, an art form so beloved of the Athenians. According to Plato, playwrights should never get ideas above their station. They must never think that 'we shall let them say things that are different from what we say.'

The children were to be imbued with the idea that the state was primary, while the individual was not even so much secondary as tertiary. The little ones were to be taught that they must be ready to sacrifice everything – but everything! – for the state. To achieve this laudable end, the children ought to be allowed to read only the books cleared by rigorous censorship. Plato did not suggest his preferred method of disposing of those tomes that did not pass muster but, as more recent history has shown, a bonfire would have worked nicely.

As to how this perfect order was to be achieved, Plato's prescriptions clearly inspired Marx's *Communist Manifesto* and corresponding Soviet and Nazi documents. Since his *polis* depended upon creating a particular mindset among its citizens, Plato accentuated brainwashing, which he coyly termed education. That was to be administered by those philosophers who, presumably, had some time left over in their busy schedules otherwise taken up by the nuts and bolts of running the state.

While most people would be enslaved, members of the ruling elite were to live in conditions of communism later described practically word for word by Marx and Engels in their cannibalistic *Manifesto*. No property was to be held individually, everything belonged to the collective. Even all women were to be shared equally, with resulting children becoming wards of the state. The poor tots would never find out who their real ('biological', in the parlance of today's social services) parents were and would have to assume that anyone within a few years of their age could be their sibling.

Where Plato diverged sharply from his teacher Socrates was in preaching that the philosopher kings must themselves stand above the law. In fact they would rise even above their own selves. As their lives were to be so wholly devoted to the state as to be fused with it, the rulers were masters of other people, but not of themselves. By their own virtue and sagacity they would set a shining example for all to follow, on pain of death.

A question arises: exactly how can we be sure that the specific philosophers running the country at present really are virtuous and sage? What if they are corrupt, their philosophy is worthless, and the state they run will soon come to ruin? What recourse shall we have then? Plato did not answer such questions. In fact, he never even asked them.

At this point it is tempting to remind ourselves that both Marxism and Nazism came to us courtesy of Germany, the modern nation most influenced by idealist philosophy. Marx, for example, started his career as a Hegelian. From then onwards he always cited Hegel as a major source of his creed. And we have already seen that Nazi apologists saw Plato as their intellectual progenitor, and not without justification.

Reading Plato's dialogues, one suspects that a causal relationship with the nastier manifestations of modernity would not be unduly hard to establish. And yet I shall not yield to this temptation, however appealing it may be. The purpose of this Appendix has been more modest: to emphasise once again that it is the metaphysical premise that skews (not to say determines) thinking, both individual and collective, and that it is thinking that skews behaviour. The amount and quality of the brainpower involved matters comparatively little.

APPENDIX 2

APES AS IDEAL DENIZENS OF THE VIRTUAL WORLD

Observing the systematic attempts to apply Darwinism to social and economic life, one could have been certain that sooner or later man would be reduced to the level of apes not only *de facto* but also *de jure*. And sure enough, as if to atone for her tardiness in abandoning Christianity, it was Spain that blazed the trail. In 2008 the Spanish parliament passed a resolution granting human rights to apes. Specifically it committed the country to the dictates of the Great Ape Project (GAP) founded in 1993 by the 'philosopher' Peter Singer, professor of bioethics at Princeton. The apes currently residing in Spain will henceforth enjoy the legal rights to life, liberty and freedom from torture.

The UN Declaration on Apes is in the works, to be adopted soon. It states that all primates, including man, are 'members of the community of equals' who are not to be deprived of their liberty without due process. The detention of great apes who have not been convicted of any crime should be permitted only where it is in their own interests or is necessary to protect the public. In such cases apes must have a right of appeal to a judicial tribunal, either directly or through an advocate.

One wonders how the framers of this document see the ensuing practicalities. For instance, where trial by jury is part of due process, who would be the ape's peers to sit in judgment? Surely they would have to be other apes (British football supporters may be narrowly disqualified). Then how would the jury follow the proceedings and then communicate their verdict? How would the defendants confer with counsel? Be sworn in? Give testimony? Launch a 'direct appeal'? And if convicted for, say, murder, how would they be punished?

As the death penalty is not an option, it would have to be incarceration in, for example, the same zoos in which all 315 Spanish apes are kept already, with no due process anywhere in sight. Illogically, the Spanish resolution states that there they can remain, although the conditions must improve, presumably in line with human prisons equipped with colour TVs and sports facilities. However, it will become illegal to keep apes in circuses, or for the purposes of using them in television commercials and films. Our 'comrades' will thus enjoy greater protection than, say, Kate Moss or the troupe of Barnum & Bailey. And in general, apes will acquire weightier rights than humans, for ours are counterbalanced by responsibilities and theirs demonstrably are not. Our right to the state's protection, for example, is contingent upon our allegiance to it (*protectio trahit subjectionem*). Since an ape cannot pledge such allegiance the balance is clearly in its favour.

Let us not forget the right to work either. Or rather the right not to work and draw welfare payments, which has become the cornerstone of government economic policies in the virtual world. It has to be acknowledged, with reluctant resignation, that, apart from appearing in circuses, apes have limited employment opportunities. However, that makes them different only from some humans, far from all. The dependent unemployable underclass, created by the state's quest to subjugate people, illustrates this point perfectly. Just like welfare recipients, apes could live in free housing provided by the state; they could be taken by their 'carers' to the social once a month to collect their paycheque. Come to think of it, simian citizens just may be the ideal that the state craves in the virtual world.

If you think this is bad, consider the track record of Peter Singer, the 'mind' behind GAP. In 2001 he allowed that humans and animals can have 'mutually satisfying' sexual relations because 'we are animals, indeed more specifically, we are great apes.' Therefore such sex 'ceases to be an offence to our status and dignity as human beings.' Good news for some shepherds, bad news for poor Mrs Singer.

Singer also maintains that the right to life is grounded in the ability to plan one's future. Since the unborn, infants and mentally disabled lack this ability, he justifies abortion, selective infanticide and euthanasia. However, even though apes are not known for prudent foresight, Singer does not advocate their cull. So his is a kind of affirmative action: he wants apes to have rights that are not just equal but superior to ours.

Now his ideas have been acted upon by the parliament of a country whose chosen recreation is watching livestock first tortured, then attacked with a sword and slaughtered. So why such touching concern for the rights of apes? On the surface of it this sounds illogical – but only until we have reminded ourselves that the logic of modernity always operates on two levels, the first virtual, the second real. Ostensibly, the Spanish parliament acted not only illogically but insanely. But the real animus behind its resolution was in no way constructive: they do not care about animal, or for that matter human, rights. Their true purpose is destruction – of the last vestiges of the first metaphysical premise. And the unique status of man has been essential to that tradition ever since Genesis 1:28. So it has to go.

Yet we cannot deny that, say, chimpanzees do look remotely similar to humans. And it is not just the appearance: humans and chimps share 99 percent of their active genetic material (the genetic distance between them is a mere 0.386). Although all decent people deplore unnecessary cruelty to animals, this makes medical experiments on apes so necessary: by responding to drugs like humans and unlike other animals, apes save human lives. Though no such experiments are conducted in Spain, the legislators banned them just in case. Yet the QED expressions on their faces are premature. For physical likeness between apes and humans creates problems for their ilk.

Biology cannot explain why, given such close proximity, apes still look rather different from humans, even those as flawed as, say,

Richard Dawkins. Anything near the same biochemical closeness produces virtual twins in other animals. For example, even though they are 20 to 30 times further apart, some species of squirrels or frogs are practically indistinguishable.

Moreover, in other species such genetic and biochemical proximity presupposes the possibility of mating so dear to Singer's heart. After all, we know of numerous examples of interbreeding not only among different species within one genus, but even among different genera or sub-families within one family, where the biochemical compositions are quite different and the genetic distances are tens of times greater than those between humans and chimpanzees. And yet these two putative twins cannot produce common progeny, for all the highly publicised scoops in the press some years ago. A mating experiment is under way, we were told, and soon a 'pithecanthropus' will be produced, proving that Darwin was right all along. The experiment failed – so do they acknowledge Darwin was wrong all along?

Other failing experiments set out to prove the intelligence of apes, allegedly so much superior to other animals', if ever so slightly inferior to man's. It is only when primatologists untainted by evolutionary afflatus became involved that any such claims were disproved. A conclusion has been reached that primates do not differ from other mammals as much as primatologists believed in the past. In fact, many scientists place chimpanzees lower on the intelligence scale than some other animals, such as dolphins and elephants.

Much has been made of the fact that apes can use a few primitive tools. After all, Engels, another demiurge of modernity, more or less equated this ability with humanity ('man was created by labour'). Yet apes are not the only nonhumans who can do this. For example, the Galapagos woodpecker (*Cactospiza pallida*) grips a cactus thorn in its beak to pluck insects out of the tree bark. Some birds of prey attack ostrich nests by dropping stones from a great height. Eagles drop turtles onto stones to break the shells. Actually, Aeschylus is said to have been killed when one such turtle-lover mistook his bald pate for a stone. And there are many other illustrations of some animals being equal, and often superior, to primates.

For example, elephants and wild dogs bury their dead, whereas apes do not. In fact the primatologist Jane Goodall shows that chimpanzees have no concept of death. Female chimps carry their dead young with them, and other siblings in the same litter continue to play with the corpse when it is already in the late stages of decomposition. Also, unlike whales who look after their aged and sick, apes often attack their defenceless old. 'It is wrong,' writes Goodall, 'to draw direct parallels between the behaviour of apes and humans.'

Here I must respectfully disagree. For moral judgement, which Goodall sees as the principal difference between the two species, is fast disappearing from the behaviour of our modern masses weaned on the second metaphysical premise. In fact, violent attacks on old people have become the norm in Western cities. This points at what the ape really is, with the theological explanation yet again much more plausible than the pseudoscientific twaddle.

Augustine refers to the devil as 'the ape of God'. To him the devil possessed some caricature similarity to the Creator in that he could perform miracles, seduce people by his spirituality and so forth. In that context, the ape is a caricature of man, the ghastly portrait in man's attic. Created in the image and likeness of God, man towers over animal; he is much more than merely its paragon, as Shakespeare believed.

Yet the further people step away from faith, the more they fall prey to shameful passions and vices, the less they resemble God. And then, as the model for the portrait grows more and more awful, the caricature begins to look just like a man. The ape was thus created as a reminder: it shows what humans will be like when they lose God's likeness – and with it their humanity. The ape is not our past; it is our future. The Spanish resolution is thus a self-fulfilling prophecy.

These days, any teacher in the West, even if he establishes unassailable atheist credentials first, will lose his job for showing that Darwinism is wrong in all its cosmic conclusions. Hard-boiled champions of this half-baked theory will mete out exemplary punishment to any critic. No amount of proof coming from the real world will change the situation.

For denizens of the virtual world are deaf to any audible signals sent by reality, and blind to the visual ones. Part of the reason is that, having abandoned the only truth worthy of the name, they do not really care about any truth any longer.